NIGHT OF DESTINY

24 December, 1944

Jack Corrigan

FaithHappenings Publishers

A Division of FaithHappenings.com

CENTENNIAL, COLORADO

Jack Corrigan/FaithHappenings Publishers
7061 S. University Blvd., Suite 307
Centennial, CO 80122

Cover design: tatlin.net

Publisher's Note: This is a work of fiction. Names, characters, places, and incidents are a product of the author's imagination. Locales and public names are sometimes used for atmospheric purposes. Any resemblance to actual people, living or dead, or to businesses, companies, events, institutions, or locales is completely coincidental.

Book Layout © 2014 BookDesignTemplates.com

Night of Destiny/Jack Corrigan -- 1st edition

ISBN 978-1-941555-00-2

Dedication

To my father, John V. Corrigan,

and to my uncles, and all the other men and women

whose sacrifices in World War II

gave all of us the chance

to live free.

Acknowledgements

Conflicts, especially ones of significance, are often viewed on an epic scale, and the events that made up what became known as World War II are no exception. In the European theater alone, operations such as the D-Day invasion and the Battle of the Bulge involved hundreds of thousands of people and tons of equipment. What must not be forgotten, however, is that war is personal. At its core, war is a story of individual actions, a tale of singular events fueled by the emotions of its participants regardless of their affiliation.

What follows is a story inspired by the events of the tragedy of the *S.S. Leopoldville*. I am indebted to my father, John V. Corrigan, for providing the framework to this story through his recollections and keepsakes. My father was a member of an ambulance squad that came ashore three days after the D-Day landings. He saw action in the hedgerows of Normandy, and travelled throughout France as a medic with the Red Ball Express, the enormous Allied truck convoy system that supplied forward-area combat units. On Christmas Eve 1944, he was nearby on the coast of Cherbourg, France, when the *Leopoldville* sunk, and he was instrumental in plucking survivors from the frigid waters of the harbor.

My father wrote home about his experiences that night but never mailed the letter due to the war department's then-strict censorship policy. That letter lay hidden in a box of WWII memorabilia for nearly fifty years. Its discovery led me to investigate the story more fully so that today's generations could envision what happened that icy night.

Like most of the survivors of this great conflict, my father rarely spoke to us about his experiences. When he became ill with cancer, I took the initiative to ask him about his wartime experiences. As a tribute, I turned those memories into a novel only because I wanted to tell it through not only his eyes but through the eyes of two other men. It was important to represent the three different perspectives of these characters because they are marked as much by their similarities as by their differences. I hoped the story's retelling would illustrate a greater principle that my father saw lived out time and time again on the battlefronts: that regardless of the horrific brutality and inhumanity that takes place during the war, there is still a fundamental humanness and compassion that survives, thrives, and even brings people together.

In addition, my thanks go Ray Roberts for his excellent memoir, *Survivors of the Leopoldville Disaster,* as well as to the writers of many other books, reports, and accounts of WW II that I used in research. The voices of those men gave me a fuller appreciation of what happened that fateful holiday evening, Christmas Eve, 1944.

Since I am still learning this craft, I am grateful for the guiding hand provided by my editor, Marcus Brotherton. He provided a firm structure to my storytelling. Also, this book would not have become a reality without the belief in its message by Greg Johnson and FaithHappenings Publishers. Most of all, loving thanks to my wife, Lisa, who has been more than patient in my pursuit at something that is becoming more than just a hobby. She's stuck now, however, because I am already at work on several new projects.

—*Jack Corrigan*
Colorado, 2014

CHAPTER ONE

9 June 1944

Omaha Beach, France

The waters of the English Channel walloped Sergeant Dan Gibbons with a salty slap. Spray doused the Higgins boat. As cold and wet and in danger as he was, Dan secretly wished the clock could be pushed back three days. He would never admit it out loud. Not even to his closest buddies. Deep inside, however, he wished he'd rushed the beaches of Normandy along with the first intrepid flood of Allied troops that had landed on D-Day, three days earlier.

Another wave hit, drenching the troops. "I thought you said we wouldn't get wet as long as we're near the front of the boat!" he shouted to his fellow medic, Gregory Martin Cunningham, who everybody called GMC for short, just like the car company.

"Who gave you that fool piece of advice?" GMC hollered back with a grin.

"You did!"

"That'll teach you to listen to me!"

Dan scanned the shoreline ahead, a strange mix of fear and hope in his heart. The Higgins, named after its inventor, was only thirty-six feet long and less than eleven feet wide. A combination of mahogany and metal, the landing craft could pull close to shore at low tide thanks to its flat bottom. Fully loaded, it traveled at less than nine knots and didn't maneuver well. He could still hear the distant rumble from artillery in operation farther inland. Nazi forces continued to roam the Normandy peninsula, and men in a boat were an easy target.

Another surge of water slapped hard against the boat. The men lurched and fought to stay standing. Dan's clothes were already drenched. They weighed him down as much as his gear and steel helmet. He tried to get his bearings before the next big wave found its mark. His stomach gurgled and spun like a washing machine.

"Sarge, you don't look so good," GMC yelled.

"Yeah, I don't feel so—." Dan stopped before finishing his sentence, turned his head quickly, and dry-heaved over the side of the boat. Nothing was left in his stomach. In the hours it'd taken to cross the one hundred miles of Channel, he'd vomited multiple times, and his stomach felt lined with tacks. A rising breaker shoved him away from the side, and he crashed against a GI behind him.

"Hey—watch what you're doing," the man groused and gave him a shove.

Dan straightened himself up and gave his fellow GI a sincere look of apology. Three dozen soldiers were crammed together on the boat. He glanced around at the helmeted faces. Most were strangers to him. He wasn't the only soldier vomiting. Some men chewed the ends of soggy cigarettes. Some checked their rifles. Most seemed lost in thought over what was to take place once they hit the sand. He stared at the distant cliffs, hoping that might help settle his gut.

Dan and three other members from his ambulance squad were riding in the Higgins boat with an infantry platoon. The arrangement wasn't his first choice. If his pick of military assignments had come about, he would have been leading the infantrymen as an officer, not assigned to bandaging their wounds. But the Army was the Army. Back in college, Dan was picked for a special officer's training program. He spent four months in the program, and then it was inexplicably canceled. He volunteered for an artillery division but was sent to an ambulance squad instead. Being a medic was a safer gig in some ways. With the circular patch of a crimson cross prominently displayed on his upper arm and the front of his helmet, the enemy wasn't supposed to shoot at him thanks to the treaties of the Geneva Convention. Still, splinting broken legs and sticking men with morphine curettes wasn't all he'd hoped to do for the war effort.

The next wall of water swept over the side. Dan took off his helmet and ran his hand through his damp brown hair. At 6'2", he was taller than the average Allied soldier. He had the clean jaw and broad smile handed down from his Irish heritage. He'd been a fine football player, a lineman. He was an All-State pick in high school even though his team had only won one game that year. That dismal record reflected his feelings about too much of his life. There were successful moments, but the limelight never seemed to shine on him in the way he hoped. Dan longed to do something significant. He reset his helmet on his head and tugged the strap tighter.

9

"Get ready, men!" an officer shouted from the rear of the boat.

The Higgins throttled back and the front ramp slowly dropped into the water. Omaha Beach remained several hundred yards away, and a forest of wooden barricades rose out of the sea between the men and the shore. Stories of heavy casualties three days earlier flitted through Dan's mind. He wondered what the men in his boat would find once they reached the sand. Hopefully, they'd do some good. Hopefully, they'd help. He knew German defenses of the northwestern coast of France were still rugged. Anything could still happen.

"Can't he get us any closer?" Dan asked GMC.

"Tide's out," GMC said. He was shorter than Dan, with a thick neck. "He doesn't want to risk a closer landing. I'm sure it's shallow here. Don't worry—."

"I'm not worried," Dan said quickly. But his voice was tight.

The noncom at the top of the ramp waved the men forward, and a line of GIs began to splash into the water in columns of two. Dan and GMC were next to each other, only three positions away from the front. It didn't take long to be their turn. Dan paused for a split second at the top of the ramp then stepped off.

Immediately he disappeared under the water. He searched for solid footing, found none, and swung his arms in a panic. The cold shocked his entire body. Briny water fought its way into his nose and mouth. He gagged, feeling as if he was going to vomit underwater. A strong hand grabbed the back of his field jacket, and Dan's head jerked from the action. In an instant, he crested the surface and sucked in a lungful of air.

"Nice and easy, big man." GMC's voice was solid. "I've got you. Take a step forward. Good. Take another."

Dan's feet found the sea floor. He exhaled water out of his nose and stood up, chagrined. He must have caught a random depression in the sand when he landed. A bomb crater maybe. The water was only chest-high where he stood. None of the other soldiers had been dunked. He murmured thanks as rivulets of water drained from his helmet and ran down his face. GMC gave him a quizzical look at what Dan said but made no reply.

The pair advanced forward, working through the waves with the rest of the landing party. When they reached the sand, they crouched low. Jagged metal defensive emplacements lay before them, half-buried in the sand. Steep cliffs guarded this section of Normandy coastline.

"Looks quiet," GMC said. "That's a relief."

"Keep watch for snipers," Dan replied in a voice just above a whisper and motioned to GMC. "Must have been a slaughter. Just look at the pockmarks on that overlook."

GMC nodded. "If that's how wildly we were shooting at them, just imagine what they dished out on us. Footing up that slope must have been a real killer."

Bobby Jepson, another member of the ambulance squad, joined Dan and GMC at the water's edge. His partner, Jefferson Davis Hardin, a freckle-faced kid from Alabama who looked about 16, followed behind. Smitty, the squad's driver, naturally had dubbed the teenager "Reb" because of his Southern background. "Y'all think it was as bad as they say, Sarge?" Reb asked.

11

"The Jerries had the high ground," Dan replied. "A lot of our guys didn't stand a chance." A Catholic, he made a Sign of the Cross on his chest. The others stared in horrific contemplation of what the scene must have been like.

"All clear!" shouted a noncom. "Move forward. Keep a sharp lookout."

An amphibious truck lay wrecked in front of them, fire still smoldering in the engine compartment. Dan saw dozens of mangled M-1 rifles, helmets, and Thompson submachine guns strewn across the beach. Pockets of the sand were stained red from blood. "They're unloading the LST down the beach," he said, breaking the silence. "The Captain and Smitty will be expecting us. That's our job for now. C'mon, let's head over."

Tanks, trucks, and other support vehicles, including ambulances, were being carried to the beachhead. In the distance, past a series of broken German barricades, Dan could see the squad's leader, Captain Abraham Levine, and their driver, Frank "Smitty" Smith, as they accompanied their truck into shore.

"There they are!" Reb called out. "I'll race y'all over. Loser owes me a Hershey bar."

The private took off at a sprint like a child trying to be first in line at a merry-go-round. Reb was the youngest of the group, and Dan worried that the boy didn't always appreciate the seriousness of their surroundings.

The rest of the medics moved at a more cautious pace. The damp yet soft beach made for tenuous footing, and about thirty yards ahead Reb took a tumble. Too eager, he slipped when he tried to stand. He rolled around in amusement at his pratfall, covering himself in sand. He was still giggling when Dan pulled him to his feet and slapped his shoulder, partly to shake the sand off, partly to tell the boy to stop being so gung-ho. They stood next to one of the barricades.

"I didn't want the race to be too easy," Reb boasted. "I thought I'd give y'all a chance to catch up."

Dan bit his lip to keep from scolding his rambunctious co-hort and averted his eyes. The sand around them didn't show much evidence of movement in the immediate area around this particular defensive obstruction. The sand was not as packed as tightly as the paths created where most of the troops made for the cliffs. When Reb had thrashed about, he stirred up the loose layer on the surface. Dan dropped to one knee and brushed sand off the boy's pants. To his left, he noticed an imperfection in the beach that appeared out of place.

"Stop being my mother, Sarge. See y'all at the finish line."

Reb took a step, ready to resume the race. Dan launched himself out of his crouched position and caught the younger man right in the midsection with his shoulder. Reb landed on his back. Dan dropped back down on all fours.

"What the hell, Sarge?"

"Don't move! Everyone!"

Dan made short, careful strokes in opposite directions to move sand away from a small bump in the beach. Into view came a small steel cylinder with a pressure sensor on top.

"Bouncing Betty," Dan said, the words catching in his throat.

Reb stood stock still. His lips quivered, and a dry swallow slid down his throat as he stared at the landmine. When enough weight depressed the plunger on the device, it would trigger a small explosion that would propel the mine up to five feet in the air. Within seconds, another explosive round would burst and send steel balls, short metal rods, and other pieces of shrapnel in every direction. That's how Bouncing Betty got her name. The men had seen demonstrations of its deadly potential during training, but that was only to prepare them for the treatment soldiers might require should they take a hit from one of these devices. Now they were the ones in danger.

Dan extracted a pair of scissors from a pouch hanging on his belt, and then lay on his chest, his nose barely an inch away from the mine. He closed his eyes for just a moment to get his heart to stop racing. The others could barely take a breath. He used the scissors to make short, vertical strokes in a tight circle. Next, he connected the holes from these thrusts with a cautious sweep around the perimeter of the mine. When the circle was complete, he removed the scissors from the sand and sat back on his haunches.

"No tripwire," he grunted. "That's a relief."

Reb exhaled.

"Hang tight," Dan muttered. "It's still live." He swiped a hand across his chin to remove some sand that was stuck in his whiskers and looked to the other medics. "Anyone remember how tall these things are?"

"Like a can of beer," GMC said. "Five to six inches. Remember that drill at Fort Riley?"

Dan nodded in acknowledgement.

GMC pulled out a heavy gauge paper clip, one that came from the handful of clips they used to keep field treatment tags together in their medical bags. "Stick this where the sun don't shine." He handed the clip to Dan.

"You're way ahead me, pal," Dan said. "Thanks."

Dan twisted the clip straight and stared at the landmine again. He searched the sensor top with a soft touch until he found his target: a small hole at the base of the trigger. He inserted the clip into the opening. A perfect fit. He stabbed his scissors into the sand on one side of the mine to a depth he thought would equal the height of a beer can and angled the instrument to get the blade under the Betty. He maintained steady pressure on the handle and worked the scissors like a fulcrum. The mine came free from the wet sand with a sucking sound. The paper clip worked just like the safety pin on a hand grenade.

GMC knelt down next to Dan. He unscrewed the sensor from the top, and then did the same with the three detonators inside to render the explosive completely inert.

"I'm glad at least one of us paid attention during those training exercises," Dan said with a grateful sigh and a slap on GMC's back.

Reb was breathing easy now. He gave a nervous laugh and glanced around at the beach, before he wordlessly started heading for the LST, again ahead of the rest of the group. This time the boy wasn't running.

"One more step by the kid and it might have been curtains for all of us," GMC said, his voice low. "How did you know to look for something, anyway?"

"Let's just say I didn't want to fall to the basement."

"What's that supposed to mean?"

"C'mon," Dan said. "Let's walk. Remember how I told you about my father?"

GMC nodded. "You said he was a smoke-eater."

"Right, a firefighter for the City of Cleveland. One day he takes me with him to work. I was maybe nine years old. We go to check out this abandoned store that's been completely gutted by a blaze. Three engine companies worked to put it out. Dad was doing the post-fire investigation."

Dan paused and glanced at the hill above them before he focused again on the sand and continued.

"Dad never said much. He just walked through the rubble. Every once in a while he'd move things out of the way with a pike. Once he knelt down and put his nose right into the debris as if he was a bloodhound looking for a scent." Dan smiled at the memory. "I remember asking him why he was so concerned because there was nothing left to the place. He looked me hard in the eye and growled in this low voice: 'When you stop paying attention to the little things, that's when you miss what's truly important.'"

"I don't get it," GMC said. "What could be so important if the fire was already out?"

"I asked him the same thing myself," Dan responded. "But he didn't say anything at first. He just kept sniffing around. I tell ya—everything in that old store was completely cooked. You should have seen the place. All these large wooden beams were completely charred. Fried clothing on the mannequins. Everything in mangled or melted heaps. After about an hour of kicking around, I was bored and about to head outside to wait in the car when my father nearly knocked me off my feet with a sudden arm across my chest. 'Don't move,' was all he said."

"He found a Bouncing Betty?" Bobby asked.

"Course not." Dan chuckled. "It was Cleveland. But he takes his pike and lifts a sheet of wood that must've fallen from the ceiling. A wisp of smoke curls out from the ashes underneath. He spreads the remains to make certain there isn't a flame still active. Then—get this: once he's satisfied, he bangs the pike hard into the floorboards. One hit. That's all it takes. This huge section of floor gives way and crashes into the basement below."

"You would have been a goner," GMC said.

"Straight through to the bottom," Dan said. "I don't know how he knew, but he did."

"Same way you knew with the kid back there," Bobby said.

"Nah, that was just luck," Dan told him. "If Reb hadn't rolled around like a dog satisfying an itch, I never would have noticed that Betty."

"Well, it saved every fool medic here," GMC said with a slap to Dan's back. "And you must've been Ohio's star lineman. That was one sweet block you put on the kid."

Dan chuckled. "Yeah, I was a real hero all right." His voice felt resigned.

Reb had reached the LST by now. He was in an animated conversation with the Captain and Smitty, telling them all about the defused landmine.

GMC rubbed his forehead underneath his helmet and nudged Dan. "Were we ever that young and rambunctious? I don't know about you, but I hope that's all the excitement we ever see over here."

Bobby piped up. "Agreed. The sooner we clean up this Nazi mess and head for home is okay by me."

Dan walked in silence for another ten yards before he spoke.

"I don't know, fellas." His voice sounded far away. "Just for once in my life I'd like to do something that truly matters."

CHAPTER TWO

14 June 1944

Camp Rucker, Alabama

Private Doug Tillman watched a bead of perspiration slide out from underneath his rolled-up sleeve. He reckoned it was at least 105 degrees Fahrenheit in the Alabama sun.

He sighed, walked forty steps forward, slowly turned around, and then walked back to where he started. He stood motionless for a minute before spending the next five minutes shifting his weight from his left leg to his right. He gave out a grunt, walked the ten steps again, stopped, glanced up at the sun, and then stared at the trees in the distance. *Guard duty in Alabama*, he thought. *Where's the enemy when you need him most?*

Another globule of sweat trickled down his arm. Doug shook it off and walked his forty paces again on the dusty path located near the north perimeter of an Army installation, his M1 rifle jostling against his leg. There was nothing to look for. Nothing to guard. Not really. He hoped his mind wouldn't sizzle up like a piece of burnt bacon and go completely numb.

19

He was 6 feet tall, muscled, with dark black hair. His cheekbones were high and solid, his complexion ruddy, and he had the chiseled good looks of a Hollywood actor. In fact, that's what all the other Army grunts called him—Hollywood. As in *Hey, Hollywood, you had any dates with Betty Grable lately?* Or *Hey there, Hollywood, hand me that mop, willya.*

It was just over two months since he made the decision to enlist. Sixty odd days since the circumstances of his life had radically changed. He was convinced that joining the military was the right thing to do, but that belief did little to relieve the tedium of training, or the aching hollow of angst he felt in his stomach.

Another large trickle of sweat slid out and worked its way down to his forearm. The drop made an abrupt turn when it reached a serpentine scar and followed its twisting path until it paused above his wrist. Regaining, its momentum, the droplet rolled through his palm and off the tip of a finger.

Doug glanced around, taking stock of his surroundings. All he could see was the sun, the trees, and the shimmering waves of heat rising up out of the ground.

He felt miserable. Absolutely miserable.

"Private Doug Tillman," he whispered under his breath. "You're one sad sack of a soldier, you know that?" A low moan of frustration escaped and he shifted his M1. "There's nothing for you now. No family. No friends." He paused, thinking hard about those last four words, and then said them out loud, his voice deeply bitter.

* * *

It was January 1939 and the buds on the orange trees in the backyard of their Hollywood Hills home hadn't yet emerged. Thirteen-year-old Doug Tillman whimpered in pain. He curled up under a blanket in the overstuffed chair at the back of the cook's kitchen in his parent's house and waited.

Consuela, the family's housekeeper, already had the telephone receiver in her hand. She hesitated when the rotary dial spun back into position after she entered the first number. She had halted two attempts earlier in the day, unsure of the consequences for attempting to telephone her employer while she was out of town. Another muffled cry came out of the boy. Consuela steeled her resolve, resumed dialing the number written on a pad next to the telephone, and prayed the call wouldn't result in her job being terminated.

"Thank you for calling the Turner Inn on beautiful Catalina Island," came the voice on the other end. "How may I help you?"

"*Por favor*, I would like to speak to Senorita Katharine Tillman ... *please*." Consuela remembered her English at the end, nervous that she was prattling.

"I'm sorry, there is no Mrs. Tillman here. The receptionist's voice was still polite.

"*Si,* of course. There is a code. What was it again... yes, the code is *Gulliver's Travels*."

There was a pause. Consuelo could hear the sound of a ledger being opened. "Mrs. Tillman has given strict orders that she is not to be disturbed. May I take a message?"

"I must speak directly with Senora Tillman.... Please tell her it is Consuela Gonzalez—her housekeeper. She will know my name. It is about her son."

21

"*Gonzalez*, you say?" The operator sighed. "All right, we'll have her paged. But you better not be from the studio. Hold please."

Consuela held, tapping her foot.

The wait seemed to last forever. Consuela drummed her fingers on the counter in an attempt to steady her nerves.

"Consuela?"

"Hello, Mrs. Tillman. Are you having a good time?"

"Sure ... yes ... but why are you calling? What's the matter?"

"I do not mean to bother you on your trip with Senor Tillman."

"Consuela—out with it. What's wrong?"

The housekeeper paused. She was having regrets again. The reigning 1939 Oscar winner for Best Actress, Kate Tillman, and her husband were on a romantic getaway, a spontaneous Valentine's Day sail to Catalina, the popular island about twenty-five miles from Los Angeles. "Senora Tillman, I am so sorry ... Senorito Doug and his amigos were playing in the trees in the backyard... and he fell ... "

"He fell?!"

"It is okay. Nothing is broken. I called Doctor Anderson to the house, and he has already come and left. There is a gash on his arm, but the doctor said he was—."

"A gash!" Mrs. Tillman's voice rose. "How big of a gash, Consuela? Did Doug need stitches?"

"It is not bad, ma'am. The doctor said—."

"How many stitches!"

"Twenty-one." Consuela's voice was meek.

"Twenty-one stitches! Oh for Heaven's sake, Consuela? When did this happen? This morning?"

"No, Mrs. Tillman, it was yesterday afterno— "

"Yesterday! Why didn't you call me then?"

"I am so sorry, Senora," she whispered. "I was going to call, but Senorito Doug insisted. He said he was okay. He begged me not to bother you and Senor Tillman."

"Look, I'm sorry to snap at you, Consuela. I really am. But just let me talk to him, okay? Is he there?"

"Yes ma'am. I am sorry. Thank you."

After a brief delay, Doug picked up the receiver. "Hi, Mom. Are you and Dad having a good time?" He attempted to sound nonchalant, but he couldn't hide the shake in his voice.

"Oh, Dougie, talk to me. How do you feel? Are you okay? What did the doctor say?" The mother's questions gushed out, then she paused and her voice turned stern. "Your father and I have warned you about climbing those trees. You're lucky you didn't break your neck."

Doug began to cry. Hearing his mother's voice was all it took to release his pent up emotions. He sniffed, trying to compose himself. "Can you come home today?"

"We're not scheduled to come back until tomorrow night, Doug. You know that."

"I know. I'm sorry."

Kate Tillman's voice turned motherly again. "Look, I'll talk to Dad. Maybe we can come back early."

"Don't do that. He'll just get mad."

"No, he won't. Tell me the truth. Would you feel better if we came back?"

"Yes."

"I'll talk with your father."

"No. Wait—."

"I'm talking to your father. We'll be home by tonight. I don't want to hear another word about it."

Doug sniffled again. "Thanks, Mom. I love you."

"I love you, too. We'll call you when we land at the yacht club."

* * *

Doug rubbed his hand across the scar in the hot Alabama sun as if trying to erase a chalkboard of memories. He understood he might never completely escape the questions, the whispered comments, the sideways looks regarding his past, but he was attempting to cope. He shouldered his rifle to begin his next circuit of guard duties.

He could walk the route with his eyes closed. This time he did. His shift would end soon, and he scrunched his eyes together and dreamed of lying down in the shade. He hadn't had much interaction with the other GIs at the camp. Not really, even though Camp Rucker had been his home for several weeks now. Located near Dothan, Alabama, the military installation was one of the hundreds across the country taking newbies and cranking them out into soldiers for the war effort in Europe and the Pacific.

Doug didn't like much at Rucker, but he knew it probably wouldn't be any different anywhere else. At least the work here in Alabama, like his basic training at Camp Blanding in Florida earlier in the summer, was better than his empty family home back in New York. The walls had grown so close together there. The rooms so empty. At night, when it was just him and the hired help in the house, Doug swore those walls could talk. He heard voices, noises, laughing, accusing. Maybe the voices were only in his mind. He only spent two nights in the house after his father's death back in April before he checked himself into a hotel. From his suite on the top floor, he could look out across miles of New York City. At night, the lights glittered like stars in the vastness of heaven. But even safe in the hotel, when he closed his eyes and tried to sleep, the images rushed back at him. So much blood. Too much blood.

He tried to read his Bible. One night in the hotel.

God is our refuge and strength, a very present help in trouble.[1]

"No!" He said the word out loud. Room service arrived. A late night snack of toast and jam. He tried to eat, but the toast stuck in his throat and wouldn't go down. *God was no refuge,* Doug thought. No sanctuary or safe haven. At least none that he could feel. God could have prevented this darkness, but God wasn't around when God was needed most. It wasn't just his mother's passing that weighed him down so heavily. It was bad, sure, but it was all the horror that happened in the years following.

The next morning he checked out of the hotel and enlisted. After his enlistment, he had been assigned to a rifle group: Third Platoon, Company B, in the 264th Regiment of the 66th Division. The nickname for the 66th was the Black Panthers, and they proudly wore a patch of the snarling ebony beast set against an orange background on their uniforms, but Doug

---

[1] Psalm 46:1.

didn't feel like much of a snarling animal. He felt like a green plant that withered and died. He came to the end of his guard route again. The hot Alabama sun felt unrelenting.

"Hiya, Hollywood," a voice called out. "You're gonna get yerself court-martialed for sleeping on the job."

"I wasn't sleeping." Doug's voice was quick on the defense.

Private Salvatore DiPrimo laughed at his fellow recruit. "If you had a cot, you'd be in dreamland. But relax. I've got next shift. You're a free man, Hollywood. Go back to the barracks or something. Try getting a real nap for once."

"Just thinking about something, that's all. And haven't I asked you a hundred times to stop calling me Hollywood?"

"Aw, don't get your shorts in a wad, Hollywood. Whaddya expect me to call you? You're the kid of big shot movie stars, a fella who's been in all the papers."

"Back off, DiPrimo."

"Look, I don't mean nothing by it. I know you had nothing to do with what happened with your old man." Sal twisted a finger into Doug's chest. "It's just a little friendly needle, that's all, so you can handle it. I know some of these bums around here look at you funny. Guys will always ask questions and say crap about you. You don't wanna be taking guff from nobody. Just fuhgeddaboudit—that's what I say."

Doug scrunched his eyes closed again. Sal apparently didn't mind, because he continued to babble. He hadn't stopped talking since he and Doug were first thrown together at Camp Blanding for Basic Training. Sal was a short kid, maybe 5"4", but he imagined himself as a tough guy, somebody who had all the answers thanks to his experiences on the streets of Brooklyn. Like a bantam rooster in the henhouse, Sal moved and talked with a braggadocio he used to offset his diminutive size.

Doug knew exactly to what Sal was referring. When the relentless probing by the Hollywood press had become intolerable following the tragic boating accident that claimed Kate Tillman's life in 1939, Doug and his father moved to Westchester County, north of Manhattan, where they lived for the next several years. They returned to the home where Big Jim Tillman had lived as a boy before he headed to Hollywood and began a decade-long career as a matinee idol of the silent film era. Questions were still unanswered as to what exactly happened to Kate, but at least the Hollywood gossipmongers were kept at bay by the move east.

Over time, a gulf grew between father and son despite the change of scenery, and that made the teenage years for Doug quite difficult. In addition, the pace and attitude of the people in New York City proved a radical change from his life in southern California. Sal was a prime example of that. The little man had decided Doug was going to be his pal almost from the moment they were assigned adjoining bunks. There was little Doug could do about it. Sal was not someone he would have chosen as a friend, but he was trying his best to make it work.

"Like I say, I only give you crap so you'll handle it better." Sal droned on. "Just like we do in the neighborhood. Get it?"

Doug opened his eyes and saw Sal staring straight at his face. "Yeah, thanks for the advice," Doug said. "What would I do without you?" His sarcasm was lost on the New Yorker, who launched into a new sermon on what he would do if he were running the Army.

Doug wiped his brow with his forearm. The sweat made the scar glisten. He reached in between the buttons of his shirt and stroked a small medallion bearing the design of a dolphin and a frog that hung on a chain alongside his dog tags. He smiled at Sal's diatribe, but his thoughts were with a time when his life was so different. A time when his family was together. A time when God still cared. It didn't matter now. Doug closed his eyes again. He was numb. Just numb.

All he wanted now was feel better. The Army wasn't going to do that for him, but at least he didn't need to be home anymore, alone with the silent walls, the voices of accusation in his head, the memory that couldn't be erased of a deep pool of his father's blood.

CHAPTER THREE

8 August 1944

The North Sea

Willy Müller struggled down a narrow hatch that led to the control room of the German submarine U-474. He had pale blue eyes and a keen Aryan face and, although he was only sixteen years old, already stood six foot three. Unfortunately, his height held no advantage in the tight confines of the U-boat. At the bottom of the hatch, Willy paused and gave a final glance upward at the azure sky. The lid on the conning tower clanged into place.

"How are we feeling today, Müller?"

Willy's face reddened at the query from Wachoffizier Karl Burtzlaff, the U-boat's second-in-command, who had emerged out of the darkness and now stood next to the boy.

"Fine, Sir. I don't know what went wrong yesterday, but I can assure you it won't happen again."

"I thought we might see a bad piece of sausage at the bottom of all your vomiting," Burtzlaff laughed heartily. "But don't feel bad. Lots of good men turn green during roll training.[2] And many of them have had far more sea time than you."

"Thank you, Sir. I still feel embarrassed. I just wished I could have done my job."

"It takes time. Rest easy, there will be no diving today. Kaleu[3] says we'll work with the torpedoes."

Willy gave a wan smile, saluted the officer, and then headed to the bow of the sub where the circular hatch into that compartment was smaller than the one connecting the conning tower to the control room. He stepped through awkwardly and needed to place his right hand on the wall above the opening to keep his balance. A cotton banner was affixed there, already turning moldy in the damp conditions. The motto for the Kreigsmarine was splashed across the flag: We follow the Fuehrer's Orders.

Isn't that what I've been doing my whole life, Willy thought, —following orders?

So far, life on the U-Boat wasn't as glorious as he envisioned. He'd snuck away last February from his Bavarian home to chase his dream of sailing the high seas for the Fatherland. He was allowed to enlist in the Kriegsmarine, even though he was underage, and was assigned to a U-boat crew. Once the terror of the high seas, German submarines had lost their advantage to the Allies' superior equipment and manpower. The attrition rate in the U-boat corps was the highest of all the Nazi naval forces. Teenagers like Willy were being used to fill the vacancies.

---

[2] "Roll drills" are when a submarine simulates turns at full speed or hurriedly dives below the surface. They are complex tasks that necessitate repeat practice.
[3] A German submarine commander frequently held the rank of Kapitänleutnant, or Kaleu for short.

His older brother, Ludwig, had left home twelve months earlier. He was the pride of the family, of their whole village of Waldberg for that matter. Smart, athletic, and personable, Ludwig could do it all. Like the others of their generation, the Müller brothers were inculcated with the Nazi worldview through their participation in the Hitler Youth (HY) programs. Ludwig was a poster child for the movement. Named the youngest sectional leader at fifteen, he posted the highest marks in various HY national competitions, and he had received special recognition from the Fuehrer himself. When a Panzer tank division, to be manned principally by graduates of Hitler Youth, was created, it was no surprise that Ludwig was selected to be the lead junior officer. Emboldened by his brother's example, Willy ran away to make his own contribution to the cause. Since 1 June 1944, Willy had been stationed in Bergen, Norway, learning how to be a submariner. The lessons had not gone as easily as he expected.

Willy pushed his way through a cluster of men to reach his bunk on the port side. The bow housed the living quarters for more than half the crew. Its small space was cramped further by racks in the aisle that held the sub's armed payloads until their placement into the launching tubes. The torpedoes were a constant reminder of how precious every inch of space was in a U-boat. Willy was uncomfortable with the weapons being so close to his bunk, and no matter the temperature in the sub, the torpedoes always felt chillingly cold.

He reached into a pocket of his trousers and removed a small, silk bag containing a crude wooden carving he made ten years earlier for the family's Nativity display. It had become his talisman since he joined the Kriegsmarine, a piece of home to keep him sane. He traced the etching on its base, placed there by his brother in the days before he left to join his Panzer unit. The etching read, Be a Leader, Not a Follower! It was typical of his brother's philosophy on life, but the message made an ironic contrast to the exhortation at the hatch of his new home.

How can I possibly be a leader? Willy thought. *I will always be following you, Ludwig.*

Sighing, he put the trinket away, picked up a large wrench at the foot of his berth and moved into position for that day's drills.

By mid-afternoon, the temperature inside the U-boat peaked at near one hundred degrees. Sweat poured off Willy and the other men, although to call it merely "sweat" was an understatement. The conditions took these green sailors to their limit. As uncomfortable as the heat might have been, it wasn't U-474's biggest problem. Forty-eight perspiring men in a confined space gave off a horrendous smell. Hygiene facilities were minimal, and potable water was too precious to be wasted on bathing or laundry, even if space would have been available for such things. The ever-present diesel fumes only added to the discomfort.

Willy's hands were greasy. He tightened a bolt, wiped the sweat from his brow with his shoulder and then returned his focus to his work.

"Whee-eew, I don't think I can take much more of this stink." Dieter Lange pinched his nose and sidled close to where Willy was working. Dieter was as wide as Willy was tall and was Willy's partner at one of the torpedo stations.

"I don't know what's worse," Willy said, "—the B.O. or that awful cologne Hesse wears."

Jurgen Hesse, the eldest crewmember, was the frequent target of inside jokes between the two teenagers, who'd formed a bond in the early days of training. With no showers, veteran submariners often used cheap perfume in an attempt to mask their ripe aroma.

"You two fools joking around again?" Hesse stood near the corner of the workstation. He shook his head in disgust and scowled at the impudent youngsters. "Just so you know…we all stink, pigs. There's nothing we can do about it. And if you don't pay attention to your business, we won't have to worry about how it smells around here because we'll all be wearing water overcoats."

Hesse was the Mechaniker, the chief mechanic, in charge of the seamen who serviced and loaded the torpedoes. Weapons work was a dirty, time-consuming job but a necessary responsibility if a U-boat was to survive. The dreary daily routine was made more monotonous because these were only training runs and not real action. Already the young sailors had grown sloppy in their duties.

"Why doesn't the Kaleu just surface so we can get some fresh air in here?" Dieter asked with a whine.

Hesse threw down his wrench and it clanged on the deck. "Why don't you just ask the Kaleu if we can paint a bulls-eye on the conning tower? That way when we surface, it will be easier for the enemy to blow us out of the water." The grizzled sailor stepped menacingly at a cowering Dieter.

Willy cut in between them. "Leave him alone. He didn't mean anything. It does stink down here."

"What stinks, beanpole, is little boys like you two fouling up what used to be something to be proud of. You kids are all going to get us killed."

"That's enough, men," interrupted Burtzlaff, observing the confrontation from a short distance away. "We've got enough to worry about with the enemy. We don't need to be fighting amongst ourselves."

Hesse turned away with a condescending wave of his arm. By the look on his face, it was clear he didn't think much of the second-in-command's constant defense of these inexperienced youngsters, but he had been in the Kriegsmarine long enough to know a sailor doesn't win when he challenges an officer.

"Pay attention to your duties," Burtzlaff said to the two boys. "The Kaleu says we'll be going topside soon and heading back to port. In the meantime, I'll see if I can get Zimmerman to play something to pick up our spirits."

The pair of teens returned to their tasks. Soon the silence was broken by music coming through the U-boat's sound system. Dirk Zimmerman, the Chief Radio Operator, often played records on a phonograph or picked up a radio station when it was in range. The crew always welcomed the diversion.

"Komm und spiel mit mir ..."

"I know that one," Dieter said. "'Come and Play with Me' by Hans Albers." The boy took a piece of chalk and made a mark on the wall above one of the torpedo tubes. "That makes the score seven to six in my favor."

"I should have caught that," Willy said with a grunt. "I saw that movie with my parents." Willy started singing along with the song. Dieter joined him. Hesse grumbled at the music but made no other comment. When the record finished, another song soon flowed from the nearby speaker. "Geg ruhig zu einer anderen ..."

"Ah, the Chilean Nightingale," Willy said. "Go Quietly to Another." He placed a mark on the makeshift scoreboard.

"Rosita Serrano." Dieter spoke the singer's name with a heavy sigh. "I'd give my right hand to see her in person. A friend at school kept a photograph of her taped to the inside of his locker. She was wearing this blouse ... you could see almost everything!"

Willy blushed like a neon sign, but he tried to act nonchalant. "My brother's got some of her records in his collection. I've seen her picture." He looked around to see if anyone else was listening, his eyes darting back and forth. He lowered his voice to a level Dieter could barely hear. "My brother has lots of records. Even Swing."

"Negro music!"[4] Dieter exclaimed too loudly.

Willy was caught off-guard by his friend's squeal, and he bobbled a part to a torpedo he was holding in an impromptu juggling act.

"Müller! Pay attention! You're getting as sloppy as Lange."

"Sorry, Hesse, I guess my mind was elsewhere."

"Get it back. That's a vital piece of equipment you've got in your grubby hands there."

"It's only a homing device. What's the big deal?"

---

[4] Listening to Swing music was looked down upon in Germany due to its association with blacks and Jews.

Hesse came closer to Willy and ran his hand alongside the smooth outer skin of the underwater bomb. He found the cavity where the homing device would be placed into position. "You respect everything about these fish, so they don't turn on you." Hesse closed his eyes halfway and for a moment looked caught in reverie. His voice took on a faraway sound as he continued, "In the early days it was easy. Just set it, put the fish in the water and hope it blows up when it runs into something. But not now."

Willy shrugged, a confused look on his face.

Hesse shot him a look of disdain. He moved over by one of the torpedo tubes where a sheet of moisture had condensed on the hull above it. "Come here and pay attention." He drew two oblong figures with his index finger. "Say this is the U-474 ... and this over here would be our target."

Willy and Dieter nodded.

"Our fish are acoustic torpedoes. When we fire one, that same homing device you're holding right now seeks the noise from the target's screws."[5] Hesse drew a line from the smaller shape in his diagram to the larger one. "But if the homing device isn't set properly, it might pick up the noise from our screw instead. Guess what happens then. Wham! The fish comes back right at us. We call that a circle runner." His finger made the line for the torpedo swing back to the U-474. With a flourish, he wiped off the submarine drawing with a closed fist.

"Is that really possible?" Willy gulped.

"You heard what happened to U-851, didn't you?" Hesse said, one eyebrow raised.

---

[5] Slang for a submarine's propellers.

"Of course. I read about it at the enlistment office when I joined. Those men were glorious in giving their lives for the Fatherland."

Hesse shook his head.

"Goebbels' goons have got you believing everything, don't they? U-851 was 'glorious' only if that means blowing yourself up. A circle runner got them, not the Allies. Some idiot kid just like you probably didn't set the homing device properly."

Willy wasn't going to let Hesse get away that. "I don't believe you. Why would our leaders lie to us?"

"You boys can think whatever you want, but I've been at sea long enough to trust only in what I can control. Mark my words—you take care with that device, or we'll be as gloriously dead as U-851." The older sailor turned away and went out the bow hatch.

Willy flipped the device over and back slowly in his hand. He stared at the mechanism with a newfound respect for its importance.

Dieter had been silent during Hesse's lecture. "I think that pain in the neck was just trying to scare us. He just wants to make sure we do everything right. There's no way our leaders wouldn't tell us the truth."

Willy replied with a smile and a punch to his friend's shoulder. "He sure had us going, didn't he? Of course our leaders wouldn't lie to us."

The two teens resumed their work in a silence that lasted nearly a half hour. Finally, Willy spoke again. "You ever wonder if he's right? You know—deep down in your gut. I mean … maybe what we're doing here is all a big mistake?"

"What?" Dieter said quickly. "That crazy fool. No way."

"I'm not just talking about Hesse." Willy set down his wrench. "I mean all of this war. Are we really defending the cause of the Fatherland, or is there something else going on we don't know about?"

"Shh!" Dieter glanced around. "How dare you doubt the Fuehrer? We're the greatest race in the world." Dieter took a peek over his shoulder and stepped closer to Willy. "Think it through, my doubting friend. Our enemies populate their countries with apes, rats, and mongrels. They placed all the blame on Germany for the last war; they tried to take over our banks and steal all our money. Now they're bombing our cities, killing our women and children." The boy scanned his surroundings again as if he couldn't trust a soul. He looked Willy in the eye. "Here's all you need to know—one word: revenge. The enemy wants you dead. You are superior to him. So you make sure you kill him first. Understood?"

Willy nodded.

Dieter slapped the other boy on the shoulder. Heartened by his own recitation of the Party line, he bent down to resume charging the battery for a torpedo.

Willy's smile, however, melted once the other boy turned away.

And a hint of doubt crept over his face.

CHAPTER FOUR

14 June 1944

Normandy, France

Sergeant Dan Gibbons lay on his belly in a tunnel of overgrown vegetation while enemy machine gun fire kicked up dirt in the road in front of him.

His body shivered from a feeling that the world was closing in on him. He felt trapped. It was mid-afternoon, but the interlaced silhouettes from the bushes and trees above him made it look more like twilight. His ambulance crew had been divided among four different infantry units the previous evening, and his platoon had pushed out before dawn, moving through the region of Normandy known as *The Hedgerows.* The locals called the area *Les Bocages.*[6]

"They've got the 'cages' part right, that's for sure," Dan muttered to himself. With a hand on the top of his helmet to keep it in place, he raised up for a cautious appraisal of his situation. Hedgerows, long dirt embankments at least three to five feet high and the same distance in width, stood guard on

---

[6] Means, roughly, "the woods," or "a rustic region."

each side of the narrow country lane where his group was stalled. The sides of the mounds were gnarled with thorn-filled shrubs, while branches of fruit trees at the top stretched out to form a thick canopy. It might have been a pretty scene, had not bullets been whizzing past.

"Well," Dan muttered again, a little louder this time, "as Laurel used to say ... or was it Hardy ... this certainly is a fine mess."

"It certainly is," another soldier called out between bursts of gunfire, giving the same reply to Dan's comment as the famous comic pair had done with each other so often in their movies.

A wry smile spread across Dan's face before he got back to business. He scanned the area, trying to see if he could pin-point where the fire was coming from. He remembered studying the region in history class during high school. The hedgerows dated back nearly two thousand years, to the time when the Roman Empire controlled the Western world. Con-structed for agricultural reasons, they also provided great military value to ancient warriors and now to their modern counterparts as well. It was difficult to detect the enemy's movements inside the dense foliage. Another staccato burst from a machine-gun, hidden somewhere in the brush ahead, planted Dan's face back into the dirt.

"Hey medic—keep yer melon down!" shouted a rifleman yards away from him. He was hidden in foliage so thick that Dan hadn't seen him.

"Why's he shooting at me?" Dan called out. "Can't he see the red cross?" He twisted the medical brassard on his upper arm, hoping to make it more visible to the concealed enemy shooter, but the response was only more gunfire. Dan rolled into some blackberry bushes where the soldier, who had warned him moments ago, was concealed.

"That old boy don't much care what y'all wearing," the soldier said. "He's gonna shoot anyone he don't know."

Despite the circumstances, Dan chuckled. "Where you from, pal?"

"Pigeon Forge, Tennessee. But I bet y'all couldn't tell."

Another burst of gunfire spattered the road. The pair ducked a falling branch that broke away when hit by German bullets.

"This is crazy," Dan said. "Crawling along, not knowing what we're up against. What kind of way to fight a war is this?"

"It's all cat and mouse with the Krauts. We push them. They push us. There's thousands of 'em still around here. Where y'all been, anyway? We've been doing this best part of a week now."

"Sitting on the beach for the past five days, if you can believe it," Dan said. "Once we landed, it took the Army awhile to sort out where they were sending us."

"Ain't that just the Army's way."

Dan grinned and pushed a branch away from his eyes. "So, if this is nothing new to you, what are we going to do then?"

"Don't worry, Sarge. I'm fixing to take care of this rascal."

The Tennessean slowly moved into a crouch, raising an M-1 to his shoulder. When the leaves in the bushes at the far end of the lane moved and smoke curled through the branches, he squeezed the trigger. The spit of the enemy's machine-gun instantly fell silent.

"Like I said, that old boy won't be bothering us no more," the soldier said while nonchalantly reloading his rifle. He wet his thumb and rubbed it across the sight at the end of the muzzle. "It's like squirrel hunting. If y'all just keep after them critters, they ain't no problem."

The Pride of Pigeon Forge moved ahead, and Dan hurried to keep up with his new guardian angel. The unit advanced fifty yards to where the lane came to an end. It was barricaded by a crossing section of hedgerow. To their left was the entrance to the next field, bordered by more mounds of brush and trees. With a seemingly endless supply of these protected pastures, the Allies' march inland was a halting movement of advances and retreats. The next piece of ground to be claimed was about three hundred yards wide and twice as long. An abandoned Sherman tank was stuck in the hedge near the entrance, and a large hole in its exposed underbelly was evidence of a fatal attempt to climb over the dirt row.

"Take cover behind that tank, boys," the platoon sergeant called. "Grab some grub or a smoke. We'll be heading out in ten."

The men sank to sitting positions behind the shelter of the Sherman. Soldiers pulled C-rations out of their rucksacks, opened tins, and munched on cold meat and vegetable stew. Others passed around Lucky Strikes. Whatever a man had, he shared with his fellow soldier. Dan took a sip of water from his canteen, peeled a paper wrapper off a chocolate bar and wolfed it down. Somehow, a tin of hash just wasn't very appealing right now. Aside from his new friend, the soldier from Tennessee, he knew nobody in the platoon. He wondered how his fellow medics, GM, Reb, and Bobby were doing in their respective assignments.

Dan glanced around the tank to survey the meadow that lay in front of them. They'd need to cross it soon to get to wherever it was they were going. He didn't like the thought of being out in the open, totally exposed and without a weapon. He slumped back against the tank.

The image of the meadow stayed in his mind. When he closed his eyes, he pictured a young woman walking along with him, hand in hand in a different field. It was back in Cleveland, and that field had changed everything.

***

Her name was Eileen Mannen, and she was just about the best thing Dan had ever seen. Actually, they'd met years earlier, when Dan was in school with one of her brothers. Since she was a couple of years behind him, he never gave her much thought. Time went on and she graduated from high school, intent on heading to college in the fall. They met again in the late summer of 1943, at a wedding just after his officer training program fell through. He was sitting glumly at a table nursing a glass of punch when she walked up to him and said, "Bob Feller or Kenny Keltner—who'd you rather buy a sandwich for?"

There was an unmistakable spark in her voice. Dan glanced up at a striking young lady, all blessed five-foot-eight inches of her, and wondered why she looked so familiar. "Bob Feller throws the best fastball the Indians have ever seen," Dan said. "But I'd take Keltner out to lunch. Any third baseman that can flash the leather like that and stop DiMaggio's fifty-six game hitting streak is worth the price of a ham and cheese and a double malted at least."

She laughed, a deep belly laugh as if she wasn't holding anything back. "You don't remember me do you?"

Dan started to say something and then paused, knowing he couldn't bluff his way forward with this girl. He shook his head.

"I'll tell you what," she said. "Instead of Keltner, why don't you take me out to lunch instead? I'll fill you in then on where you know me from. Tuesday?"

Dan nodded.

"But ... you need to ask me first." The girl looked at him expectantly, saying nothing more.

Dan paused, a brief show of consternation swept over his face before he clued in to what she meant. He gave her his broadest grin. "Would you have lunch with me?"

"I'd be delighted." The girl laughed again, kindly, and tossed back her shoulder-length, mocha-colored hair. "You know Mawby's at Cedar and Lee?"

"Know it? Those burgers with the grilled onions sprinkled with paprika. I lived on those when I was at Carroll."

"Noontime? Good. I'll see you then. But if you're secretly a Yankees fan," she added with a mischievous grin, "I'll never speak to you again."

Then she was gone, just like that. She didn't look like the type of girl who'd ask a boy out on a date. Technically, she hadn't. She'd allowed him to ask her, and she did it so sweetly, with so much fun in her eyes. Dan knew that any girl who liked sandwiches and baseball was going to be a girl he absolutely needed to get to know better.

They'd been together ever since.

She came from a large family—her, a little sister Mary, and five brothers. That's how come she wasn't afraid of joking around with boys. Being the elder daughter, by eight years, she helped her mother with a lot of the work around their home. Her mom was a sweet woman but suffered from migraines. When the really bad ones left the poor woman lying in bed for days, the burden of the household fell onto Eileen. She shouldered the responsibility with grace and a grin. Even still, Dan could tell she longed for something else.

"A house of my own one day," she said flat out one afternoon when he asked her. "Mary will be old enough to look after herself soon, and Dad ... well, he's always figured out a way to get along. Mom will be okay because there'll be fewer of us in the house. I just think it's time for me."

Eileen didn't resent the responsibility growing up; Dan could sense that. It was more that she wanted the freedom to be in charge of her own life. She was old enough now to be her own person. Marriage would provide that environment for her, even though she'd be making decisions with a life partner. Dan had no doubts about her affection for him, and he knew she liked him for much more than just being a gentleman. He could tell it when they kissed.

One of their last dates before he headed overseas was at Edgewater Park, a recreation area along Lake Erie where Dan had spent so many days with his brothers during his childhood. Walking on the beach, tossing stones into the water from a bleached piece of driftwood, the two of them didn't say much, but it was evident how they felt about each other. They climbed the hill from the sand and found a large, open area of grass just beyond the sandlot where a game was being played. If it wasn't for the sight of the Terminal Tower off in the distant skyline, the spot might have looked just like a meadow out in the country. They held hands and looked deeply into each other's eyes.

"Promise me you'll come home," she said.

"I promise," Dan said.

"Promise me you won't try to do anything heroic."

Dan looked at her a long time when she said that. He didn't give her an answer.

"Promise me, Dan. Don't volunteer for anything that puts you in harm's way. I don't care if you do big things over there or not. I just want you home alive."

Dan looked around. At the seagulls flying overhead. At the small whitecaps on the lake, caused by the breeze. It seemed an eternity went by without a word between them.

Finally, he took her face in his hands and spoke. "I love you, Eileen."

When he said that, her eyes sparkled but words would not come immediately. It was almost as if she was too overwhelmed to respond. At last, she reached up and caressed Dan's cheek. "I love you too."

They held each other for a long time, there in the meadow, both thinking of the future, both worried about the unknown.

***

"Hey you muttonheads, shake a leg!"

The noncom's voice broke into Dan's thoughts and snapped him back to Normandy. The soldiers stood up behind the tank, rechecked their gear, and loaded ammo into their weapons. The next piece of French soil needed to be taken.

"Let's head out!" the sergeant called, and the unit began pushing into the meadow.

The soldiers walked in single file with good spacing between them in case of drawing fire. Dan's eyes darted back and forth between the lines of bushes on the distant perimeter. The field provided little cover. A few scattered boulders and haystacks. It was an easy place for a man to get mown down.

The first shot rang out, clear and cold. A bullet hit in the grass just ahead of the private taking the point.

"Take cover!" the soldier yelled, and the men scrambled to do so. Dan flung himself on the dirt. Another bullet zipped overhead. Machine gun fire broke out. *Rat-a-tat-tat.* German gunners were nested in the brush on both flanks. The Americans were caught in a crossfire.

"Back to the opening!" He heard a yell and felt someone smack his helmet. Dan found his feet and sprinted back to the abandoned tank. He was one of the last ones there. A quick count told him they hadn't lost a man. Fire still rained down on the field.

The men huddled together. Bullets pinged against the other side of the tank. "Damn Krauts," the platoon leader screamed aloud what everyone else was thinking. He looked up at the sky and assessed the position of the late afternoon sun. "We got to get to the far side to hook up with the rest of the unit before it gets dark."

The sergeant dropped to one knee and drew a diagram in the dirt as if designing a play on a sandlot. He scratched out a rectangle with a crooked twig.

"Judging from where we're drawing fire, I'm guessing the Jerries are here and here." He marked two circles along the longer sides of the rectangle to indicate the enemy positions and then made a third for their place behind the tank. "Okay, here's the plan. We'll send one patrol through the brush this way. Another patrol will go the other way. The two patrols will flank the Krauts and take them out." He waved the stick along the sides, and with dramatic strokes, made a large X over each of the enemy circles on his dirt map.

Soldiers voiced their desire to volunteer, and men were quickly selected to take part. When the dust had settled, the platoon leader turned to Dan. "Sergeant," the fellow noncom said. "You stay here with the others until I give the all clear sign."

Dan nodded. He had no desire to try and outflank the enemy when he couldn't even carry a weapon. He had found it idiotic to have taken firearms instruction during basic training and now not have even so much as a handgun to use. Captain Levine had been adamant, however, about following the prohibition against medical personnel being armed.

The two attacking groups hurried through the brush and tall grass to take out the snipers. Dan reclaimed a seat alongside the tank, the ground comfortably soft from earlier rains. One of the remaining GIs, a private with hollow circles under his eyes, peeked over the front end of the Sherman. Bursts of gunfire from distant fields could be heard at irregular intervals. Dan unhooked the medical bags hanging from his belt to take inventory of their contents.

"You a real doc?" the private asked.

"Not even close. I was getting ready for law school."

"Then how did you ever—"

"It's a long story," Dan said with a shrug. "Let's just say what the Army had in mind didn't work out as planned."

The private grinned and then took another nervous peek over his shoulder toward the open field. He fiddled with the bolt of his rifle, engaged it, and then pulled it back. When a surprisingly loud volley rang out in the distance, he dropped his M-1.

"Not like training is it?" Dan asked.

"I ain't been through anything like this," the private answered, red-faced.

"Me neither. Just stick together and do what we were taught. We'll be fine."

The private smiled, tight and uncertain, and returned to his watch of the field.

Dan picked up one of his supply bags. The pouch was filled with Emergency Medical Tags (EMTs). When a medic worked on a wounded man during combat, he would affix an EMT to the soldier, detailing the treatment that had been provided. Sometimes an EMT would need to carry the tragic news of the cause of death. He was carrying an ample supply of these tags.

His other bag, at least a third larger than its partner, carried most of his medical materials—tools of the trade such as bandages, scissors, and vials of medicine. He recalled his initial days at Fort Riley when first aid work felt foreign to him.

He became more comfortable as training progressed, but now the potential for working on a wounded soldier was never more real. He couldn't help but wonder how he would react. He touched the breast pocket of his uniform. Inside lay his most important piece of equipment, at least in his mind anyway. Nestled there was a small leather pouch that contained a rosary. It had been blessed by his recently-ordained brother, Tom, and the rosary was a comforting reminder of life back home. His thoughts were interrupted by a noise that sounded like a woodpecker hammering at a tree trunk.

"What's that?" Dan asked. The staccato beat had the same pace as when the larger machine-guns were fired but not with the same tonal intensity. The frenzied activity was startling, but then just as quickly, the field went silent.

"Burp-gun," the private told him. "Maybe you medics didn't cover that in training. It's like a machine pistol. It means our guys have closed in, because it's too hard for the Jerries to use their bigger guns."

Then ... "You hear that?" Dan said.

All was quiet.

"I think we got 'em," the private said, his voice low.

A series of whistles, two long and one short, rang out from one side of the field, followed shortly by its echo from across the way—the signal from the patrols that it was safe to advance.

Dan and the remaining soldiers moved into the meadow. The front of the group advanced about thirty yards when the raiding soldiers emerged from the brush to reconnect with their mates. Dan was at the rear of the pack, barely into the field, when a shriek raced across the sky.

"Incoming! Hit the deck!"

A mortar shell smashed into the ground and exploded. Dan and two infantrymen sprinted back to the entrance. A second payload struck moments later where they had just vacated, and it was followed by a third that set a haystack on fire.

"Medic!"

The painful cry rang across the pasture.

A knot twisted in Dan's gut. He grabbed his bags and was ready to sprint out into the open field, but another artillery shell landed only yards away. Dan removed his helmet and ran a forearm across his brow. He needed to do something ... and fast.

"Guys, can you give me some cover?" Dan asked the soldiers who had retreated with him.

"Sure, Sarge. What's your plan?"

"They'll be focusing on any movement, so we need to give the Jerries the old razzle-dazzle."

"Give it to us square. What do you need us to do?"

"Just like in football. Fake one way and then go another. We'll start off with you bracketing me, but then we'll dazzle them the other way."

The soldiers stared at him, confused.

"You two take off away from where our man is down. Have your guns blazing, but aim high because we don't want to hit any of our boys in the bushes. Run in zigzags ... just like they taught us. That should be enough to draw their fire and let me get safely to where your buddy is."

The men checked their weapons to make certain they were fully loaded. With a nod, the soldiers moved into the meadow, firing rapidly.

The timing chant of one thousand one, one thousand two resounded in Dan's brain. In his mind, he was back in college again.

***

The 1942 John Carroll Blue Streaks were in a timeout, players huddled around their coach. The scoreboard at the back of the end zone displayed an 8 to 3 advantage for their archrivals, the Case Tech Rough Riders. The football rested on Case's fourteen-yard line. The back judge of the officiating crew was ready to call the game. His pistol was in the air, set to signal the game's conclusion the moment Carroll's final play was complete. The Blue Streaks were seconds away from a difficult loss.

"Boys, this is what we're going to do," Coach Lenny Brickman announced with a shower of tobacco juice from the large piece of chew in his cheek. "It's time for the old Razzle-Dazzle."

Dan's face went white. His coach loved to create trick plays with colorful names. Dan knew the play but it had never worked before in practice.

"You sure, Coach?" Dan asked. "Wouldn't we better off having Scottie pass it to Anthony?"

"Nonsense." Brickman chuckled. "That's just what those stinking Rough Riders think we're going to do. You're our captain. You lead us to victory."

The players grunted in the huddle. They put their hands in for the cheer, ran back onto the field, and moved into formation on the muddy turf.

Dan took his position at right guard, hoping the defender across from him couldn't tell his heart was racing. The Carroll quarterback aligned several yards behind the line and barked out signals. After the quarterback yelled "Hut" and received the ball from his center, the rest of the backfield crossed in front of him and headed right. The line of scrimmage disappeared as the two teams surged into each other. The capacity crowd at the annual season-ending game between the two bitter adversaries rose to its feet and cheered in anticipation.

All the men on the field were moving ... except Dan, who didn't come out of his lineman's crouch. The snap from the center to the quarterback was a ruse; the ball lay on the ground not more than a few feet from where Dan was positioned. As the backfield behind him moved to his right, the left guard and tackle pulled from their positions and ran past him in the same direction, supposedly to be the escorts around the end.

One thousand one ... One thousand two... Dan counted to himself. The numbers thundered in his head. He fought to keep from starting too soon as he had done every time they attempted Razzle-Dazzle during practice. *"Remember,"* he heard coach's voice in his head, *"get them to think we're going one way, and then go the other."*

The noise from the crowd climbed higher as the Tech defenders closed in on the Carroll quarterback racing towards the far sidelines. Time was up.

Dan reached down, snatched the hidden ball and dashed in the opposite direction.

***

Dan sprinted forward on the Normandy ground toward the wounded soldier.

With each step he could feel the rush of blood through his veins. His body tingled with equal parts of exhilaration and terror. *This is crazy,* he thought. *I'm going to get us all killed.*

A mortar shell exploded near the soldiers as they moved off to his left. They changed their path and kept moving. Dan's plan was working.

After several more strides toward the injured man, however, his right foot stepped into a soft spot and sank above his ankle into the mud. As he furiously tried to extract himself, he could feel his foot coming out of its boot. He stuck both hands into the mire, and with panicked pulls, tried to work his shoe free. The delay gave the Nazi mortar men a chance to spot him in the unprotected area.

They discharged their next round. The high-pitched whine of another treetop flyer drew closer. Dan's tugs became desperate. With a mighty whoosh, the mud released its hold, putting him flat on his back, helpless as an overturned turtle. The enemy's aim was long, fortunately, and the explosion only showered him with a light cloud of debris.

Back on his feet, he resumed his dash to the wounded man. He might have been a lineman, but he ran with the broken field skill of the cleverest halfback. With a dive, which proved unnecessary when the mortar position was taken out by one of the men from the raiding units, he reached the fallen GI.

"Help me! It hurts so bad!" The soldier's leg was a mess of blood and bone.

"Relax," Dan said. "You're going to be okay. We're going get this bleeding stopped and get you out of here."

A quick splash from his canteen washed away the mud on his hands. After he pulled a tourniquet from his pouch, he applied it just above the man's knee to stem the blood gushing from an exposed artery.

If he was nauseated by it all, he didn't show it. He didn't have time to consider his own discomfort. A shot of morphine was administered to the soldier's abdomen, followed by an application of sulfa powder to curb infection around the wound. The tourniquet did its job in slowing the flow from the wound. With cloths from his pouch, he soaked up the blood that covered much of area around the injury and then constructed a crude bandage. Finally, he scribbled notes on an EMT and fastened it to the soldier's shirt to have him ready for transport to a field hospital. In a whirlwind, he handled his first crisis with a quiet calm despite the nervousness that churned his insides.

Two soldiers manned a litter to take their injured comrade back to a safer area. The platoon leader radioed their location to headquarters.

The rest of the unit proceeded, clearing the field and two more to the east without further incident. They reached a highway, alive with activity, and halted to wait for their rendezvous with other platoons from their regiment.

"Nice work," his fellow sergeant told Dan as they sat in the brush along the edge of the road. "Those were some nifty moves. You must've played football in your day. You looked like a pretty good scatback out there. "

"It was nothing," Dan said. "But I was just one of the grunts up front."

He'd never say it out loud, but in his heart Dan beamed with pride. He'd received his first taste of why he was here. To do something that mattered.

Cheers from a distant stadium echoed faintly in his head, and he longed for more.

CHAPTER FIVE

1 September 1944

Camp Rucker, Alabama

Doug Tillman hit the ground, and the buzz from the crowd of soldiers behind him grew. He bent his elbows and spread his arms for balance to steady his M1. Finally comfortable with the setup, he nestled the stock of the rifle into the hollow of his shoulder and aimed at the target.

"C'mon, Hollywood!" Sal yelled. "We're all counting on you."

A momentary look of chagrin washed over Doug. Sal could rattle him like that even when the comment was well intended. Doug focused on the range, ready to squeeze the trigger at the appropriate moment.

The 264th Regiment was in a holding pattern at Camp Rucker. The time to ship out to Europe was imminent, but the uncertainty as to exactly when had led to sloppy training and an increased edginess among the soldiers. Colonel Clifford Garrison, the regimental commander, decided to stage an Infantry Skills Olympics to break up the monotony. Relay races with full packs, contests on weapons assembly, even a challenge to see which squad could build the best foxhole produced spirited competition. The winning platoon was going to get a 3-day furlough, and Doug's unit was tied for first. A kid named Egins was the top shooter from First Platoon. It all came down to his performance versus Doug's.

"Attention, men!" The bellow from Colonel Garrison brought his charges under control. It was hard to tell what commanded more respect: his rank or that he was six-foot-seven and weighed more than 250 pounds. "This final competition will decide the winner between First Platoon and Third Platoon."

"No sweat, Hollywood," Sal called out. "I bet that guy couldn't hit the latrine if he was standing right in front of it." Sal's dig drew laughter from the soldiers standing near him, but something less friendly came from First Platoon.

The remark also did not please Colonel Garrison. "That's enough, private. Do you want me to disqualify your shooter?"

The threat muzzled Sal, although his apish expression still offered an invitation that he was ready if anyone from First Platoon wanted to mix it up with him.

"The rules for this last round are simple," the colonel resumed. "There are targets at 100, 200, and 300 yards. Our two shooters will get an opportunity to make their mark at each distance."

The entire regiment was gathered on a small rise, watching. In the field below, wooden silhouettes in the shape of soldiers sprang up at different spots before being hidden again in the tall grass and bushes.

"Points will be given for accuracy and the speed in which a shot is executed," the colonel added. "A kill shot in five seconds or less will produce a score of fifty points"

The noise from the soldiers reinvigorated. Cheers were raised for their favorites, even from those who didn't have any direct connection to either one of the two rifle platoons.

"Gentlemen, it's your show," the colonel announced with a wave of his massive arm.

Doug won the coin toss and elected to go first. Confident of his ability, he wanted to put the pressure on his opponent. *Keep it slow,* Doug thought … *just a soft, easy pull. Isn't that what you always said, Dad?*

The first target rose from behind a myrtle bush off to his left. Doug confidently squeezed the trigger. The paper target attached to the plywood mannequin was pierced at what would have been mid-chest. Doug's response time was just over five seconds. Judges assessed the result and transmitted the score with signal flags.

"A kill shot in 5.1," the colonel cried out. "That's worth forty-nine points."

Doug's mates whooped and hollered; his score was one point short of a perfect round. They shouted friendly catcalls at Egins, the other shooter, as he moved into place. First Platoon's contestant was equally accurate, a hit center-torso on the target. The execution time was two-tenths slower than Doug's, however, and that gave Third Platoon a small lead.

"Your call, Private Tillman," the colonel said. "You've got the lead, so it's your decision. First or second?"

Doug pondered his option. A breeze fanned the leaves of a nearby sugar maple tree. It was a new element to consider. "I'll let my opponent go ahead of me this time, sir," he said.

"Fine!" the colonel bellowed. "Major Atkinson"—he motioned to an officer on his right, "take over for me for a few minutes, will ya." The major took the colonel's place and instructed Egins to set up his shot. Doug focused his eyes straight ahead, envisioning what he would do when it was his turn again.

"I thought you'd look for the early advantage again." A familiar voice sounded behind Doug's ear, although this time it wasn't yelling; it had more of a friendly tone to it.

It was the colonel. The officer had come alongside while the soldier from First Platoon made his preparations. Doug nodded and then turned back to the targets to keep a watch on the line of trees surrounding the meadow. He wanted to gauge what effect the crosswind that had kicked up might have on his next attempt. Slowly he spoke. "My dad always told me to be certain of your surroundings before you pulled the trigger, sir."

"Big Jim Tillman." Colonel Garrison gave a low whistle. "So the man could actually shoot, eh?"

Doug made eye contact with the officer. "Dad hated it when people said it was staged, sir. He did all of his own stunts, including the shooting. We went to the range all the time."

"When I went to the picture show as a teenager, it was always to see your dad save the day," the colonel said. "I tell ya, Big Jim was a natural in whatever picture he was in. Western, war movie, whatever. And I must say you are his spitting image. We're glad to have you in the regiment."

The intended compliment produced the opposite effect on Doug. He dropped his head and offered no response.

The veteran Army man put a hand on his shoulder. "I've read the papers. I won't pretend to understand what happened with your parents ... but I do know Big Jim Tillman will always be one of my heroes. Try to remember the good times you had with him, son."

"Yes, sir ... thank you. It's just ..."

"It's just *what*?"

Doug looked at the ground again. He said nothing.

"You've just lost your father," the colonel probed, "and now you feel like you've got nothing left?"

"I guess you could say that, sir. Maybe it was the way he went. And before that my mother. Nothing's the same as it once was."

The officer looked at the trees, and then back at the private. "I know it's not easy, son, but you just keep at it. You keep wrestling with everything you're feeling. You'll get it right. In the meantime ... let's see if you can make Third Platoon proud."

Their attention was drawn back to the field by the retort from the rifle of Doug's competitor. Again, the First Platoon shooter hit his target in the chest area, this time from 200 yards. His reaction time was a little slower than his first round, but that was to be expected at the increased distance. Doug would need a similar effort to maintain his lead.

Autumn was approaching, but it was still hot in Alabama. The thermometer had hovered around ninety degrees for more than a week and afternoon showers were a regular occurrence. Thunderheads to the southwest promised another soaking was on the agenda. From his prone position, the rising wind twirled a lock of Doug's hair hanging down his forehead. He took no notice. The target rose from a patch of Christmasberry bushes on the far right perimeter of the range. The wind intensified as he swung his weapon, took aim, and fired. The shot was a good one, but a little closer to the shoulder than the chest. Doug knew it wasn't what was needed even before the judges signaled back the score. The colonel had returned to his place and taken over for the major.

"Private Egins wins the second round with a score of 48," the colonel announced. "He now has 95 points. Private Tillman scored a 46, so he also has 95. It's a dead heat, men."

The First Platoon shooter, by virtue of the higher score on the last round, now controlled the order, and he decided he would make the first attempt in the final round. With a weekend furlough on the line, the competing platoons grew more passionate in their support.

"This poor sap doesn't even know he's already lost!" Sal called out to Doug. "Put him out of his misery, Hollywood, so we can go hit the town."

"Put a sock in it, pipsqueak," a man from First Platoon shouted back.

"I'd tell you where to put it! Sal shouted back. "But you'd probably need directions to know how!"

The barbs between Sal and the soldier grew into harsher insults. The competing groups moved towards each other, and MPs stepped between them to maintain order. Meanwhile, the First Platoon rifleman prepped to hit a target at a distance of three football fields. Trees were staggered in and around the starting position. The trees' convoluted limbs and branches took the wind, now steady, and made it swirl rather than travel in a specific direction.

Colonel Garrison peered at the target area through his binoculars, awaiting a signal from the judges that they were ready. A captain raised two green flags and waved them back and forth.

"Proceed, Private Egins," he instructed, the binoculars never leaving his face.

A target popped out from behind a patch of red sorrel in the center of the field. Egins fired his M1, striking his objective with enough force that splintered plywood poked through the paper target. The judges transmitted the score back to the colonel.

"Right center in a time of 5.1," Garrison intoned. "That's worth a score of 49. Private Egan's total is 144."

"Your boy is toast!" a First Platoon man yelled. "Mr. Movie Star Kid won't be able to handle the pressure."

There was no response from Sal. He glowered and acted as if he wanted to start something, but it was all show. His confidence had taken a hit. "How's Hollywood gonna beat this guy?" Sal moaned in a low voice to himself. "A rich kid like him's never had to handle the heat."

Doug did not watch when his rival made his final attempt. Instead, his attention was riveted on the wind as it moved through the trees. He concentrated on a black tupelo that stood near the targets at the three hundred yard distance. The movement of its leaves indicated a steady crosswind from east to west in that area rather than the erratic pattern he felt where he was standing.

"*Just play the breeze,*" he thought. "*She's blowing pretty good.*"

Doug dropped to his knees, but he was not going to take his set position until he was certain about his calculations. Speed was going to be just as essential as accuracy since his opponent completed his shot in 5.1. He decided he would gamble and eliminate one-half of the range for the sake of time. The first target he shot was only one that had been on the left during the competition; the other four were in the center or to the right. He smiled as he worked into position and shouldered his weapon.

The crowd hushed.

"Ready, sir," he said, his voice barely above a whisper.

Doug took a deep breath and slowly released the air so he would be as still as possible when it was time to fire. The target rose out of some tall grass exactly where he guessed it might. He squeezed the trigger. The echo from the bullet's release rang through the range.

"He missed!" called a man from First Platoon. "Ha! Your golden boy missed the whole thing!" Others from his group began to celebrate their upcoming liberty.

Doug brushed himself off and walked over to Colonel Garrison, who still had his binoculars up against his face. When the colonel pulled them away, he wore a shocked look. "How did you do that?"

Doug gave just a hint of a smile, but his eyes sparkled. "Mom always said when something feels right, you should trust your instincts, sir. I figured the target would be on the left since there hadn't been one there since the beginning."

The judges relayed Doug's results from the field with their signal flags, but Garrison had already seen enough.

"But the shot? I've been in this man's army a lot of years, but I still don't understand your technique, son."

"Kentucky windage, sir ... that's what Dad called it," Doug answered, his smile wider. "When it kicks up like this, you have to compensate. 'Play the breeze,' he would always tell me."

Sal and the rest of Third Platoon were still crestfallen. They couldn't see what the colonel saw. How could Doug have missed the target completely? The rejoicing by their opponents only heightened the disappointment until ...

"Here is the official score for Private Tillman," Garrison called out in a loud voice and turned to face the spectators. "In a new range record for that distance with a time of 4.7, we have a center mass kill for a perfect—."

The colonel never got the chance to finish. Third Platoon erupted in boisterous cheers. First Platoon looked shocked as the implications of the colonel's words became apparent. Doug's bullet had struck the target so cleanly that the plywood never moved. What looked like a miss was actually a furlough-winning shot.

"That was the greatest! I ain't never seen nothing like that," Sal kept saying over and over as he pumped Doug's hand and slapped him on the back. "You can shoot a lot better than your old man ever could."

The loudmouth from First Platoon, irate over his sudden change in fortune, heard what Sal said and felt compelled to make a response. "I just hope he can swim better, too."

Doug whirled to confront whoever made the comment, but Sal was faster. The little man jumped on the back of the soldier and rode him to the ground like a cowboy taking down a bull. Sal landed punch after punch until his arms became entangled with others joining the fight. The melee was finally subdued.

"No way some jerk is gonna get away saying something like that to my friend," Sal crowed as an MP carried him away. A small bump was forming on his forehead, but he was in better shape than his opponent. "I got your back, Hollywood!" he added with a shout and a salute.

The gesture was returned with an ironic smile. Too often, Sal was a pain in the backside, but his loyalty had never wavered. The colonel's kind words, as well as the new enthusiasm of his platoon mates, gave Doug a feeling of comfort that he hadn't felt in years. For the first time in a long time, he felt supported. Like someone cared about him, like someone was on his side.

CHAPTER SIX

5 September 1944

135 nautical miles from Bergen, Norway

The North Sea was completely calm. Thank goodness U-474 was not a sailing vessel, otherwise she would be caught in a dead zone.

U-474 was built in the shipyards at Kiel and launched on 12 February 1944. She was assigned to the 11th Flotilla, based in Vagen Harbor at Bergen, Norway. Germany had controlled Norway since April 1940. Kapitänleutnant Erich Marquardt had worked his inexperienced crew in the relatively safe waters of the North Sea since the first few days of June. If U-474, a Type VIIC submarine, was an automobile, the U-boat would still have a new car feel.

It was just past 1700 hours, and the bright northern sun paled the sky into an azure color that matched the glassy water beneath it. The Kaleu surfaced the submarine and then shut down the diesel. He wanted to test the engine crew's ability to get it restarted quickly. Training was constant for the men under the command of Captain Marquardt, and he especially liked to conduct exercises near a shift change when he thought his crew's concentration might be waning.

Hesse, meanwhile, frustrated by the constant inefficiencies of his young charges, only wanted them out of his sight. He ordered Willy and Dieter topside with buckets and mops to swab the wooden decking at the rear of the U-boat. The boys were the only ones sent outside. It was a senseless exercise when not at port, but the sea veteran wanted to make a point to the teenagers. He was in charge, not them, and they needed to do whatever he ordered.

"That old bear is punishing us for no reason," Dieter said with a whine. "You know what I'd like to do to him?" The corpulent sailor brandished his mop like a sword, but then slipped on the wet boards. The safety cables that framed the planking kept him from slipping overboard.

Willy ignored the false bravado; there was little likelihood there would ever be a confrontation between his friend and their crew chief.

"Why's he so mad at us anyway?" Dieter righted himself, stuck his mop into the bucket at his feet, and leaned against the pole.

"Oh, I don't know," Willy said. "Maybe because you dropped that big wrench on his foot?"

Dieter snickered.

"Actually, I'm glad he sent us out here." Willy grinned. "Just being in this fresh air is worth it." He let his mop fall to the deck and raised his hands to his forehead to shadow his eyes from the sun. He made a slow circle to survey their position. Nothing was moving, not even scavenger birds flying overhead as they usually did when U-474 surfaced close to Bergen. For a boy from Bavaria, the absence of any movement in the water or in the sky was a remarkable sight. A breeze was always blowing at his childhood home, and the area was normally alive with wildlife. Even so, this fresh air was heaven in comparison to the stifling air inside as they did monotonous drill after monotonous drill. Too often, the tight confines inside the U-boat played on the psyche of a boy who loved to be outdoors.

The diesel engines reignited with a rumble, startling Willy from his musing. The engines shut down again just as quickly.

"That was strange." Dieter's voice quivered. "You think everything's alright?"

A surge went through the boat again before Willy could answer, but this time, her power platform remained alive. The sub began to move. It made a slow turn in the still water and looked to set her heading to the east and back to port. In the midst of coming about, the sun glinted off the Flotilla's insignia—a large polar bear at the helm of a U-boat—that was painted on the conning tower. Now aligned to her destination, the U-boat's pace made a gentle increase.

"I don't like this," Dieter said. "Maybe we should go back inside. What if they've forgotten about us and begin to submerge?"

"Relax. The Kaleu would never let that happen. Look busy or Hesse will have another reason to get on you." Willy was not totally convinced himself of the Kaleu's knowledge that they were topside, but he tried to sound confident.

On the advice of his friend, Dieter dragged his mop across the boards. Perhaps to steel his confidence, Dieter began to sing under his breath. His pitch was far from perfect, and Willy smiled at the off-key drone. He reloaded his own mop with water from the pail and swabbed the area at his feet with long, smooth strokes.

Several minutes went by. Willy noticed Dieter's attempt at singing had grown louder and with a more distinguished whine to it. What was odd, however, was that the noise seemed to be coming from behind him even though his friend was several feet in front of his spot.

"Dieter, what are you doing? What kind of song is that supposed to be?"

"What are you talking about?"

"That noise ... how are you making that noise?"

"I think the sun is getting to you, Willy. I haven't been singing for a couple minutes now."

The humming didn't stop. It grew in volume while the two friends stared at each other in puzzlement. Willy turned around to see if the noise might be some kind of echo coming from the diesel. The sun blinded his vision for a moment, but when it cleared, he spotted the source, far off in the distance. A dark spot seemed to have sprung out of the sun, and it grew in size as it moved closer to them. When it got within several hundred yards, they could see it was an airplane. This was a first for the boys. It was rare to see an aircraft aloft in these waters, even when they were much closer to port.

"Hey ... hey!" Dieter shouted up at the plane as he waved his arms back and forth. "Can you see us?"

The plane banked right to make a wide turn around the U-boat just before it reached the rear of their vessel. It appeared to be accelerating as it made the maneuver.

"That's a Messerschmitt Bf109," Dieter boasted. "You may know music better than me, Willy, but I know my airplanes."

It was terribly bright, and with all the reflection, Willy found it difficult to identify the plane despite Dieter's claim. The plane banked to the left again then righted itself. The glare lifted for a moment, and Willy spotted the insignia on the underside of the left wing: a circle comprised of blue and white rings with a red spot in the middle.

"That's not a Messerschmitt." Willy's voice was low. "It's a—."

"Spitfire!" Dieter shouted. "Alarm! Alarm! It's the enemy."

Willy quickly scanned the sky for additional aircraft, but the Spitfire appeared to be going it alone. U-474's position was far from Royal Air Force bases on the east coast of Scotland, but rumors of an Allied invasion of Norway had been a regular topic of conversation among the men since the enemy had landed at Normandy. The lone plane's pilot might have been just as surprised to see the U-boat as the sailors were to see him. In a flash, when the plane got to a 12 o'clock position, the Spitfire stopped its turn and headed back to the boat. The plane dropped from the sky to no more than fifty feet above the water.

"Hit the deck!" Willy shouted. "He's coming after us!"

Dieter was frozen in place, even when the bullets from the Spitfire's machine gun gouged chunks from the wooden decking. Willy pulled him down just before the spray passed by where they were standing. Somehow, as he yanked at his friend, he was able to grab a safety cable and keep both of them from sliding into the sea. A claxon shrieked from a speaker on the conning tower as the crew below realized they were under attack. Nevertheless, they would be of little help if the enemy plane wanted to make another pass. They wouldn't submerge until Willy and Dieter were back below. Sure enough, the Spitfire banked for his second strafing runt.

"Here! Willy said. "Hold this and don't let go." Willy locked Dieter's hands around the cable. "Keep your head down," he added. Willy scrambled to the front of U-474 where an 88mm gun[7] was located. He pulled back on the bolt.

"You know it's not loaded, don't you!" Dieter shouted.

"I know! But maybe I can scare him off." Willy raised the barrel to pose a threat to the Spitfire. It would only move upward about 30 degrees. He was fairly sure the pilot wouldn't know that the gun had no ammunition, so he waved the gun back and forth rapidly and simulated he was returning fire.

The enemy plane spit another volley, only to stop and climb away from what he thought was being sent his direction. Willy could see the pilot's face when he passed over. The man had a perplexed look, as if he couldn't figure out why he wasn't getting any flak from the deck gun.

"There it is, men!" the Kaleu said and pointed. He and three sailors, armed with rifles, had come through the hatch at the top of the conning tower. They fired at the departing plane. The sub's captain knew the gesture would cause little if any damage, but he hoped the show of force would be enough to send the plane back to its airfield.

---

[7] The 88 wasn't an anti-aircraft weapon; it was used by U-boat crews to finish off any boat they had wounded with torpedoes.

The hunch proved correct. The Spitfire waggled his wings at the U-boat and kept moving westward until it disappeared into the shimmering rays of the lowering sun. Willy remained at the deck gun while Dieter clung to the safety cable with a death grip.

The captain watched the plane disappear, then looked at Willy and asked, "What's your name, son?"

"Müller, Kaleu."

"You're part of the torpedo unit, aren't you?"

"Yes sir," Willy said.

The captain chuckled. "You know there is no way you could have fired that gun? It takes three men to operate it, and the shells are in one of the lockers below deck." U-474's leader displayed a broad smile of yellowed teeth through his whiskery face. "That was a brave thing you did, son. Sometimes the best defense is to make the enemy believe you're on the attack. We'll never know for sure what sent him away, but I'm going to believe you made all the difference."

He slapped Willy on the back and gave a patronizing look to Dieter. "Gentlemen … unless you plan on holding your breath until we get back to Bergen, I suggest you join us back below so we may submerge." The captain and the three sailors with the rifles departed through the hatch.

Willy went over and helped his partner to his feet.

"You're a hero," Dieter gushed. "Captain said so. Just like your big brother.

Willy nodded without much of an expression, but inside he was bursting with pride. *Wait until Ludwig hears what I did,* he thought.

He continued down the ladder and forward to his bunk in the bow room. It was time for his break and he wanted to write to his parents and his brother while his showdown with the Spitfire was still fresh in his mind.

CHAPTER SEVEN

22 September 1944

Chartres, France

The ambulance hit another pothole, jolting Dan out of his sleep. He pitched upward, hit the roof of the truck, and bounced down again into his seat.

Most of the Army medical vehicles were converted weapons carriers with hard-roof rear compartments, built by the White Motor Company. The unit's regular truck was in for repairs, and this canvas-topped Dodge spared Dan from a repeat of an incident in August. On that run, he hit his head on the metal top with his helmet, and the contact left his ears ringing.

Dan yawned from sheer boredom as much as a lack of sleep. It looked like they were in for another long night. He glanced around the truck. The other members of his squad looked to be still asleep—or at least trying—slumped on each side of the Red Cross wagon as it rode along with an overnight convoy on the Red Ball Express. Across from him were Bobby and Reb. GMC was alongside Dan. The ambulance's cab was the domain of Smitty and the leader of their mobile medical detachment, Captain Levine. Any one of the squad could have driven the truck, but since Smitty had been a cab driver in New York before the war, it just seemed natural he should be the one behind the wheel.

The night was warm and the rear flaps of the truck were open to let air circulate in the compartment. Dan gazed at the dark French countryside trailing away behind them, his thoughts far away. The truck sent him airborne again, and his helmet pressed against the canvas roof. The roadway was a disaster. The constant stream of supply trucks moving to the front and the Germans bombing raids trying to stop the flow caused extensive damage. Traveling at night on these narrow highways with headlights dimmed by covers, called cat's eyes, made it impossible for Smitty to avoid the potholes no matter how good of a driver he was.

Dan was no longer assigned to an infantry outfit. Once General Omar Bradley's First Army broke through the German lines at St. Lo in July, American forces raced through the French countryside and secured Normandy. Bradley led the First, and along with General George Patton and Third Army, they joined other Allied forces in reclaiming Paris by late August. There was no stopping the push against the Nazis. The front lines now stretched more than three hundred miles from the main supply depots back along the Atlantic coast. Allied bombs had destroyed most of the French rail lines to impede the Germans' retreat, so another way was needed to keep gasoline, ammunition, and other essentials moving forward.

The Red Ball Express ("red ball" means to ship nonstop in railroad lingo) was devised to carry the supplies in convoys.

Scores of trucks, painted with red circles on their sides for identification, kept the First and the Third well-fortified. The procession would move one way on a northern route, designated by signs with similar markings as the trucks, and then return by a southern route carrying salvaged shell casings, POWs, wounded GIs or the remains of the dead back to Normandy. The trucks rolled twenty-four hours a day, and at its peak, the Express involved more than one hundred and forty truck companies and better than six thousand vehicles.

Dan's ambulance squad had been traveling with the Express since late August, and this trip found them in their usual position at the rear of a convoy of twenty trucks. The vehicles were ordered to maintain sixty yards of space between them and the next truck, and not to travel at more than twenty-five miles per hour. There wasn't always a strict adherence to these demands, especially on the night runs, but it still meant that convoys of this size became a snail-crawling line that could stretch out almost a mile in length. Fortunately, contact with enemy forces had diminished once Paris was liberated. For Captain Levine's squad, most of their medical attention was given to injuries suffered in traffic accidents when the truckers drove too recklessly or fell asleep at the wheel. The squad's work was deemed important, and it spared them from the dangers of the heavier fighting, but it was not exactly what Dan expected to be involved with when he joined the Army.

Smitty stomped heavily on the brakes, sending the ambulance into a skid until he could get the Dodge under control. The sudden stop threw the dozing quartet off their seats in the back.

"What going on, Smitty?" Reb said. "Where'd y'all learn to drive?"

"In a hack, kid. You gotta problem with that?"

Reb didn't attempt a comeback. Everyone knew Smitty had a short fuse.

"Looks like trouble ahead," Levine called back to them as he pulled open the canvas curtain that separated the two compartments. "Sergeant, come with me. They may be in need of our services. The rest of you stay ready. Corporal, if things go bad, get this thing off the road as quick as you can."

Dan gathered his gear, climbed out the rear gate, and accelerated his pace to catch his superior. The captain was already moving past the trucks in the stalled procession. Dan checked his watch; it was nearly midnight. The First and Third Armies were swallowing more than 80,000 gallons of gasoline daily, and the need for supplies was constant. Somewhere behind them, another convoy was on the move, with another on the road ahead of them.

"What do you think happened, Captain? I didn't hear anything."

"Hard to say ... but whatever it is, I don't like sitting still. If I'm going to be a target, I'd rather be a moving one."

The countryside was bathed by a full moon. Even moving in and out of the shadows cast by the supply trucks, the two men were targets for any snipers that might be nearby. The tree-lined road was no more than twenty-five feet wide. Dan glanced around nervously. The Allies controlled the area, but sabotage was still an everyday threat. The sooner they found out what was wrong and got things moving again, the better both men were going to feel.

"It's at times like this I wish I had a rifle," Dan said. "Or least a pistol."

"We'll be fine," the captain assured him. "Besides, if we run into any trouble, I don't think a weapon is going to do you much good, unless you know how to take out a Stuka[8] with a handgun."

The two men took cautious steps forward in the moonlight. Dan alternated between watching where he walked and scanning the cloudless sky for any sign of aircraft. Dive bombing, mortar attacks, and land mines were the principal tactics employed by the enemy in their efforts to slow down the steady stream of supplies being ferried by the Express.

When they got to the front of the convoy, they spotted the trouble: a jeep nose down in a ditch and a supply truck spun sideways. The two-and-a-half ton vehicle, carrying a full load of ammunition, blocked the roadway. The driver's ability to keep his truck upright had prevented a potentially more serious situation from taking place. The truck straddled a small crater in the pavement. A land mine planted in the packed clay was the cause.

"You take care of this one," Levine ordered as he continued up the road. "I'll see about the jeep."

Dan climbed on the running board of the truck.

"Everybody all right in here?"

The two-man driving team appeared to be uninjured, although there was a hole in the floorboard and the soldiers were covered with dirt. The man sitting in the passenger seat held up a rapidly emptying sand bag. "We're okay ... thanks to these."

---

[8] German dive bomber and ground attack aircraft.

The floor was covered with sacks, barely allowing space for the stick shift and pedals.

"I saw our lead swerve off the road," the driver explained, "and then Luther and me felt this thump. We started to spin, but I kept this baby on its wheels."

"That's a nice piece of driving," Dan said.

"Friends call me Red," the trucker said with a grin, doffing his helmet to reveal auburn hair that offered quite a contrast to his dark complexion. "Been driving since I was fourteen."

"Well, these bags probably saved your--"

"That's all thanks to Luther here. It was his idea. Now a bunch of us are doing it."

"You guys look good," Dan said and climbed down from the cab. "Just let us know if something begins to bother you. Can you still drive this thing?"

"I'll get her going," Red promised out the window. "We sure don't want to stick around here."

Dan waved good-bye to the industrious pair and hurried to join the captain. When he reached the accident scene, a man from the disabled jeep was climbing up from the ditch.

"You okay, sir?" Dan asked, noticing the second lieutenant's gold bar. The officer hardly looked old enough for the part.

"I'm fine, Sergeant ... just a little shook up." The young officer looked back down into the ditch. "I hope Corporal Benson's going to be all right."

"Don't worry, sir. He's in great hands with the captain. What happened?"

"We received reports of increased sabotage activity in this area." The lieutenant gestured at the tree lines flanking each side of the road. "Freddy—uh, that's Corporal Benson—and me were on the lookout for anything suspicious, but even with the cat's eyes, it still was awfully bright with that full moon. We decided to drop our windshield so that it wouldn't pick up a reflection. Then the wire got us."

"I don't understand," Dan said.

"It's a Kraut tactic. We thought it was isolated, but we should have known better. They string piano wire across road to disrupt the convoys. When a windshield is down, the wire can do some serious damage to whoever's in the cab." The young officer ran a forearm across his mouth before continuing. "Have you seen some of our trucks with the big hooks on the front bumpers? That's to catch the wire. Hate to say it, but our jeep doesn't have that protection. We were almost on top of it when I saw the wire glinting in the moonlight. I yelled to Freddy and ducked."

The lieutenant took off his helmet to examine a scratch left on it by the sharp cable. "It caught me right here and, boy, did it snap my head back. But I was the lucky one ... Freddy wasn't wearing his helmet." The bravado in his voice trailed off, and the younger officer swayed and his knees buckled. Dan grabbed him in a bear hug and eased him to the ground. He took an ammonia capsule from one of his pouches and snapped it open between his thumb and forefinger. He waved the chemical under the officer's nose.

"Wow," the lieutenant said. "That'll clear your head. Thanks. Thinking how close I was to buying the farm ... I guess I lost it."

"You'll be fine, Lieutenant."

81

Back on his feet, but still wobbly, the officer staggered to one of the nearby trucks. Dan slid into the ditch on the passenger side of the jeep. Levine was straddling the injured driver. Dan went jelly-legged at what he saw. Blood was everywhere.

"Soak up some of this," the captain instructed. "I can't see what I'm working on."

Dan pulled cloths from his supply pouch and began to blot the blood. Remarkably, the corporal was still conscious, his eyes blinking rapidly, wide with fear.

Dan quickly found his bearing. "Don't worry, Mac," he said, "You've got the best sawbones on the Express taking care of you. Where are you from anyway?"

Levine glanced at his helper with a bemused smile but kept on working. Learning to ask questions like a soldier's hometown was a procedure they had been taught as part of the training for the medical corps. A distracted patient was likely to be a more cooperative patient, and the ever-inquisitive Dan enjoyed employing the technique.

"Massachusetts, sir." The man coughed, his eyes still wide. "Plymouth."

"Don't bother with that 'sir' stuff," Dan chuckled kindly. " ... I'm just a plain old sergeant."

The soldier closed his eyes for a moment, and when he reopened them, a little less fear was there. Dan held the man's shoulders to keep him from moving too much.

"This isn't as bad as it looks," Levine said calmly. "Plymouth, Mass, huh? Well, I don't know if your ancestors landed at the Rock, but you look like one who might have run into some unhappy Indians." He lowered his voice, turned to Dan, and added, "Sergeant, see if you can find me some better light, would you. There's one in my bag."

Dan kept a grip on the patient with one hand. With his other, he pulled out a flashlight. He cupped his palm around the front end to focus the beam where the captain was working and to shield it from any snipers that might be in the area. Dan could see the extent of the wound better. When the driver made an unsuccessful attempt to get below the wire, it sliced into him at his hairline. He had been scalped.

The captain's hands worked efficiently to reposition the thin layer of skin and hair that had been peeled halfway back on the man's head. Almost magically, a needle and thread appeared and the scalp was skillfully secured in place.

"I'll finish up with the bandages," Captain Levine said, "but we need to get this man back to our truck. Go get Hardin and Jepson and bring a stretcher."

Dan climbed out of the ditch and moved double-time to the end of the convoy. By the time the trio returned with the litter, Captain Levine had dressed the wound and attached the EMT tag to the soldier's shirt. They carefully lifted the soldier into the carrier, and despite the tight quarters, they were able to get him up on the road in a matter of minutes. Bobby and Reb went off with the stretcher to the ambulance. Dan soaked a bandage with water from his canteen and helped Levine clean his hands.

"I don't think I've ever seen that much blood before," Dan said. "Is he going to make it?"

"He should," the captain told him. "Head wounds tend to be bloodier than most, even when they aren't serious. That was one lucky young man. A little lower and we'd be looking at the headless horseman."

Dan shuddered at the thought. "That was remarkable what you did, sir. I know I couldn't do anything like that"

"I'm sure you would have handled it the same way, if it was necessary," Levine said. "You've been a good student. That's why I rely on you. The rest of them are fine, but I know I can count on you to get it done right."

"Thank you, sir."

They collected the damp, bloody cloths and began the walk back to their ambulance at the rear of the queue.

"Did you get any emergency room work at med school?" Captain asked.

"Excuse me?"

"At medical school ... before you enlisted."

The color of Dan's face matched the stained bandages. "I was headed to law school, not to be a doctor."

"That's the Army, I guess." The captain shook his head in disgust.

"My military career has not been what I expected, to say the least," Dan said, then added almost as an afterthought, "Not that it hasn't been great working with you and the others."

"Well, you haven't let disappointment affect who you are. I wouldn't have had a clue that being a medic wasn't what was planned for if you hadn't told me."

Dan smiled in appreciation.

"The way you go about things," Levine continued, "I would have thought you were the most contented soldier in the world. Except, of course, for being stuck in all of this traffic."

Dan grinned. "We all want this war to be over, but as long as we're here, we might as well make the best of it. I can't say that driving up and down these roads day after day is all I'd hoped for, but I figure I'm here for a reason, and whatever that is, I'll be ready."

"You dreamed of doing more than riding along in the Red Ball, huh?"

"Didn't you?"

The captain nodded and then sucked air through his teeth. "I'm happy to be here to help out a kid like we did tonight. But there are a lot of days of twiddling your thumbs, that's for sure."

They passed the munitions truck, now back in proper alignment with the rest of the convoy, and he waved to the men inside the cab. The soldiers responded with a thumbs-up sign.

"I take it they're okay, then," the captain said. "I should have asked earlier, but I figured you would have told me otherwise."

"Get this…" The grin on Dan's face grew and his gestures became more rapid as he spoke. "They lined their cab with sandbags. They could barely move around, but it probably saved their lives when they ran over a land mine." He stopped walking as if he didn't think he could make his point with his captain without such emphasis. "It's funny. You never know when you can learn something, or who you get to know, and since we've been over here, I've sure gotten an education from some interesting people."

85

Levine tilted back his helmet. "You're remarkable, son. You always seem to see the best in everybody."

"I guess I get that from my family, sir ... from my mother. My Pa's a rock, but it was Ma that taught my brothers and me to be open to everyone. She said we should always to be ready to help anyone in need."

"And if they didn't respond in kind?"

His chest swelled. "Offer it up." His display of pride intensified and the words came out faster. "Ma says if you offer it up, God will reward you someday. My big brother says it's being a man for others. All I know is I'm just trying to be who Ma taught me to be. That's why I want to do all I can while I'm here."

"She must be some kind of lady."

"Yes sir, she is, sir."

"Tell you what ... when it's just the two of us, forget the 'sir' and just call me Abe."

"Thank you, Captain ... I mean, Abe. Sorry, sir, I'll get it right one of these times. Say, can I ask you a personal question, Abe, if it's not too much?"

"Anything."

"How old are you?"

The doctor laughed, probably louder than he intended. "If you must know, I'll be forty-five in February."

"The reason ... uh ... I asked is ... uh ... you don't find many guys your age doing what you do. I don't mean being a doctor, but doing what we're doing here. Did you tick off somebody to get stuck with us?"

Levine laughed, even harder than before. "Hardly ... and I consider it a privilege to serve with you and the rest."

Dan loved listening to him. It was an educated voice, but colored with a Bronx accent.

"To be honest," the captain kept on, "I never thought about the Army until one day I just got fed up with everything going on over here. I shut down my clinic, walked into a recruitment center, and badgered a poor young man until the Army let me enlist." The medic's teeth clenched; his voice lost its sophistication. "Because, you know, somebody's gotta stop that idiot Hitler, and I decided it might as well be me." He pulled his helmet down on his forehead. "And I hope I'm around when that schmendrik[9] gets it."

"Me, too, Abe ... me, too."

They finished the walk in silence, both men alone with their thoughts.

---

[9] Yiddish for "a jerk."

CHAPTER EIGHT

28 September 1944

Bergen, Norway

U-474 eased back through the harbor's mouth, aiming for the pier below the Bergenhus Fortress. A gaping hole was visible in the Norwegian medieval structure, the result of an earlier explosion from a ship that had been carrying more than one hundred tons of TNT in its hold. Despite the damage, naval operations were still ongoing in the building. Willy could see people passing back and forth behind the opening the blast had caused.

The crew was on deck as the U-boat glided towards her landing position. It was a gorgeous Indian summer afternoon with temperatures in the upper fifties thanks to warm winds from the Gulfstream. The aquamarine water of the Hardangerfjord to the south of the harbor splashed into lush, green valleys that wound down from the umber-colored peaks above. The scene was beautiful for these sailors eager to see anything that didn't look like the inside of a submarine. Willy loved the view of Bergen unfolding before them whenever they returned to port. The mountains girdling the city reminded him of Bavaria.

Yet for all of Bergen's beauty on this day, he was melancholic. In his most honest moments with himself, he knew his childhood dream of a life at sea for the Fatherland had become a nightmare. Service on U-474 was dirty and boring, and he had a growing fear over the uncertainties that lay ahead.

A small detail of men on the pier worked to tie fast the lines, and the U-boat's engines began their shutdown process. Beyond that, no notice was taken of the submarine's return.

"You should've seen how it used to be, Müller." Burtzlaff, the U-boat's second-in-command, jolted Willy from his reverie.

"What are you talking about?"

"The Kaleu would demand we make ourselves as presentable as possible," Burtzlaff said, "and when we pulled into the harbor, we stood in lines so straight it would have made a draftsman proud."

Willy looked around. There was no such organization for this landing. The crew was in a rugby scrum at the gangway, anxious to disembark.

"A band would be playing," Burtzlaff continued, "banners flying everywhere, and you should have seen all the people. My goodness, I miss those days."

"We'll have them again, won't we, sir?"

"I've been three tours at sea, my boy. Reality means we are simply trying to survive."

"Sir?"

89

Burtzlaff gave Willy a sincere smile. His young charge, inculcated with Nazi doctrine from his Hitler Youth lessons, probably can't comprehend the possibility that the Fuehrer's plans would not succeed. "Trust in the Kaleu, Müller," he offered in placation. "He will do everything in his power for us."

Heartened by Burtzlaff's words, Willy's spirits brightened. "I know what you mean about a grand show. When my brother, Ludwig, and I became part of the New World Order, we had bands and parades and a huge crowd. I even got to meet the Fuehrer."

"That must have been quite an honor," Burtzlaff replied with an impressed look. "You actually met Adolf Hitler?"

* * *

The city of Nuremberg was pulsating with energy from the disciples who had come for salvation. Hundreds of multi-hued flags and pennants of different shapes and sizes formed a contrasting rainbow over the marketplace and its monochromatic stone buildings. Stalls were jammed one on top of another throughout the giant plaza, and vendors hawked merchandise bearing the Nazi swastika or the image of Adolf Hitler, and sometimes both. Succulent smells from oversized food tents on various corners were hypnotic, drawing crowds to sample from steaming vats filled with sausage, bratwurst, and sauerkraut. Others satisfied themselves with frothy steins of the best from local brewmeisters, who kept the golden liquid flowing like the Rhine.

Among the revelers were the young Müller brothers—Ludwig and Willy. Only months earlier they were initiated into Hitler Youth and now they had been invited to be a part of the Rally for Greater Germany. It was the tenth edition of the annual meeting of the National Socialist Party, and the Nazi leaders wanted it to be the most majestic display yet of their power.

"Stick close," Ludwig ordered. "Mother would kill me if I let anything happen to her precious little boy."

Willy threw a punch at his older brother but it was easily deflected. They were traveling without their parents for the first time, and Ludwig was enjoying being in charge. He caught the younger boy's second swing in his hand.

"Take it easy," Ludwig said. "I'm just teasing."

Willy twisted free, but not from his own effort. A group of drunken men, in a rush to refill their steins, inadvertently pushed them apart. There was a moment of panic for these country boys in the big city until Ludwig was able to snatch him back out the path of more merrymakers.

The older brother gave the younger a fierce hug. "Mother was right when she said this wasn't going to be anything like Würzburg."

The Müllers' village of Waldberg was so small that their April induction into the Nazi youth programs had taken place in Würzburg, the nearest larger town. The ceremony in the city of sixty thousand was a kaffeeklatsch in comparison to the events that would take place in Nuremberg. The marketplace was teeming with people. Ludwig tried to appear unconcerned by the crush, but he reflexively tightened his hold on his brother. The organizers for the Rally decided to include children from Hitler Youth groups across the country in the celebration. The invitation for Ludwig was not surprising, not after his performance at their initiation. Willy's inclusion, however, did not sit well with some back in Waldberg. Technically, he was not yet old enough to be an official member of Hitler Youth, but he was specifically mentioned in the official request. Rudolf Schmidt, the HY leader for their region in Bavaria, was assigned as their chaperone, and the boys found him at a nearby streetcar stop. Space was already a precious commodity for the thousands seeking a ride to the rally, and the chaperone fought to find the three of them seats.

"Herr Schmidt..." Willy asked as the brothers moved alongside their temporary guardian.

The chaperone barely glanced at him. The eleven-year old had raised a litany of questions from the moment he met the brothers at the Würzburg depot. "What is it this time, Willy?"

"Will we get to meet the Fuehrer?"

"Oh, that will be easy," the chaperone sneered. "I'll just talk to my good friend, Herr Himmler, and I'm sure he'll arrange it. And, maybe, you'd like to speak with Admiral Donitz, too?"

"Can we?"

Schmidt stared at him and then threw up his hands in exasperation. He went back to his search for room on the streetcar.

"You're unbelievable," Ludwig said to his brother with a laugh. "Do you really think we could get anywhere close to the leaders?" He grabbed Willy by the back of the shirt, and with an effortless pull elevated the younger boy into the last available seat. He jumped on the running board just below. Willy wanted to say something, but Ludwig's attention was already fixed elsewhere as the trolley pulled away towards its destination, Zeppelin Field.

Twenty minutes later, they exited at a staging area outside an immense stadium. A seemingly endless sea of children was gathered there.[10] Herr Schmidt scanned the surroundings and then hurried them to a spot underneath a placard attached to a long pole. In the midst of the organized chaos, Ludwig recognized someone. "Fritz ... Fritz Stahl. It's me, Ludwig Müller from Waldberg."

The young man's face lit up in recognition. "Ludwig! Of course, how are you?" He and Ludwig had been the top winners at a Hitler Youth sports festival in the boy's hometown the previous month.

The boys shook hands vigorously. Willy stood at Ludwig's side, proud and yet a little envious. Everything seemed to come so naturally for his older brother.

As the boys moved into a formation with the others, Ludwig removed a cloth band from his pocket and secured it around his upper arm.

"What's this?" Willy asked as he twisted the armband. "How come I don't get one?"

"I have no idea. Herr Schmidt told me to put it on, but he didn't say why."

Ludwig straightened the armband, which had markings similar to the Hitler Youth insignia, but with the addition of a silver eagle holding lightning bolts in its claws. He shrugged his shoulders and chuckled. "It probably means I'm going to be on the cleanup crew."

---

[10] Newspaper accounts later would estimate as many as eighty thousand young people took part in the celebration.

Finally assembled, their group stepped out smartly toward the stadium. The edifice was a testament to the artistry of Albert Speer, Hitler's chief architect. The Nuremburg arena was not constructed in the typical circular fashion for an outdoor sports venue. Speer took the classic design and split one side of the oval. The structure was then opened and extended outward to form a giant, arcing line. Tall pillars, at least fifty feet high, rose from the main body of the building. Red banners, trimmed in black and gold and bearing the Nazi swastika, filled the spaces between the columns. The superstructure was made of rich granite blocks, each weighing several hundred pounds. They gave the stadium an air of magnificent indestructibility.

"Ludwig ..."

"Can't you ever stop with the questions? Pay attention to what you're doing. You keep bumping into me."

Chastened, Willy looked down at his feet, measuring his steps so that he wouldn't catch the heels of his brother. Finding his rhythm, and eventually his courage, he tried again.

"Ludwig?"

"Good grief, Willy. What?"

"I just wanted to thank you and say how lucky I am to be here. I know all of this wouldn't have happened without you."

Ludwig smiled, almost paternally. "Well, I'm glad you're here with me, too."

"The Müller brothers ... no one can top us!" Willy added.

"Calm down and pay attention to what you're doing," Ludwig snapped, but his voice wasn't unkind. "When we begin our maneuvers, make sure you follow my lead."

"At your command, Herr Müller." Willy gave his brother the Nazi salute.

Ludwig grinned and playfully pushed his brother's arm away causing him to stumble. A boy marching alongside shoved him back into position with a dismissive grunt. When the boy turned away, Willy stuck out his tongue at him.

Zeppelin Field was used as docking space for the giant dirigibles of the German air industry when not involved in events like the rally. It stretched more than fifteen football fields in length and its width was nearly as much. The parade of children progressed into a tunnel underneath the section of the massive stone structure where the rostrum for Hitler and the Party leaders was situated. Seating for thousands of spectators spread from each side of the center stage. When the boys emerged from the passageway, they were struck silent by the sight of the parade grounds filled with children. Every inch seemed to be occupied by youthful apostles of the Aryan Way.

Selected units would be performing routines, including the Müllers' group. Willy pulled out a piece of paper from his pocket. It was filled with notes he made for himself on the program his unit would be doing. He prayed silently that he would remember what he was supposed to do, and then folded his cheat sheet and put it in his pocket. The spectators and Party officials responded with roaring ovations for each presentation of intricate weave patterns and high-stepping footwork. Flags, flapping in the gentle breeze, and long silk ribbons, twisted in rhythmic patterns by young artists, added to the spectacle.

Willy and Ludwig's group was the last of twenty-some acts to perform, but the crowd remained enthusiastic. Willy tried his best to stay in step with the older boys around him. At one point, Ludwig looked back and flashed him a smile that helped him relax. At the completion of their performance, the unit aligned in the front row of the field, to the left of the main stage. Fireworks exploded above the cornice of the grandstand to signify the end of the children's efforts, and the crowd reacted wildly.

Still huffing from the exertion—and his nerves—Willy gazed up at the men assembled near the podium. He recognized familiar faces from the newsreels and his schoolbooks: Hess, Speer, Goebbels, and, of course, the Fuehrer himself. The hierarchy of the Party sat in regal chairs of Black Forest maple and crushed red velvet, but the majesty of the seats was outdone by the men's uniforms festooned with medals and ribbons. The scene was completed by a stone carving of a large swastika towering above the platform. A man from the side opposite Willy rose and walked to the microphones at the center of the stage. It was Rudolph Hess, deputy Fuehrer of the Nazi Party.

"Heil, Hitler!"

The children responded with a wave of sound that exploded against the grandstand. Hess kept repeating the command. The children raised their arms in salute, shouting out their loyalty at each prompt. He seemed as if he would never stop until he made a dramatic pause. The disciples all went silent. Hess slowly turned his head from one side to the other. The tension, the anticipation, was palpable. At last, he raised both arms to the sky.

"Let me present our exalted leader, our supreme commander, Adolf Hitler!"

The reaction was incredible. Noise cascaded back and forth between the children in formation and the spectators in the stands. Hitler stood calmly at the podium, raising his right arm perfunctorily as he recognized his followers' adoration. When he raised his left arm as well, the crowd fell silent with sudden swiftness.

"My children ... my people ... my Germany!"

The rise and fall in the tenor of the Fuehrer's voice, his dramatic gestures, and the fire in his eyes mesmerized the crowd. He could control the masses simply by a wave of his arm, by the sound of his voice. The speech lasted forty minutes, but no one noticed its length. The adults found in him a reason to be proud to be Germans again, while the children had raised him to divine status. This slight man was the answer to their prayers. When yet another sustained round of applause subsided, Hitler spread his arms, looked down at the children, and concluded:

"You, my youth, are our nation's most precious guarantee for the future. Your destiny is to be the leaders of a glorious new order. Never forget, one day you will rule the world!"

The crowd roared in prolonged adulation until it was replaced by the collective gasp from the children. Hitler had descended from the platform to inspect the formations on the giant parade grounds. Children pushed forward for a closer glimpse, only to move back quickly when admonished by their leaders. Willy was frozen in fear. If the Fuehrer continued on his same path, he would pass right in front of them.

Willy felt his knees giving out until Ludwig supported him with a comforting squeeze of his arm.

Hitler nodded and smiled as he moved along the front row of his Youth, occasionally making an obligatory acknowledgment to salutes and cheers. He stopped abruptly at the spot where the Müller brothers stood and glanced over his shoulder at an officer in his entourage.

"Is this the young man?" Hitler asked Baldur von Schirach, the leader of Hitler Youth.

"Yes, Mein Fuehrer, he is the one."

The Hitler Youth initiation for Ludwig took place on his birthday in April, a birthday he happened to share with the Fuehrer. Recognition of that fact was made at the event, and Ludwig had led the gathering in a rendition of "Deutschland, Deutschland" at the end of the ceremony. Everyone was struck by his poise.

"What a fine example of German youth!" Hitler exclaimed as he grasped Ludwig's hand.

Photographers and filmmakers scrambled to capture the moment. Ludwig smiled and tried his best to give a calm response to the leader's questions.

"And this must be his brother," the Fuehrer continued, reaching out to tousle Willy's hair. "What do you think of all this?"

Willy tried to make his mouth work, but no sound was forthcoming. Hitler was amused at the boy's bashfulness and was about to move on when Willy blurted out a response. "I only came because of my brother. I just follow my brother. I do everything he tells me."

The German leader bellowed a hearty laugh, almost too large for a small man. "Such loyalty, such devotion! If I can get these children to believe in me like this boy believes in his brother, then I will indeed rule the world."

Hitler ran his hand through the boy's blond curls a second time and resumed his inspection of the other groups.

Willy was stunned, but Ludwig's wink told him everything was okay.

* * *

Even years later, the words still poured out in a rush.

Willy was as breathless in telling the story to Burtzlaff as if he had just finished the choreographed marching he did that afternoon six years earlier in Nuremberg. His excitement was so pronounced, his hands shook and he was bouncing up and down on the balls of his feet.

Burtzlaff watched with amusement as Willy removed his cap to pat the top of his head.

"And can you believe it," Willy said, "… he touched me!"

"I think I remember reading something about that in the newspapers. So that was you, was it? You're one of the famous Müller brothers."

Willy's grin was impossibly wide and his eyes blazed with pride. U-474 was finally at rest in her landing place, so with a gentle shove, Burtzlaff sent him down the gangway. "Go with your mates and have some fun. It won't be long before we take her out for real."

Willy ran to catch up with Dieter and the others, all of them eager to enjoy some freedom on the streets of Bergen. First stop was a small corner café where they wolfed down a local favorite of smoked salmon and scrambled eggs. They spent the rest of their time at a pub trying to attract the attention of the local girls. The young women flirted and the boys wooed mightily, but despite their best efforts, they were still out of luck by evening's end. Now curfew was approaching, and they needed to hurry if they were to return to the barracks in time.

"I think that one girl liked me." Dieter wore a silly grin, fueled by far too much alcohol. "The blonde with the red lipstick. Such a lovely mouth."

"Sure she liked you. She liked you because you kept buying beer for her and her friends."

"You're just jealous, Willy. I think she picked me out right when we walked in. If that big farmer hadn't kept barging in, I know what I'd be doing right now."

Dieter wrapped his arms around himself and kissed his imaginary partner. He staggered down the road, lost his balance and fell onto the pavement, giggling like a small child. Willy yanked at his portly friend several times before he could get him back on his feet.

"Burtzlaff told me we may be going out soon," Willy announced as they resumed their rush back to the compound.

"Finally. When?"

"He didn't give a date, but he said it wouldn't be long."

"I can't wait," Dieter huffed, the quickening pace too much for his overweight body. "I am so tired of doing the same thing over and over." He picked up a small stone and

100

hurled the pebble at a metal sign hanging from a storefront. The missile found its mark. "Hit! A direct hit!" he exclaimed with arms raised. "Before you know it, we'll be out there chasing the enemy ... sinking their ships."

Willy didn't share in his friend's exuberance; training had dulled his ardor. His thoughts, of late, had been concentrated on his brother rather than some future battle with the enemy. "I wonder what Ludwig is doing right now," he whispered aloud.

"Who? Your brother? He's with the Panzers, right?"

"Somewhere in France," Willy confirmed with a nod.

"Is he the one who likes swing music?"

"I've only got one brother."

Dieter began whistling a popular tune. He made a sloppy attempt at doing the Lindy and nearly fell again. Willy grabbed one of his arms, and then the other in an awkward attempt to keep him upright. To a passerby, they might have resembled a couple taking their first dance lesson. "That combo at the pub could really swing," Dieter slurred.

"Hardly. Ludwig says nobody does it like the Americans ... especially Glenn Miller and Benny Goodman."

"Keep your voice down." Even as drunk as he was, Dieter was still horrified. The overt endorsement of American jazz musicians, particularly with Goodman's Jewish heritage, stiffened him into a moment of sobriety. "You and your brother are going to get into real trouble if you go around talking that way to the wrong people. American music is subversive. It's created by inferior people."

"I said the same thing to my brother once," Willy countered, "but he told me you can still be a good German and like the music regardless of where it came from." He turned quiet as his thoughts wandered back to those discussions with his brother.

His bravado gone as quickly as it had arisen, Dieter walked along in silence until his friend was ready to say something else.

"Ludwig has never led me wrong," Willy offered at last. "So if that's what he says, then I believe him with all my heart."

"You know what I believe with all my heart?" Dieter wiped his mouth with the back of his hand.

"What?"

"I believe that when that blonde said no to me at the pub, it was the biggest mistake of her life. I would have *loved* to have led her wrong." The boys laughed for a long time.

***

The pair arrived at the barracks just before lights out, and Dieter was asleep as soon as his head hit the pillow. He began to snore, and Willy pushed him onto his side to short-circuit the snorts. The respite was temporary. The nocturnal serenade resumed with greater vigor, in chorus with the others already asleep.

Willy moved to his bunk where he was surprised to find a letter from Ludwig laying atop the blanket. He opened it and read it with keen interest.

September 10, 1944

Dear Willy,

Greetings from Belgium. Sorry it has been so long since I last wrote, but we've run into some tough going. There aren't many of us left, and we're not doing much more than trying to survive until they bring us reinforcements. I'm not sure when you will get this, but I wanted to let you know that I'm fine for now.

Did you notice the date at the top? Do you remember? I didn't plan it this way, but it's quite a coincidence, don't you think? That seems so long ago now when we were in Nuremburg. Sometimes, people ask me about meeting the Fuehrer because they had seen the newsreel or heard others tell the story. I just say that it was a tremendous honor and try to leave it at that. What I liked best was riding with you on the train back home. Remember? It is memories like those that keep me going. I pray that soon we will all be back together, laughing and sharing more great adventures.

I don't want you to be overly concerned, but we have been under constant fire almost from the moment we jumped into the action at Normandy. That's why I haven't written to you for all these months. The days are long and the food is terrible. I wish I could tell you more about what has been going on, but I have to be careful because they've been reading our mail before it's posted.

Sorry to say, but I do not have a good feeling about how this is all going to turn out for our great country.

Keep me in your prayers as I do for you. Mother's last letter said you were still in Norway. Mother and Father are going to need you.

Be well, my brother.

Ludwig

Willy read the letter a second time, and then a third, trying to make sense of its pessimistic tone. It was completely out of character for his older brother.

Mother and Father are going to need me? he thought. *What did that mean? And where was Ludwig going to be? And why would he be so worried about someone reading his mail?"*

CHAPTER NINE

30 October 1944

Bergen, Norway

"Mail call, men," Burtzlaff hollered. "... the last we're going to get for a while." The U-boat's second-in-command stood on the rear deck of U-474 just below the conning tower. Three rows of sailors faced him, each man hopeful that one of the letters in Burtzlaff's hand had his name on it. He began to pass out the mail. "Wolf ... Huber ... Schroeder ... Müller ..."

Willy raced forward and snatched the letter, eager for any word from family. This letter was from his mother, her first correspondence in more than a month. He wanted to open it right away, but the Kaleu had strict protocol against such activity. To avoid hard feelings for the men who did not receive something, no sailor could read his mail except at his bunk. When Burtzlaff finished the litany of names, he ordered the men to their stations in preparation for departure. After months of training, U-474 was embarking on her first tour.

Willy was in the first work rotation, and he took his place in the bow room. The latest news from home would need to

105

wait until he finished his six hour shift, the standard time segment for work details on a U-boat. His torpedo group did maintenance work in the initial hours after departure, and with the letter burning a hole in his pocket, the shift seemed to last forever. Twice Hesse barked at him for being inattentive, and the chastened teenager fought to keep his focus.

His detail finally ended, and although he tried to appear casual as he retreated to his bunk, his heart raced. He removed the crumpled envelope and traced a finger over the lettering on the front as if he could feel his mother's touch through her penmanship. He was desperate to see what she had written, but he removed the letter with slow, loving care. Inside were multiple pages, and curiously, some were blank.

October 9, 1944

Dearest Willy,

My beautiful boy! I hope this letter finds you safe. Your last letter home said that you might be shipping out soon, so I am concerned you might not get this. I worry about you constantly. I don't know why you were so determined to be in the Kriegsmarine. The ocean is no place for a boy from Bavaria, but your father says you are fine and they could have put you someplace worse. I don't know of any place that would be safe except right here with us. I pray I can one day again see your face and hold you close.

He flushed at the sentiment even though no one in the area would know the reason for it, and kept reading.

What am I about to tell you is the hardest thing I have ever needed to do. It is all so painful. Be brave, my son. Your father and I are beyond words, but we know you would have wanted to know as soon as possible.

Yesterday, we received the tragic word that your brother has been killed in action.

Willy's scream could be heard over the whine of the engines. He jerked forward and accidentally slammed his forehead against the hull. The blow cut off his cry and a bump swelled. Nearby sailors were surprised by the outburst, but when nothing else happened, they resumed their duties. If it didn't affect them, there was no reason to be concerned.

Apparently Ludwig's unit was under heavy artillery fire on September 11th at a place called Namur. The soldiers in his unit who didn't die were captured, so the details of what exactly happened are sketchy. They found his field pack, but there was no other sign of his body in the rubble.

Another moan escaped, but Willy muffled his despair by forcing a fist into his mouth. He reached into the cubbyhole near his bunk and retrieved the letter he received from his brother in September. He stared with incredulity at the date. It had been written the day before Ludwig's Panzer unit was overrun.

He said things were tough, Willy thought, *but it can't be true ... he can't be gone.*

107

The earlier letter fell from his hand, landing on his stomach without a sound. He returned to his mother's correspondence.

The officer told us artillery assaults went on throughout the day they were searching for him. That made it difficult to find any remains. The only personal thing in his pack was a letter he had written to us, dated September 11th, the day he went missing. He must have written it that morning, but never got to post it.

Willy sank deeper into his pillow, totally at a loss.

I have sent you several blank pages that came with the letter. Why your brother would want you to have them I have no clue, but he was insistent about it. He said something about a train ride from Nuremberg and the two of you playing leapfrog. Do you have any idea what he was talking about?

Willy pulled the blank sheets away from the rest of the letter. His heart pumped in erratic beats as he held a page toward the light hanging by his bunk. *What did Ludwig want only me to know?*

He finished the final paragraphs, tucked his mother's letter in its envelope, and placed it along with Ludwig's in his cubbyhole. He took the blank pages and headed to the latrine. Crewmen worked on the diesels near the toilet, but they hardly gave him a glance. He swiveled his head fore and aft anyway to see who might be watching before he grasped the door latch. Satisfied no one was paying him any attention, Willy climbed into the cramped booth, locked the door, and pulled on a cord to illuminate a light bulb hanging naked from its wire. The place had a putrid smell even though U-474's tour had just gotten underway. He fought the urge to vomit and focused on Ludwig's secret message. He held the first sheet up to the light, close enough to warm the page but not so near that it might scorch.

Jg zpv dbo sfbe uijt ...

Random letters blossomed on the page, just as they had done that September evening six years ago. Willy knew exactly what they meant, and a furrow of concern creased his brow.

* * *

Jammed with participants from the earlier events at Zeppelin Field, the overnight train steamed towards Würzburg. Herr Schmidt snored loudly on the other side of the aisle, but the boys were too excited to sleep after their meeting with the Fuehrer.

"I'll never wash my hair again," Willy gushed. "I can't believe he touched me."

"Mother might not share your sentiments about hygiene." Ludwig replied.

"But wasn't it something? In front of all those people, the Fuehrer spoke to us!"

"Yes, it was a great honor." Ludwig feigned a yawn and tried to act as if he wasn't just as excited as his brother was.

"I'm sure it is something we will long remember, but right now I think we should try and get some sleep."

Willy squirmed in his seat, his energy boundless. "I'm not tired or anything. Let's do something."

Ludwig reluctantly agreed and searched his rucksack. His books and magazines would be of little interest to his younger brother, and apparently, he did not bring a deck of playing cards as he thought he had. Inspiration came when a passenger several rows ahead of them cleared her throat with a series of rhythmic coughs. "Doesn't that woman sound suspicious?" Ludwig said.

"I don't follow you."

"I'm telling you there's something funny about her. Look at her hat."

The woman was one of a few onboard not dressed in a Party uniform. She wore a conservative tweed suit, forest green in color, but her millinery choice was extreme. The hat was a mishmash of feathers and ribbons without pattern or regard to hue.

"Who else would dress like that?" Ludwig added. "I bet she's a spy." He made an exaggerated wink at his younger brother.

"Oh, now I see." Willy responded with a face-splitting grin. "I bet she's got secret documents hidden under that crazy hat. And what about that man with the limp coming down the aisle? Maybe he has a hollow wooden leg and he's smuggling plans for an attack?"

The brothers chuckled at the thought, and the man glowered as he passed their seats.

"We must get this information to headquarters," Ludwig whispered, reclaiming command of their operation. "... but we can't let the enemy know we are on to them."

"What can we do?"

"It's simple. Hand me that carton of milk."

Ludwig poured a small amount of the liquid over the wooden armrest of his seat. Some of it dripped to the floor, but a tiny puddle of milk remained on the maple where a hollow had been carved out by its maker. The boy removed a sheaf of papers from his rucksack and pulled away a paper clip that held them together. He straightened the clip to use it like a pen tip and wrote a few words with the milk on a small piece he tore from one of the pages.

"I can't see anything," Willy complained. The white liquid on the similar colored paper had dried without a trace.

"Just watch ..."

Ludwig removed the small shade from a lamp, affixed to the wall just above their seats, and held the slip of paper close to the exposed light bulb. As the page heated, the words in his message reappeared as if by magic.

"Wow," Willy said. "That's great. How did you do that?"

"I learned it at one of my meetings."

Willy took the paper and looked furtively at the other passengers. "But if we know how this works, our enemies might, too. We need a secret code."

The boys snickered again, but hurriedly stifled their enthusiasm to avoid too much curiosity from the other passengers. After all, they were spies.

"I agree," Ludwig said, "we need a code. Any ideas?"

"Me and my friends use one at school to keep out of trouble for passing notes. We call it Leap Frog. All you do is skip ahead one letter in the alphabet to disguise a message. It's simple but it works."

"Ah, brilliant," Ludwig said. "So, if I wanted to write the words 'enemy spy', it would become 'fofnz tqz'."

Both boys delighted in the ingenious way they would be able to keep their information from being discovered. The remaining time on the train was spent passing notes back and forth, many of them producing more laughter.

* * *

In the quiet stink of the U-boat's lavatory, Willy found it hard to take a breath as the letters revealed themselves from the warmth of the light bulb. The secrecy of blank pages and using the Leap Frog Code was troubling enough, but the tenor of his brother's words intensified his fear.

> *If you can read this, Willy, then you remember our secret code. I don't want anybody else to know what I am going to tell you.*
>
> *My time is short. The enemy has us pinned down, and I don't think we have any way out. Word came this morning that Kurt Meyer, our commandant, has been captured as he tried to escape. He is a coward and I am not surprised he would desert us.*

The words dripped with cynicism. The lack of respect wasn't something Willy was used to hearing from his brother.

He set aside the first page, the letters disappearing as soon as they were removed from the heat. He picked up the next sheet.

I have always been proud to be a German, even if I didn't agree with everything the Party stood for. That began to change in Normandy when we captured some Allied soldiers at Caen. An order was issued that there were to be no wounded prisoners. We were told to shoot them right there. I knew as well as all the men in my squad did that this was not right to do. But—and here I'm ashamed to say it, brother—we followed orders.

Other Allied prisoners on the march back to our headquarters were run over with trucks. It was a bizarre to watch such a scene of total disregard for acting humanely. Some in my squad averted their eyes, but other men laughed like it was a game. Two days later, more prisoners were captured and they were beaten with rifles and slashed with bayonets. Some were tied to poles because otherwise they would not have been able to stand for their executions.

Willy dropped the sheet as if it were contaminated. He wouldn't have believed it if it had come from anyone other than his brother. Nausea swept over him. He did not want to read anymore, but he was compelled.

I don't know how long this would have gone on if senior officers hadn't finally put an end to it. I should have spoken up, I should have said something earlier, but to my everlasting regret, I said nothing. That is not how Mother and Father taught us to be.

Since Normandy, our division continues to fight bravely, but too much so I'm afraid. It's sad to see what has happened. We were fifteen thousand strong at Beverloo, but now I think there are less than six hundred of us left. The officers don't care how many have been lost. Day after day, they continue to send us out to meet certain death. The hardest thing is watching so many die just because that's what they thought they were supposed to do.

Disbelief permeated every part of Willy's body. He slumped on the toilet, his despair absolute. Thoughts raced through his brain. *All the meetings, all the slogans that instructed us to follow the Fuehrer, to do it for the glory of the Fatherland, were they nothing but lies? No wonder Ludwig didn't want anyone to know how he truly felt.* Willy held the final page near the bulb.

I better end here. The enemy's artillery is getting closer and we are just about out of ammunition. I have tried to convince my men that death is imminent and it would be better to surrender, but most are still blinded by their fanaticism. I know my best chance would be to run away, but you know that's not me. I will stay until the end because that is what I am supposed to do.

But—and this is my strongest encouragement for you, dear brother—you don't need to! There is nothing left for you in this war, nothing to be gained and everything to lose.

Find a way to get out before it is too late. Forget everything the Party has taught us, because it just isn't true. Go back home and live the life that was supposed to be for you and me.

I pray that you make it, my brother; it is my final wish. Someday, we will be together again.

Tears flowed unchecked as Willy imagined what his brother must have experienced in those final, chaotic hours. Ludwig had always been there with the right advice during their childhood, but his timing was off this time. Willy wouldn't be able to get away ... it was too far to swim.

He gave out a sardonic laugh and pounded the wall with his fist. The laughter soon turned to wailing, his chest heaving as he sobbed.

CHAPTER TEN

18 December 1944

Rheims, France

"Pack up a fresh round of supplies quick as you can, boys. Captain says we're moving out on the double."

"Hang tight, Smitty," Reb said. "I was fixing to take a little nap and y'all are going to spoil it."

Smitty scowled. Reb scampered away to fetch his kit.

"What's up?" Dan asked. "Where are we going that we have to move out so fast?"

"Sounds bad." Smitty said. "Nazis launched a last-ditch offensive. Looks like all the action's up in the forests near the Ardennes."[11] The squad's driver took a deep drag from his cigarette. "You know how we're spread out all over this part of Europe. The captain says our lines are thinnest there. He thinks Hitler's hoping he can split our defenses, and then they might be able to get all the way to Antwerp."

---

[11] Mountain range that covers parts of Belgium, Luxembourg, France and Germany.

"That's a strategic port," Dan said. "I can see why that'd be their target, but what's that mean for us?"

"Tenth Armored's dug in at Bastogne, and Captain says there's at least a division of Panzers heading right for them. They're gonna need help fast, and plenty of it. Our trucks are going to run in the guys from the 101st."

"The 101st! The brass can't be serious." Dan groaned. "You saw what those boys looked like when they straggled in this morning."[12]

"Oh, they're serious all right." Smitty grunted and flicked his spent cigarette away. "They need every warm body with a rifle they can get."

"I suppose that goes for us, too."

"Well, they want us along for the insertion anyway."

The ambulance squad didn't need long to get ready, but the fatigued men of the 101st moved at a pace only slightly faster than erosion. By late afternoon the caravan of jeeps and trucks, numbering in the hundreds, was finally ready to begin the trip. A driving rain fell. The medics hopped in the back of their truck, and the race up the muddy road to Bastogne began. Hours passed. Dan looked at his watch. He knew it should only take about six or seven hours to get there, but sleet soon replaced the rain, and everything slowed down. The

---

[12] The 101st Airborne had been going non-stop since their deployment into France as part of the D-Day invasion. In September 1944, they were assigned to an area in the Netherlands between the lower Rhine and Waal Rivers. The paratroopers derisively dubbed it 'The Island' because of its isolation from the main Allied forces. They faced fierce opposition for the better part of three months. When the calendar page turned to December, they were finally allowed to regroup at Camp Mourmelon, about twenty miles southeast of where Jack's unit and other support teams were in a holding pattern. The respite for the 101st was short-lived. Orders came down early on December 18 that they were to marshal together with the others in Reims for a race to Bastogne.

rapid shift in weather created fog banks that accentuated the foreboding atmosphere. The moisture-heavy snowdrops mixed with remnants of the disintegrating roads to form a sloppy path that made it difficult for the drivers to stay on course. As darkness fell, all the men felt the tension.

"We're never gonna get there at this rate," Reb said. "We're gonna miss our leave time for Christmas."

"You know, Reb, sometimes you're an idiot," the usually quiet Bobby replied with a look of disdain. "This may be as important as D-Day was, and all you can do is complain that it doesn't fit your timetable."

"Easy, boys." Dan stuck his brawny arm between the two combatants. "Everyone just keep your cool."

Bobby made a throaty grunt and turned away. Reb looked as if someone had taken away his favorite pet, and he dropped his head in embarrassment.

With each passing mile, the speed of the column slowed even further. Dan did some math in his head. He reckoned at this rate it would take them more than double the time to get where they needed. The sheer number of vehicles and the pace of no more than twenty miles per hour stretched the motorized line to a length that would have been dangerous if the Luftwaffe was flying in the area. Fortunately, he knew that wouldn't be an issue this night because the Allies enjoyed air superiority, and in these foul conditions, there weren't any planes aloft from either side.

The trucks continued to bounce along. The wind grew stronger; the storm was a snarling beast that blew the precipitation in horizontal swipes. This trip through the Ardennes wasn't as rugged as it would have been if they were traveling through the Alps, but the relatively flat terrain rose as they moved east to almost two thousand feet. The roadway's rising grade made their destination seem more distant. Dan hated to admit it, but Reb wasn't far off in his pessimistic assessment.

"Whaddya think we're gonna find when we get there, Sarge?" Reb was alive again; the chastisement by Bobby had been put out of his mind.

"I'm not sure," Dan told him in a voice that he wanted to sound soothing, "but it must be something important if we're moving a group this big."

"It's always a big deal for the brass. They've been telling us that since we got over here. Bastogne? Never heard of it."

This mindset was not unusual for Reb. If a subject was unfamiliar to him, he often dismissed it as unimportant. Dan knew better and trusted his experience. He took off his helmet and wiped his brow even if there wasn't any sweat there because of the cold temperatures. It was time to provide a little education.

"Reb," he said. "I want you to picture your home state for a minute." History had been Dan's favorite subject in school, and he was avid student of the Civil War period. As a boy, he had consumed book after book about those times from the public library near his home. He was especially fascinated by biographies on Confederate generals like Stonewall Jackson and Jeb Stuart. His interest made the geography of the South as familiar to him as his home state of Ohio.

"My pleasure," Reb said. "Nothing better than dreaming of 'Bama, especially in this lousy weather."

"What city you from?"

"Tuscaloosa. Nothing else can touch it."

"So think of it this way. Since everything you care about is in Tuscaloosa, what would you need to do if you were facing an enemy coming at you from, say ... Chattanooga?"

Reb scrunched his eyes shut as if he needed to prevent anything from disturbing his focus as he pictured the scenario in his mind. He got along with the others in the squad—except, perhaps Smitty who didn't always have the patience for his constant chatter—but he had a special appreciation for how Dan looked after him and helped him through rough patches. He wanted to find out where all this was headed and he was eager to please his tutor. Reb opened his eyes and said, "That'd mean the enemy was coming from the northeast. I'd say the best way to go would be right through the Magic City. You know where that is?"

"Birmingham."

Reb grinned. "Yeah, Birmingham all right. I wouldn't have expected a Yankee to know that Southern slang."

"Okay. Now that you've got that picture, think of what's happening here this way," Dan said. "I had a conversation with one of the truck drivers before we pulled out of Reims. He told me that Bastogne's important because it's a cross-roads town. He said there's something like seven or eight highways in the Ardennes region that run right through it, all of them big enough to let an army roll in and take over. Whoever holds Bastogne controls the flow of troops and supplies throughout the area. The Germans need to have it, and we need to stop them. So ... to go back to your original question about Bastogne, it'd be like we were trying to protect Birmingham and everything around it like Tuscaloosa. Ike and the rest of them know we have to hold that town."

"Like General Allen had to stop Sherman in the Alabama Campaign," Reb said with a rise in his voice.

"Absolutely ... just like William Allen."[13]

"So we're trucking in our boys to stop the Jerries, just like the pride of 'Bama put it to those damn Yankees." Reb caught his remark, and then quickly added, "Sorry Sarge, no offense meant."

"None taken." Dan smiled. At least, Reb had paid attention in his Alabama History classes. "10th Armored's hanging on, and we need to get the 101st there before it's too late for them. Maybe even for all of us."

The last comment pushed the boy into some fearful contemplation of the danger that might be faced at Bastogne. GMC and Bobby rustled in their napping positions as if in response to the warning but said nothing. Dan pulled out his rosary and fingered the beads in silent prayer. The tires sloshed through the snow and mud and the ambulance rattled each time it hit a pit in the pavement, but nothing broke the quiet in the compartment for the remainder of the journey.

***

Word came back along the convoy in the early hours of the 19th that the head of the elongated column had reached the outskirts of Bastogne. Three hours later, Dan's truck rolled into the city. Another hour would pass before the entire procession of trucks and jeeps found its way into town.

---

[13] Born in Montgomery, Alabama, Allen rose through the Confederate ranks during the Civil War. He led a brigade of cavalry, and eventually an entire division, in trying to slow Sherman's march through the South. He survived several serious wounds, and he is considered one of Alabama's top military leaders.

The arriving trucks gathered in the wreckage of what was once the west side of the city. Stone and brick lay in disarray. The walls that had girdled the city since the fourteenth century were no match for the modern firepower they tried to withstand. The sun was smothered in blankets of clouds. Smitty picked his way through the rubble and parked the ambulance near the rear of a column of halted trucks.

Dan climbed out and stood at the front fender. Since the medics didn't have any specific duties while the trucks were being unloaded, he could do some people watching. He spotted a soldier among a group of paratroopers milling about. The 101st were veterans of the European theater of operations, but the reality of combat losses dictated the need to mix in raw recruits with seasoned men. Dan's paratrooper in question was one of the newbies. He was an angular young man, so thin it appeared the next blast of wind would knock him down. He was standing off to one side as if ostracized from the others, although there was little interaction among the GIs in general. Most wore the numbed expression of those who had seen more than they wanted and felt no need to talk about it. The adolescent soldier removed his helmet and adjusted a stocking cap underneath. He had a shock of blond hair like corn silk, and if there were any whiskers on his face, they were invisible. An artillery round landed within earshot. He flinched even though the explosion was not close. He kept checking the strap of his headgear as if he wanted to concentrate on anything but what might be coming, what could be advancing through the forests beyond the crumbled walls.

"Get a move on, soldier," came a call from an NCO.

The young paratrooper fumbled his helmet at the bark from his platoon leader, and the headgear filled with snow when it hit the ground. His cheeks reddened and he mumbled angry words as he shook it clean. Back on his head, he reached for a rifle leaning against a truck's tire.

"Hey, kid."

The soldier turned in the direction of this new voice.

"Keep your head down." Dan said, a small grin on his face. It wasn't really a smile, just a movement of his lips meant for encouragement. With a nod and a crisp salute, the soldier was gone. For the remainder of the morning, except to grab a cup of coffee for some warmth, Dan watched the 101st make preparations. He helped out wherever he could, carrying boxes, unloading supplies, but there wasn't much to unload. The entire operation had been organized so quickly, most men arrived with only a weapon and the clothes on their backs. The clothes weren't meant for winter, a point made quite clear to Dan as he fought off the cold with his own gear. He shook his head and let out a low whistle through his chattering teeth. He kept his eye on the action.

Some troops organized into units that would head into the nearby woods to harass the advancing enemy. Others checked equipment or built temporary fortifications out of the rubble to protect their positions. German artillery fire increased while Dan kept watch. The noise became deafening, and time and again, he felt the ground quake from the impact even though the shells were still falling outside the city limits.

"Let's wrap this up." A voice came from out of nowhere, interrupting his thoughts. It was Dan's turn to be caught off guard by Captain Levine.

"The forecast doesn't look like it's going to be getting better anytime soon," the captain said. "I don't want to get stuck in this town."

Dan saluted his superior, more out of habit than necessity. Levine rarely bothered with military ceremony. "We're leaving?" Dan's eyebrows rose.

"Our orders were to ride up with the men," the captain, "and then ride back. We're an ambulance squad, that's all, so let's go. It's going to be a rough ride back to Ste. Mère Eglise, but I'd certainly rather be there than here."

Dan frowned, turned up the collar of his coat, and rewrapped the knitted woolen scarf from his mother around his nose and mouth. It didn't seem right. The Army needed every able bodied man on the line. In his mind, that meant the ambulance squad, too. The snow crackled underfoot like crinkling cellophane as he retreated to the back of their truck. A gust whipped its canvas sides when he reluctantly climbed in to join the others.

"Dang, it's cold," Reb whined, stamping his feet on the floorboards. He had not left the back of the ambulance other than to get something to eat since they arrived in Bastogne. "This has got be about as cold as any of y'all have ever gone through."

GMC rubbed his gloved hands together rapidly. "I don't know. Back in Petoskey[14] it would start getting cold in October, and we usually had snow on the ground from November until spring."

"And you stayed there anyway?" Reb asked.

---

[14] A small town in the northern part of the Lower Peninsula of Michigan

"It may be hard to believe," GMC said, "but not everyone thinks Alabama is the only swell place to live."

Before Reb could deliver a comeback, Dan interrupted. "You get used to the cold and snow in the north ... I've always had more trouble with the gray skies day after day during the winter."

"Try living in Seattle," Bobby put in, the cynicism obvious in his voice.

Small talk about the weather continued until Smitty put the ambulance into gear and joined the line of trucks moving out. The conversation fizzled, almost as if the energy used for talking would take away from the strength needed to stay warm. The men watched through the split in the rear canvas while white flashes of German artillery whipped across gunmetal skies. Answering American guns mixed in, and the concussions shook the vehicle.

"I hope them boys make it through this all right," Reb said. Too much silence was unnerving for the boy, and he rarely missed a chance to fill it with chatter. "...cuz I heard there's a bunch of Panzers sitting out there."

"This is probably Der Fuehrer's last shot," GMC speculated. "You gotta figure he's going to send just about everything he's got at us. I hope we've got enough men to handle it."

"Just wish we were staying here," Dan muttered.

A particularly loud chorus of competing gunfire briefly halted the back and forth.

"Sarge, are you nuts?" Reb asked. "I'm happier than a fox in a henhouse to be heading the other way."

Dan stroked his chin and looked thoughtfully at the canvas wall. "No, not nuts," he said. "But I'd give anything in the world to be in Bastogne right now. Our boys are doing a mighty important work up there, and I'd like to be with them."

"Well, y'all must have ice flowing through your veins to say something like that. Doesn't anything scare you, Sarge?"

Dan was quiet for a moment. Reb's comment had sparked the interest of the other medics, and they were all staring at him intently, waiting for an answer. Dan let another moment of silence pass before he said, "Well, there's one thing that scares me, sure. In fact, it scares me a whale of a lot more than getting shelled ..." A lump slid down Dan's throat.

The other medics stayed silent for a few moments, expecting Dan to continue. When he didn't, GMC gave him a brotherly punch on the shoulder.

"That's okay, big man," GMC said. "If it's too hard to talk about, you just keep it to yourself."

* * *

"Go get it," Eileen called. Her hair looked amazing in the early September sunlight.

"Nah, you get it," Dan called back with a grin. "You were the one who threw it wide."

"And you were the one who missed it. C'mon—chivalry isn't dead."

Dan and Eileen playfully argued at the edge of Lake Erie while a football bobbed in the waves beyond them. It was Labor Day weekend, 1943, and Dan was home on weekend leave from his special officer's candidate program. The family came often to Cedar Point, a resort west of Cleveland, whenever his father had free time during the summer. Pete knew Dan's inviting Eileen on this excursion was no coincidence. Dan wanted everybody in the family to get to know her better, and Pete was pleased as punch with the girl Dan was seriously dating.

The amusement park rides at Cedar Point were a draw, but the park's popularity was built on its wide, pristine beaches along the Lake Erie water that was usually bathtub warm by summer's end. Extensive sand bars were situated only yards into the waves, and these long stretches meant almost anyone, regardless of their aquatic abilities, could play in water that remained shallow.

The banter between the young lovers provided amusement to Pete as he watched from a nearby beach chair. Eileen caught his eye, and he smiled warmly at her. "Hey!" Dan's father called. "A perfectly good football is going to float its way to Canada if you two don't settle this."

Dan's older brother, Tom, was home for the weekend from his final year at St. Mary's Seminary, where he was studying for the priesthood. He was sprawled on a beach blanket, his glasses on, his nose in a book. Even on breaks, he needed to keep studying.

"I'm serious, Eileen." Dan voice neared a shout. "You threw it, so you get it."

The strange tone to his voice made Eileen wrinkle her brow. She was about to say something back, but a stern look from her boyfriend froze her tongue.

Dan looked beyond the football to the western horizon where clouds were gathering. "It looks deep out there," he said.

"Nonsense," Eileen said. "It can't be more than up to your chest. She curtsied. C'mon—I know you're my knight in shining armor, but you won't rust. Hurry up. It looks like it might rain soon."

The weather had been perfect, but a swift drop in the temperature was turning a lovely day into a threatening one. Puffy white clouds had grown into darker thunderheads in the distance, and the wind gained in strength. Other sun worshippers had begun their retreats from the menacing weather. The air had that feel where it had to rain.

"I'm going to take your mother and little brother back to the hotel," Dan's father called out as he gave a worried glance to the skies. "Tom—you staying awhile longer?"

"Just to the end of this chapter," Tom grunted and looked up. "Hey Dan—that's the ball I gave you for your birthday. Quick, get it before we lose it."

Dan exhaled loudly and made a face. He looked at his girlfriend again, this time with concern, took off his tee-shirt, and began wading out to reach the football. The ball had drifted out even farther from the shore than when Eileen first tossed it into the waves. Goose pimples rose on his arms. The water of the great lake seemed colder than he remembered from earlier in the day. A hard winter had given the lake a chill that was still present even at the end of summer, but now it felt even worse. The breakers rushed shoreward and packed a punch that had been absent when he and Eileen had waded in the water before lunch. He shuddered.

He navigated along one of the sand bars, and although he was some seventy-five yards out, the water was still only chest high. The waves continued to grow, and periodically one would rise up and drench him. The football danced in the lake just beyond his reach. He walked out farther and made a grab, but the ball slipped from his grasp and floated away. Another wave crashed down. Dan was knocked off his feet. When he came back up, his bearings had been knocked a kilter by the water's impact. He floundered in the water, righted himself, and continued out deeper. Eighty yards. Eighty-five. Ninety. The water was now even with his shoulders.

"Tom!" Dan called back toward the shore. He arched his hands over his eyes looking for his brother, hoping to improve his focus. Tom was still deep in a book. Dan made another grab, but the football teased him and slipped off to his left. He was a hundred yards from shore now—the length of a football field. He lunged toward the ball again, but this time he plunged under the waves. The sand bar had come to an end. Dan surfaced in a panic and struggled to find his footing. He could feel a pull on his body. The undertow caught him and was carrying him away from the beach.

"Help! Tom!" It was hard for Dan to keep his head above the crests. "Please! Somebody help me!"

On shore, Dan's cries were lost to a crash of thunder. The clouds, now inky black, hung low in the sky. Eileen shaded her brow with the back of her hand. "Tom," she called over her shoulder. "Do you think your brother's all right? I can't see him. How hard can it be to get a ball anyway?"

Another dunking followed, and this time Dan was barely able to gasp for air when he broke back through the surface. "Help!" he called. "Help! ... Oh, God ... please help!" The thrashing of his arms and legs to stay afloat sputtered to a halt. A huge wave hit, and he sank beneath the surface.

"Tom!" Eileen's voice rose in alarm. "Tom—quick! Dan's in trouble!" She sprinted into the water and dove in headfirst when the water reached her knees. She began making broad overhand strokes in Dan's direction.

Tom threw his book aside, splashed in after her, and dove into the chop. Tom had always excelled at swimming—his lanky frame was perfectly suited for it. He quickly passed Eileen and reached the spot where the football bounced in the breakers. "Where is he?" Tom called back to Eileen.

Eileen looked all around. She tread water, twenty yards away from Tom. "I can't see him anywhere," she shouted.

Tom dove beneath the surface, arching his arms and legs in every direction in an attempt to make contact with something solid. His head bobbed up again. "It's impossible to see anything under there! Eileen—swim for shore. Go get something that floats and bring it out here—quick!"

Eileen began swimming for shore. Tom moved in a circle, and then dove under the water again. Nothing. Tom dove again. On his third plunge, he felt Dan's arm. With a mighty pull, he brought his brother back to the surface. A swell took them ten yards closer to shore where he was able to gain footing for a moment, and then shook his brother by the shoulders. "Dan? Dan! Talk to me!"

Dan coughed, sputtered, and opened his eyes. He was disoriented, but when he recognized his brother, his energy reignited. The undertow was still a major concern; they needed to keep moving. Tom hooked an arm across Dan's chest and they worked their way with back and forth moves almost parallel to the beach. The storm let loose with a furious wind. Heavy rain began to fall. A spastic burst of lightning jolted in the distance. In time, they broke free of the water's pull and reached one of the sand bars where they could stand again. Dan kept his arm wrapped around Tom's waist.

Eileen rushed through the water to where the brothers were standing. She threw her arms around Dan and hugged him tightly, and then backed away and hit him in the chest with an open hand. She spoke through a gush of tears. "Dan! What were you doing out there! You gave us such an awful fright. You nearly—"

Tom held out his hand. "It's okay. Give him some air, Eileen. Let's get out of this water."

The trio collapsed by the water's edge. Dan was still struggling to breathe. He reached over, grasped Eileen's hand, and held it tightly in his. "It's okay everybody," Dan said at last. "I just misjudged where that sandbar ended. That's all."

Tom slapped him on the back and tousled his hair. He glanced at Eileen and chuckled. "I'm going to go get this girl a towel. By the way, Eileen, there's something important you need to know about my brother, but I'll let him tell you …" Tom's voice trailed off. He stood up and headed toward the chairs where a towel hung.

"What?" Eileen looked at Dan for an answer. "Tell me!"

Still panting, Dan started to say something but paused, as if thinking of the right words to say. He kissed her on the cheek, and then spoke. "When I was growing up I was always way more interested in playing football than any other sport."

"What's that supposed to mean." Eileen shook her head. "You nearly drowned out there today."

"It means ..." Dan took a deep breath and kissed her again, this time on the lips. He backed away and looked her in the eyes. "It means your boyfriend never learned how to swim."

* * *

In the back of the truck heading down the road from Bastogne Dan shivered at the memory, but the other medics thought it was just from the cold.

He opened his mouth again as if to speak, but GMC shook his head, and Dan stayed silent. The barrage of artillery gradually faded into echoes, just like the conversation. The focus returned to the attempt to stay warm and pass the time with a little sleep. Still, Reb had to get in one more comment.

"Well, Sarge, at least you won't have to worry about anything for a while. A nice break back at camp. Maybe we'll just sit out the rest of the war safe and secure in reserve—wouldn't that be a peach?"

Dan made a tight smile, tightened his scarf, and shoved his hands as deep as he could into the pockets of his coat.

CHAPTER ELEVEN

20 December 1944

The Ardennes

Levine's concerns about the weather were justified. Conditions deteriorated as the convoy slogged its way toward the safety of the Allied rear lines to the west. The tight organization during the slow push into Bastogne was lost on the return.

The trucks, fully loaded with their consignments of GIs and equipment, had torn apart the roads on their ingress. Now empty, the trucks endured frequent spinouts on the shredded pathways slicked with ice and snow. Switchbacks and highways laid out like a maze were further impediments. A full-blown blizzard mixed its wall of snow with fog banks that had not completely disappeared from the previous night. The weather and the damage to the roads broke the original long chain of vehicles into smaller links, and more often than not, the new configurations were left to find their own way back.

Their ambulance was second in line with a band of seven General Motors trucks, or 'Deuce and a Halves' as the soldiers dubbed them in recognition of their weight of two and one half tons. At a fork in the road, the lead truck took the right-hand path, but Smitty stopped short of the dividing intersection.

"Why aren't we moving, Corporal?" Levine demanded. "We don't want to lose contact with them." Levine's trust in the driver's judgment was absolute. Perhaps, it was because they were both from New York City. Maybe it was a simple matter of Smitty's experience as a cabbie in civilian life. Separation from the trucks, however, tested the doctor's faith. Smitty scowled and pounded the steering wheel in frustration.

"Begging your pardon, Captain, but those idiots in front of us don't know what in the Sam Hill they're doing." He wiped at the frost on the windshield. The taillights of the lead truck were barely visible ... and moving away from them. "See that stump over there? The one with the long piece that's sticking up like a spear?"

"The one up on the left?" Levine said.

"Yeah, that one. This is the third time we have passed it in the last hour. These morons have been going round in a circle." Smitty mumbled a series of obscenities before he turned and pointed to the opposite side of the road. "And somebody's been messing with that signpost. I swear those arrows were going in different directions the last time we went by."

The captain pushed back the sleeve of his coat to check his watch. He chewed on his lower lip while his brain churned to find a solution. "Corporal ... This storm doesn't look like it's ready to let up. It's going to be dark soon." He leaned in close and spoke just above a whisper. "If we aren't going to follow those truckers ... what *are* we going to do?"

Smitty yanked at the gearshift. The transmission grinded in response. He swung the ambulance onto the left-hand fork. This part of the highway looked less traveled than its partner. The snow cover was deeper, and the tires slipped on the icy layers underneath. Smitty plowed forward.

While he and the captain kept a lookout for what may lay ahead, the quartet watching through the rear flap of the ambulance could plainly see a fearful reality: no one else was following them. GMC took a peek through the front curtain. When he turned back to the others, his face was as white as the snow. "We're out here on our own. What the hell's going on?"

"The Captain and Smitty know what's best for us." Dan tried to reassure all of them. "They've got some kind of plan, I'm sure."

GMC wasn't mollified, and neither were Bobby and Reb. The enemy could be in the area, and they were alone and un-armed. Bobby lit a cigarette and pulled on it as if he was trying to draw in all the smoke it offered in one big inhale. Reb covered his face with his hands and rocked in his seat.

"Was there a man dismayed," Dan recited slowly through a sly grin. "Not tho' the soldier knew someone had blun-dered…"

GMC gave him an 'are you kidding me' shake of his head, but he picked up the next line.

"Theirs not to make reply."

"Theirs not to reason why," Bobby jumped in, almost in unison with GMC.

"Theirs but to do and die," all three of them recited. "Into the valley of death rode the six hundred!"

"What in the tarnation is going on with y'all?" Reb asked.

"*The Charge of the Light Brigade.*" GMC said. "Alfred Lord Tennyson. Didn't you learn it in school?"

"Not in Tuscaloosa. The three of y'all must be going crazy."

"Maybe you can offer a quick history lesson for our young friend," Dan suggested.

GMC nodded. "The poem's about a British cavalry unit fighting the Russians during the Crimean War nearly a century ago."

"You trying to tell me that the Limeys and the Russkies used to be enemies and now they're friends?" Reb's eyebrows rose.

"Alliances come and go," GMC said. "Who knows...maybe someday the Germans and the Japanese could end up being our friends."

"No way!—I gotta think about that some." Reb jammed his eyes shut and held the sides of his head as if this latest bit of information was going to make his brain explode.

A skid on the ice fishtailed the back of the ambulance, and Smitty strained to keep control. His stream of obscenities sounded throughout the truck, but with a twist of the steering wheel to the left, to the right, and then back to the left, he kept the ambulance kept rolling ahead. The tension eased in the back compartment.

"So ... I get that enemies can become partners," Reb said, a small amount of conviction back in his voice. "Like you Yankees...y'all aren't the worst boys for a son of the South to be stuck with." He scratched his head through his stocking cap as if he was trying to light a fire. "But it's like I'm treed by a bear. I am stuck trying to figger what a poem about the Russkies and Brits has to do with us?"

The other three laughed. Dan reached across and patted Reb on the knee. "*The Charge of the Light Brigade* is a perfect poem for people like us," he said. "Those soldiers knew they were in a bad way, but it didn't make any difference. They were going to do their best because that's what was expected of them." He made a sweeping gesture with his arm. "All of us...the Captain and Smitty, too...we've got a job to do. Whatever is going to happen is what was planned for us. We're going to do it to the best of our ability no matter how bleak things may appear."

"Amen to that," GMC said. "It's why we're here. To do what is necessary."

"Y'all might feel that way," Reb said. "But I ain't sure if I'm up for that when the time comes."

"You'll know what to do." Dan tried to give the frightened teenager as much assurance as possible. "Just keep an eye out, that's what my Pa would tell me. Be ready for anything."

The ambulance went into a prolonged skid until it came to a jerky halt. A new squall had dropped the visibility to near zero. It was blind luck that Smitty spotted a jeep in the middle of the road and slammed on the brakes in time. A large pine tree was sprawled across the highway, the jeep's front end shrouded by its thick branches. A man with officer's bars on his coat walked back to where the ambulance idled. Captain Levine dropped his side window.

"I am certainly glad to see you men this evening," the stymied soldier told them. His voice was crisp, his words measured.

"What happened?"

"We were driving along slowly because of the storm when this tree came crashing down and nearly crushed us. My corporal and I could have been killed."

"Where's your driver?" Levine said. "Does he need medical attention?"

"No, the man is fine. I sent him to get assistance." The officer blew into clenched fists covered by woolen gloves and hopped up and down. The soldier appeared to be in his late twenties. The shoulder of his overcoat bore the patch of a rifle crossed by a pickaxe on a background of pink and white stripes. Dan could see him through the window of the cab. He was struck by the fact that the man's boots appeared almost new. He shook off the thought; the officer's unit must've been able to resupply somehow.

"Well, why don't you climb into the back with the others to get out of the cold until your corporal returns."

"Thank you, but no," the officer said. "I am more interested in seeking your assistance in moving the tree in order that we all may proceed again."

"Sarge," Reb whispered, "is it just me, or does that fella sound a little funny to you?"

"Everybody whose mouth doesn't sound like it's filled with molasses sounds funny to you," GMC interjected. "You're right about one thing, though, kid. This guy's so formal, it's like he's got a broomstick stuck up his ass."

"Check out his boots," Dan said. "It's a wonder—"

"C'mon, men," Levine shouted. "Let's move this tree off the highway." He began to fish around at his feet for a flashlight.

The medics climbed out of the back of the cab. Dan sidled up to the truck's side window and leaned inside to where the Captain still sat. "No sense us all freezing our fingers off," Dan said. "You and Smitty stay in the cab. Rest of us can get it."

Levine nodded and handed Dan the flashlight. "Fine by me," Levine said. Smitty mumbled something about wanting to help, but he remained behind the wheel.

Dan padded through the snow to where the other men joined the stranded officer around the tree. They looked like a gathering of steam locomotives. Clouds of frosted breath floated above them each time they grunted in unison from the exertion. The steady snowfall dusted their shoulders and the tops of their helmets.

Ten minutes of strenuous pushing and pulling achieved only incremental success. The footing was slippery and it was difficult to find leverage. Dan was just about to head back to the cab and change his tune about the Captain and Smitty joining them when the officer suggested they take a short rest. He put a cigarette to his lips and then offered the pack to the others. Reb, Bobby, and GMC each took one and made of nod of gratitude. Dan didn't smoke. The officer ignited the Lucky Strike with a Zippo. Each man took a long pull after they were lit. Dan was struck by the way the unusual way the officer held his cigarette. He seemed a man more inclined to be standing next to a roaring fireplace in a parlor than be a combat soldier out on a mission.

"Just curious," GMC said between drags on his smoke, "why would you send your man off while you stayed here?"

"There were several trucks in front of us," the officer said. "I was of the opinion that he might be able to reach them before their distance became too great."

"There he goes again," Reb murmured.

Dan ignored the observation. "Where you headed anyway?"

"I am with the 298th Battalion of Combat Engineers. Our orders are to return to Ardennes, along the Meuse River. Apparently, Headquarters believes that the enemy might sabotage the bridge located there. They would like us to be present to aid in a reconstruction if it proves to be necessary."

"Excuse me, sir," Reb said. "But y'all sure talk different."

The officer attempted a hearty laugh, but it didn't have much depth. He cleared his throat. "I have been told that more than once in this man's army. My family moved from Krakow when I was a small boy. I guess my English is still a work in progress." He motioned to the fallen tree. "I believe we should return to our task."

"Don't worry about Reb, sir," Dan told him. "He thinks everybody should speak like they're from the Deep South."

The officer smiled nervously but offered no other response. He stood between Dan and GMC on one side of the tree trunk, with Bobby, and Reb on the other. Smitty wandered over and smacked his hands together. "You boys need a real man pushing here?" he said.

Dan laughed and nodded. Smitty took his place at the tree. One trio pushed with as much force as their footing allowed while the other gripped branches and pulled. Almost imperceptible at first, progress came in inches and then a few feet.

They needed to stop again; Bobby looked to be near exhaustion.

"I think if we all get on one side the next time," Smitty huffed, "... we should be able to move it enough to get through."

All agreed, but they were grateful for a chance to recharge before making the next attempt. Reb was sent to fetch a canteen, and the remaining men took seats on the tree. Smitty and the officer had another round of cigarettes. Dan wondered how they could smoke; his lungs were burning from the effort in the cold air. He was bent over at the waist and it was difficult for him to raise his head. The way he sucked in deep breaths would have been worrisome if the rest of them didn't look just as spent. Nonetheless, his brain was still buzzing. "I don't want to sound as nosy as our young friend, but can I ask what city you're from, sir?"

"Ah. I was about to ask all of you the same question. My name is Casimir Kalisewski. My acquaintances call me Caz. I am from Chicago...a large Polish neighborhood on the South Side."

"This here's Smitty from New York," Dan said. "Bobby Jepson from Seattle. GMC from Michigan. The kid that went to get the canteen. That's Reb. He's from Alabama. And I'm Dan Gibbons from Cleveland."

Kalisewski nodded each time Dan identified a man and shook hands with all of them when the introductions were complete.

"You a baseball fan, lieutenant?" GMC asked.

"Who in this army isn't?"

141

"That means you must be a big Phil Cavaretta fan," Dan suggested.

"You have been trained well, Sergeant," Kalisewski said with a chuckle. "But how could I follow the feats of Mr. Cavaretta? In Chicago, the Northsiders follow the Cubs, but the good people on the South Side only root for the White Sox."

"Ah," GMC said. "So you're a Luke Appling fan then? Me, I like the Tigers. Hank Greenberg is about as good as it gets in the American League."

The lieutenant scowled. "Hank Greenberg ... not for me. Now, Luke Appling ..." The officer took a short puff on his cigarette. "I wish 'Old Aches and Pains' could stay healthier, but in my mind, he is the best player in the League."

"Yeah, if my Hank wasn't helping us win this war, my Tigers would be too much for your White Sox," GMC boasted. "There's nobody better than Hank Greenberg."

Kalisewski made another face, but quickly replaced it with a tight smile. Reb returned with a canteen and he passed it among them.

"C'mon, let's get this thing off the road," Smitty said after wiping a gloved hand across his mouth. "It's freezing out here."

Dan set up next to the lieutenant as all six of them aligned on one side of tree. He figured what GMC was up to, so he wanted to ask a question of his own. "I've got family in Chicago...in Bridgeport right by Comiskey. We would always go to a place called Twin Anchors after a Sox game. They've got the best ribs in town. Ever been there?"

"Of course." The officer heaved against the tree. "Twin Anchors. A fine establishment. I have been there many times." Jack gave him a warm smile.

The men pushed together. With renewed vigor, they were able to move the large fir several more feet to the side of the road. Finally, there appeared to be enough room between the tree and a deep ditch on the other side to squeeze through both vehicles. The men congratulated each other as they walked back to the jeep. Kalisewski climbed behind the wheel and pumped the accelerator several times. The motor roared to life as soon as he turned the key. He gave a formal salute to his rescuers. "Your assistance was invaluable, gentlemen. I know this area well. Instruct your captain to follow me. I will make certain we all reach our destination safely." Kalisewski reversed his jeep several feet to maneuver past the tree. He gave the okay to the ambulance by making a circle with his thumb and forefinger and then drove forward.

The squad climbed back into the ambulance, all except Dan. He grabbed Smitty by the shoulder, pulled his ear close, and whispered to the man. Dan jumped in the back. Smitty into the cab. He engaged the clutch and shifted, but when he stomped on the accelerator, the ambulance made a ninety degree spin in reverse and then raced away in the opposite direction.

"Corporal!" Levine said. "What are you doing? Follow that officer. He knows where he's going."

"Sorry Captain," Smitty said. "Nothing doing." The ambulance hurtled along the snowy road.

"Why not?" Levine asked.

"Because we're medics." Smitty snarled.

"Have you lost your mind?" Levine screamed.

Smitty reached the fork in the highway, hit the brakes, and swung the steering wheel with a violent twist to his left. Whether it was a miracle, or just a cab driver's skill, the ambulance made a perfect turn just short of ninety degrees. Smitty was headed forward on the new road almost before the maneuver was complete.

"I need an answer, Corporal," Levine demanded. "Why aren't we moving ahead?"

"It's ahead that I'm worried about," Smitty grumbled.

"Then stop this vehicle. That's an order."

"Sorry Captain. That's an order we need to disobey." Smitty shifted gears and stomped down hard on the accelerator. The truck fishtailed back and forth, nearly going into the culverts on the sides of the road, but Smitty never reduced speed until the taillights of the trucks they abandoned thirty minutes earlier were once again visible. He downshifted to a slower pace, and for the first time since he executed his stuntman move, Smitty loosened his white-knuckled grip on the steering wheel.

The Captain's face was scarlet. "Of all the insubordinate acts. You know I don't care much for all the military formality, but what makes you think you can disobey my direct order?"

"Ask the Sarge," Smitty said, pointing with a thumb over his shoulder in Dan's direction.

Levine sat for a moment as if trying to lower his blood pressure. The pulsing vein in his neck indicated that was not working. He pulled back the curtain behind his seat with such force that it tore away from the hooks holding it in place.

"Sergeant! What did you say to Corporal Smith that would cause him to place all of us in such jeopardy? We might have been killed."

"How did Smitty explain it to you, sir?" Dan asked.

"All he said was 'because we're medics.'"

"Right," Dan said. "And medics don't carry guns."

"What in the world are you talking about?" Levine said. The rest of the men in the back of the ambulance were staring at Dan. All except GMC. He just grinned.

"Actually, sir, we might have been killed if we had stayed with that officer," GMC said. "I had my hunches, but it was the Sarge here who figured it out. Tell 'em, Dan."

"It was the shiny boots that first made me suspicious," Dan explained, his face earnest. "But let me walk you through my fuller case. Question one: any of you seen the Captain here go anywhere for long without at least one of us close by? That's one of the reasons Smitty stayed in the cab as long as he did."

The group, including the Captain, nodded in agreement.

"Question two: when a regular guy has a cigarette, how does he hold his smoke? Between the index and middle finger, right? That guy held it with the tips of his thumb and index finger."

"You heard him say about moving from Poland when he was a kid," Bobby interrupted. "He probably watched his parents do it that way and he's just copying them."

"That's what I thought at first," Dan said. "But I knew he was full of it when GMC started talking about the Tigers. The guy made a face each time GMC bragged about Hank Greenberg. That wasn't a baseball thing. That officer plain hates Jews."

145

"Not every anti-Semite is a Nazi," Bobby countered. "I know folks in America who feel the same way. Isn't right, but that's how it is."

"True," Dan said. "If my mother hadn't raised me to be a gentleman, I swear I would've punched him right in the nose."

The truck fishtailed on some ice, and Smitty let off the gas to right its direction.

"Go on," Levine said. "How were you so convinced?"

Dan cleared his throat. "The officer said he was from the south side of Chicago, so that means he could only be White Sox fan, and not the Cubs. No self-respecting Southsider would root for the Cubbies."

"GMC asked him if Cavaretta was his favorite player," Bobby offered. "The officer said he wasn't because Cavaretta played for the Cubs. That was the right answer. That proved he was a Sox fan."

"Nope," Dan said. "It only proved that the officer had been well-drilled by German headquarters to know which players were members of which Chicago team. Just before that last push to clear the tree, I asked him if he went to a restaurant called the Twin Anchors after Sox games. It's a ribs joint I've been to with my cousin, Eddie, who lives in Chicago."

"Ribs," Reb said. "My kinda place."

"So the officer likes to eat," Bobby said. "You can't fault the old boy for that."

"But ... Twin Anchors is right around the corner from Wrigley Field."

The revelation was as if a bomb had gone off inside the ambulance. The men all knew no White Sox fan would be caught anywhere near the home of the Cubs.

"Well done, Sergeant," Levine said. "Well done." [15]

Dan leaned back against the canvas wall of the rear compartment.

"How come y'all so smart?" Reb said. "I sure wish I had some brains."

"It's not smarts necessarily," Dan said. "It's just being watchful. Like my father always said, when you don't pay attention to the little things, you might miss something important."

He stuffed his hands back into his pockets and nestled inside his coat. It was another taste of helping people out, of doing something that matters. The glow of satisfaction kept him warmer than the woolen clothing ever possibly could, and all he could think about was doing more.

---

[15] During the wait in Bastogne while the 101st deployed, stories circulated about Germans impersonating GIs. Sabotage and obfuscation were as real as the Panzers moving west. In uncertain times, even rumors could become powerful weapons against any army. The possibility of the enemy posing as fellow Americans was difficult to consider for many Allied soldiers, but real nonetheless.

CHAPTER TWELVE

24 December 1944

Twenty-one hours before midnight.

A drop of condensation fell from the hull and stabbed the back of Willy's neck like a dull knife. He jerked and dropped the tool he was using on a torpedo. It had been fifty-four days, seventeen hours, and forty-one minutes since U-474 set sail from Bergen, and there were nineteen minutes to go before this shift ended. The upcoming six-hour respite would not provide any relief. The breaks never did.

His depression was interrupted by a resounding reverberation, followed by a hissing intake of air. Pain exploded in his left ear. The clatter was from built-up pressure in the schnorchel, the ventilation pipe affixed alongside the periscope on the conning tower. Even when the noise gave him a warning, there was nothing he could do but accept the punishment and hope the throbbing would subside before it became inhibiting.

A schnorchel provided fresh air when a German submarine was submerged but still somewhat close to the surface. Its length was nearly the same as the periscope, approximately sixty feet. That shallower depth kept the U-boat in the potentially rougher surface waters, and in the early days of the tour, the top portion of U-474's schnorchel snapped off during a North Sea storm. They were able to jerry-rig a solution during one of their nighttime surfacings, but the accident created a new problem. The valve that prevented water from entering through the tube would close on occasion without any reason. When that happened, the airflow reversed and caused a change in the pressure throughout the sub. The first time the valve clamped shut improperly back in November, Willy felt as if the top of his head had been blown away and his ear was on fire. Subsequent malfunctions gradually but consistently diminished the hearing on his left side to almost nothing.

* * *

"Mister Richter!" the Kaleu said. "Give me some good news."

Kapitänleutnant Marquardt was growing impatient with Klaus Richter. The submarine's navigator flinched as he plotted their course with a grease pencil on a plate of glass lying over charts in the control room. The Kaleu paced behind his junior officer, stopping only when he would press close to peer over Richter's shoulder. A band of sweat formed on the route-finder's forehead. Several beads rolled off the tip of his nose and landed with a splat on the glass. U-474's objective was to get into the shipping lanes of the English Channel by a specific time, and the submarine was behind schedule. Calculations were made off to one corner of the glass and then erased with furious swipes of a closed fist. Each computation and subsequent removal increased the irritation of the sub's leader.

"Mister Richter ..."

"Sorry, Kaleu, I have been working through this as best as I can and we cannot reach our destination point on time as long as we keep traveling at this speed." The U-boat was forced to throttle down to no more than six knots when submerged in order to prevent their air pipe from breaking again. "I know we have weather issues and the reconnaissance planes, but we are not going to reach our target unless we go at least several knots faster."

"Which means on the surface?" the Kaleu questioned to an answer he already knew.

"Yes, sir. It's the only way."

"Then, we will increase our speed by going up top. Very good."

* * *

The schnorchel malfunctioned again, but the pressure change was not as troublesome as before. Alone with his thoughts, Willy continued to toy with a bolt he had tightened and loosened multiple times in the last hour. His chore felt like aimless busy work; a tour of two months without any confrontations had removed all the urgency from the crew's preparations.

"Hey beanpole," Hesse snapped, "...take your break."

Willy was bent over, still at work on the fastener.

"Beanpole. Shift change. Now!"

When Willy made no reaction, Hesse jerked him by the shoulder. "When I say now, I mean now? Understand!"

Willy brushed by him without comment, stored his wrench, and retreated to his bunk. The monotony of his existence was unchanged except for a fatalistic sadness that had grown more oppressive each day since they set sail.

"Whew, I'm glad that's over." Someone from behind gabbed his arm. "I said, 'I'm glad that's over.'"

"What do you want, Dieter?"

"Didn't you hear me? I said I was glad our shift is over."

"Sorry. My brain feels like it's paralyzed from doing nothing."

Dieter pressed close against his friend. "But it's like you don't hear anything anymore."

Willy turned his head, unconsciously tweaking his left ear with his little finger like a swimmer trying to clear water. He did not want Dieter to know about his hearing loss. It shamed him, and he didn't want his friend telling anyone else about it. Dieter could never stay quiet.

"I overheard Zimmerman tell Hesse he's been picking up more traffic on the radio," Dieter continued. "Maybe we're going to see some action soon."

Willy gave him a wan smile. He wasn't looking for the enemy. He would be content to keep sailing around without finding anything. All he cared about was returning home to Waldberg. The war had ended for him fifty-five days earlier when he received his mother's letter.

"Do you want something to eat?"

Willy sighed, his stomach rumbling. "Sure, but you're going to get into trouble again. You heard what the Kaleu said.

Supplies are dwindling. He'll kill you if he finds out you're sneaking food again."

Dieter grinned. "Never mind that. I saw some apples near the galley. I'll grab us a couple."

"Just don't get caught."

Dieter went off on his search, and Willy climbed onto his bunk. With his good ear, he could hear the Kaleu voicing his displeasure over another delay. Zimmerman cranked his phonograph through the sub's sound system to provide a temporary diversion. He played a tune from Charlie and His Orchestra, a musical group formed by Josef Goebbels in an attempt to give a Nazi touch to the popularity of swing music. Ludwig had scoffed at the notion. The music wasn't anything like the real thing from Miller, Goodman, and the other American bands he had told his little brother. The tune playing was titled *You're Driving Me Crazy*.

"At least the song's appropriate," Willy whispered, a light mist coating his eyes. He stared into the hull just above his head.

Five minutes later Dieter returned and dropped an apple on Willy's midsection. The pair gnawed at the fruit in silence. Willy declined the offer of a slab of Swiss cheese—mold was visible on its edges—and Dieter was delighted to be able to pop all of it into his mouth. He didn't even bother to strip away the offensive sections. "I'm going to take a nap." Dieter sprayed tiny morsels of cheese onto Willy's pants with his comment. The boy waddled down the cramped aisle between the beds and the torpedoes in their racks and fell into his space at the bottom of a column of three bunks. The springs groaned as they sank to the deck below.

Willy brushed away the crumbs and then retrieved his Nativity figurine from its hiding place. He rubbed a finger along the etched message. Returning it to the silk pouch, he extracted the blank pages that came with his mother's letter. He flipped through each sheet. Smudges dotted the papers and the edges were tattered from constant handling. Part of him wanted to rip the letter into pieces, but the knowledge they were all he had left from his older brother made them as valuable as the ornament with which they shared space. He covered his eyes to hide the tears. The papers fluttered to his chest like leaves falling in a primeval forest.

Willy wiped his eyes. Through his mind ran two thoughts. One was to heed his dead brother's warning. To get out of the military as quickly as he could, somehow, someway. The next time the U-boat went to shore, he could run away and hide in some back alleyway. Little by little, he'd make his way back to his village, to his family and safety. They'd obtain forged passports and cross the border into Austria or Switzerland, maybe even into France. There, they'd live a long life in peace.

CHAPTER THIRTEEN

24 December 1944

Nineteen hours before midnight.

It was still dark when the troop train pulled into the railway station at Southampton, England. The smell of the nearby ocean hung in the air. The trip to the port city during the overnight hours seemed to have been fueled more by uncertainty than coal or diesel. Sleep had proved an elusive goal for most of the soldiers.

Private Doug Tillman stretched and opened his eyes. "You catch any winks?" He rapped Sal DiPrimo on the shoulder. "Man, I don't think I got more than an hour total."

"Out like a light bulb." Sal yawned and shook himself. "But what I wouldn't give for some chow right about now. My gut's rumbling. You hear anything about breakfast?"

"Not 'til we get on the boat—that's what I heard. Might be a while." When their holiday feast back in Piddlehinton was cancelled, the only meal for them ended up being a box of C rations on the train.

"So where's this boat then?" Sal banged on the side of the train." Hey, Sergeant! Let's get this show rolling." Sal was already wide awake and operating at full capacity. The rest of the soldiers cursed the noise. They looked either too weary from the trip or too self-absorbed to answer.

Doug and his mates from the 66th Division had left Alabama and been sent across the Atlantic. They'd been in the English village of Piddlehinton since Thanksgiving, repeating, ad nauseum, the same drills as the ones they did in Florida and Alabama. Of late, their thoughts about the deployment to France had been replaced by plans for a Christmas Eve feast and a holiday furlough.

All that had changed eighteen hours earlier when Sergeant Bill Zoller, their platoon leader, delivered the orders that they were to break camp. The Germans' thrust west had not been blunted, and the 101st was cut off at Bastogne. Allied Command made a hurried call for reinforcements. The Black Panthers of the 66th Division were finally heading into the action. Sergeant Zoller looked as if steam was going to come out of his ears over Sal's attitude, but he let it go for the moment. Instead, he concentrated on herding his men off the train.

Doug blinked in the early morning shadows. "There's the boat. See it?" He pointed down a still-darkened road to where the smoking stacks of a large steamer could be seen under the amber glow of distant spotlights.

Sal dropped his overloaded duffel bag with a thud. "That's a long way to walk. How far do they expect us to carry all this crap?"

"Maybe to Berlin." Zoller's voice blistered from behind. "The brass is tired of all your griping, DiPrimo. Now pick up your gear and get moving."

Sal shrugged, while Doug allowed a small grin to surface. The men gathered field packs, duffel bags, and weapons—more than one hundred pounds worth of gear for each of them—and fell in with other soldiers marching to the waiting ship. A rifle or helmet seemed to be lost every few steps, which meant setting down the rest of the equipment to retrieve the dropped items. The procession was going nowhere fast. The sun was just beginning to rise, and its rays competed without much success against gathering storm clouds. By the time they arrived at the rusting steamer that was to take them across the English Channel, the air was gray and moist. Doug set down his duffel and field pack, laid his rifle across his gear, took a seat on the pavement of the pier, and looked at Sal. "I hope things are better organized here than they were on the train."

"It's the Army, Hollywood. Whaddya expect?" Hundreds of soldiers meandered on the dock, waiting for someone to tell them what they were supposed to do next. Sal surveyed the disorganization on the docks. "Man, what a complete SNA-FU."[16]

Doug leaned back against his duffel and made himself comfortable. If this was like everything else he'd learned so far from his time in the Army, then nothing was going to happen soon.

"Hey, you boys see what I see?" one of the squad members, the always-hungry Gerry Dugan, noticed. "Across the pier. Red Cross truck. Bet they've got something to eat."

"And girls!" Sal said. "C'mon boys, I'll race ya there!"

---

[16] Slang for *Situation Normal All Fouled Up* (coarser words are sometimes substituted for *fouled*).

Doug wasn't inclined to move, but his stomach was growling too. He forced himself to join the group of soldiers massed around the food wagon. Sure enough, the boys found donuts and pretty girls. Doug smiled at a blue-eyed volunteer who handed him three donuts and a cup of coffee. "You're cute," she said, and handed him three more donuts. A few years back, he would have hung around the Red Cross truck as long as possible. He would have sweet-talked the girl and asked for her address to write, but today he only smiled politely at the extra food and kept walking.

"Orders are in," Zoller barked. "Report to the lieutenant at the opposite end of the dock. The sergeant pointed south. A long queue of GIs snaked toward a checkpoint set up at the foot of an extended gangway. Doug looked at the sea, stuffed the last of donuts in his mouth, and scowled.

"Don't worry, Hollywood, things will be better inside the ship." The encouragement came from Rich Novak, another member of the rifle unit.

"It's not the ship I'm worried about," Doug said.

Novak gave him a puzzled look but didn't press the matter.

Doug kept his thoughts to himself. It wouldn't do any good blabbing what was on his mind to the rest of the boys.

Their transport to France was to be aboard a Belgian liner, the *S. S. Leopoldville*, a deteriorating hulk of a ship that seemed to groan each time a soldier climbed onto her main deck. Hundreds of private vessels had been commandeered to help with the Allied war effort, and the *Leopoldville* was part of that fleet. Launched in 1929, she looked older than her years. The steamer was long overdue for a paint job, and multiple patches were slapped on her hull above the water line.

She didn't seem capable of making it out of Southampton Harbor, much less across the Channel.

The soldiers lined up, passed around smokes, and ate whatever they could scrounge. Occasionally an off-color joke was told, but mostly the soldiers just stood and waited. The registration process went as smoothly as a root canal with a dull drill. The squad didn't reach the checkpoint until 0730. Once everyone was mustered, Zoller marched them up the entrance ramp and then across the main deck to a hatch near the stern.

The original layout of the *Leopoldville* didn't provide enough accommodation space for her wartime duties, and modifications had been made throughout the ship. The rifle squad was assigned to Compartment Four on the F Deck, the second lowest of the seven levels on the ship. A group of hatches, approximately forty feet square in size, dotted the main deck. The shafts ran down all the way to the hull. Wooden planking was installed at every level within the hatches; a small section in the center removed to allow for a series of stairs. The narrow steps were set in a crisscross design.

The unit labored down multiple flights before they finally reached their compartment. They were among the final ones cleared through the checkpoint, and their assigned area was already filled beyond capacity. This part of F Deck served as the mess hall under normal conditions. Multiple dining tables were affixed to the floor throughout the level. GIs had already staked claims to most of the flattops, and gear that wasn't being used as pillows was piled haphazardly on the floor.

Doug found it difficult to move. Rows of bunks, already filled, lined the outside walls, and hammocks were strung from the poles that supported the deck above them. Most of those were occupied, too. Bob Bristol, the "nervous Nellie" of the squad, searched the faces of the soldiers around them, his eyes darting back and forth. "Where's the rest of our company? I thought we were supposed to stay together?"

"I'm sure they'll get us all sorted out once we get there," Novak hollered over the noise. "C'mon, let's find a spot."

Bristol seemed assuaged and joined in the quest for a few feet of space to claim for their own. Eventually, they were able to stow their gear under one of the tables and sprawled on top of their duffels. Bristol stuck out his head from their hiding place and let loose an elaborate whistle that cut through the din. The familiar sound of his unique call drew the others from their unit to the temporary home. Before they could settle in, the steamer lurched.

"Hey, we're moving ..."

The *Leopoldville* left Southampton and sailed away from her mooring in the company of another troopship, the *HMS Hotham,* and three escorts: the French frigate, *Croix de Lorraine,* and two British destroyers, the *HMS Brilliant* and the *HMS Anthony.* With a precious cargo of more than two thousand men, she initiated her twenty-fifth crossing of the Channel. The sounding from her massive horns stilled the hubbub below. Hot, stale air hung over the huddled men like a misty shroud. The length of the voyage—likely eight to ten hours—would only worsen the circumstances before their arrival in Cherbourg.

"Anybody knows what's next?" a voice finally spoke out in the semi-darkness.

"We're supposed to meet on top for lifeboat drills," came a response. "Probably the same crap they put us through when we came over."

"What time?"

"Around ten hundred."

Doug glanced at his wristwatch; it was nearly 9:45 a.m. His nap would need to wait.

The drill topside proved a waste of time as the Belgian crew did not speak English—or chose not to—and they made just a token effort to demonstrate how to launch the lifeboats. Judging by the number of GIs that came topside, it appeared that fewer than twenty percent of the soldiers even bothered to participate.

Back below, Doug managed to fall asleep, missing the journey's first meal at noontime. Several hours later, he crawled out from his hideaway. A queasy sensation percolated in his stomach.

"Hey, Sleeping Beauty! So glad you could join us." Sal jabbered like a magpie.

"I don't feel so good," Doug said with a moan.

"Well, don't stay around here. It smells bad enough already. Go up top."

Doug bent down to retrieve his coat. The move made his head spin. He picked his way through the other soldiers and sped up the stairs as fast as the narrow flights would allow. A cold wind hit him in the face when he came through the hatch on Deck C. The wind mixed with mist off the choppy waters of the Channel, and bile bubbled in his throat. He sprinted to a nearby railing. Most of the coffee and donuts from breakfast made their escape. Much to his regret, he found he was facing into the wind. He wiped his face with a sleeve and ran a hand through his hair to remove some of what had been returned by Mother Nature's ironic cruelty.

The weather had him vexed, but something else dark stirred inside his thoughts. Everywhere he looked, his surroundings reminded him of blackness. Doug dared not tell the rest of the boys.

What caused his grief was no more than the simple fact he was at sea.

* * *

A large bank of clouds on the horizon appeared to be moving straight toward them with increasing speed.

It was 1939, and Consuelo's phone call about Doug's injury had pushed Kate Tillman into cutting short her Catalina getaway with her husband, Big Jim. The couple's afternoon departure meant they would not make it back to the mainland until after the winter sun would set.

Once they cleared Avalon Bay, the waters and the wind grew rougher. Kate showed no concern as the sailboat knifed through the burgeoning waves. Her focus was riveted on getting back to her injured son as quickly as possible. Besides, she was no stranger to sailing.

The conditions had Big Jim's full attention, however, and his face was paler than the sail that billowed above him. The clouds were moving closer, growing in size and darkening in color. He staggered to keep upright on the pitching deck. The movie hero reached inside his shirt to caress a small medallion Kate had given him the day before as an anniversary gift. The small effort at fortification wasn't enough. Big Jim wished he were anywhere else.

Kate's red hair was pulled back, and the wash from the waves gave her face a glistening sheen. Her hazel eyes were alive with purpose as she worked at the helm. "Do you know what sailors used to call this run?" she shouted above the gale.

"A bad place for a vacation?" Big Jim offered meekly.

"Hurricane Gulch. It was because of how quickly the winds could come up."

"My," he said. "What an encouraging thought."

Water splashed over the boat, drenching both of them. With a deep-throated laugh, she wiped off the Pacific's slap. A crest propelled them into the air before crashing the boat back down with a fury. The canvas strained against its riggings and the wind took on a menacing, whistling tone. Losing his battle for balance, Big Jim dropped into a seated position on the deck, the remaining color now gone from his face.

"We should turn back and let this blow through," Big Jim pleaded. "The people back at the dock said things could get really bad for us. Doug will be okay if we don't get there until tomorrow."

"I couldn't turn around now even if I wanted to," Kate said. "We'd be going right into the teeth of this thing if we did. We're better off just trying to stay ahead of it and letting it blow us back home."

Big Jim shook his head. He was unconvinced of the strategy, but he knew his wife wouldn't be dissuaded. The skies were now completely dark. Rain mixed in with the ocean waves and buffeted the sailboat. The strongest gust yet suddenly unleashed a mainsail line from its hook, sending it into a twisting, fluttering frenzy.

"Quick!" Kate ordered. "Grab that before it gets tangled with the others."

"I don't know if I can ..."

"Do it, Jim! We can't let the lines get tangled."

He tried to move to the starboard side, but when another swell elevated the boat, he sank back into his immobile position. The wind was living up to its hurricane nickname, and the guide ropes that enabled Kate to pilot the sailboat through it were becoming increasingly snarled. Accommodating his fear was no longer a consideration. He must help her correct the problem if they were going to survive.

"Okay, try this," Kate offered. "Work your way back toward me and take the tiller. I'll go forward and secure the lines."

"I don't know ... No, I can't ... I can't move."

"Sure you can. Just hang onto the rail there and slide back toward me. I'll help you." She gave her husband her warmest smile, hoping it would help him summon the courage. Things would get treacherous quickly if she didn't get the mainsail back under control, but he mustn't know how perilous their situation could become.

Big Jim inched his way along the port rail, hesitating each time the boat was tossed by a wave. The clouds, now ebony more than steel gray, hung so low they appeared to have become attached to the churning sea. When they set sail, Kate calculated they could stay ahead of any trouble, but the storm had risen much faster than anticipated. The rain's intensity increased, not in developing drops, but in sheets of moisture. Jim finally reached her side at the helm.

"Here, take this and hold it steady." She wanted her voice to be calm and soothing, but in the rain and howling wind, she needed to shout to be heard.

"Kate! I don't know about this." The wind all but swallowed Jim's croaking words.

"No problem, my love," she said with a smile. "This will make the backdrop for a great movie someday. Just keep it as steady as you can. I'm going to get that sail."

Kate kissed him lightly on the nose and scrambled along the starboard side to deal with the lost lines that cost them control of the mainsail. With her feet wedged against the cabin and her backside pressed against the rail, she manipulated the ropes this way and that to get them free. Her hands grew cold, buffeted by the wind and water, and the roughness of the cords made her palms red and raw. When the two lines finally worked free, one was snatched by the wind and flew out of her grip. No amount of stretching could reach it. She would need to get to her feet.

With a smile at Jim, she slowly stood. The line still darted away from her. The sailboat rose on the apex of another wave, and the momentum was just what she needed. With a triumphant whoop, she claimed her prize.

The wave providing the helpful boost threw the sailboat downward with savage intent. Kate staggered momentarily, but stayed on her feet. Proud of herself, she smiled and made an exaggerated stage bow. At that moment, the wind shifted, sending the boom of the mainsail from the port side across to starboard. The heavy wooden beam caught her on the forehead just as she was rising. Kate tumbled over the rail and into the stormy seas.

"Kate! KATE!"

One moment she was there, and in a flash, she was gone. Hanging hand over hand onto the rail with a white-knuckled grip, Jim crawled forward to search for any sign of his beloved. He spotted her floating on her back in a swell not more than twenty feet from the boat. Her eyes were open and it looked as if she was smiling, although she had suffered a large gash on her forehead and blood flowed from the opening.

"Kate ... Kate! Are you all right?"

There was no response.

Jim quickly found a preserver ring on a line and threw it over the side. The float landed near Kate, but she made no attempt to reach for it. He grabbed a pole and tried to hook her clothing, but she remained beyond his grasp even when he leaned as far over the side as his fear would allow him. When another large wave tossed the boat violently, he fell back in horror.

"Kate! KATE! KATE ..."

His screeching croaks soared in an unending litany as he pulled his knees tightly to his chest. The unconscious first lady of Hollywood bobbed in the waves. Her traumatized husband was paralyzed, powerless to do anything.

* * *

Doug pushed back his right sleeve to reveal the jagged scar running between the bend of his elbow and wrist.

His stomach was still churning from the Leopoldville's rise and fall across the Channel. The scar emitted a reddish glow while the rest of his exposed arm paled from the cold. He ran his hand across the bumpy skin in an erasing action that had become his tic whenever emotion got the better of him. The skin soon became raw and painful. He covered his arm with a rough pull on his cuff.

In anxious times like these, he once would have prayed. But Doug remained at the rail in sullen contemplation while the wind and the water's spray mocked him. He pulled the medallion hanging with his dog tags from underneath his shirt and traced the shape of the dolphin and the frog on its face. He raised it to his lips, lightly kissing it. A tear slid down his cheek and he quickly wiped it away.

The bouncing main deck and the rickety steps back down to F Deck made Doug's return a cautious one. The deliberate pace allowed the stain on his coat to develop an unpleasant odor by the time he reached his unit among the hundreds of GIs.

"Hoo boy, what did you do to yourself?" Sal groaned.

"No offense, Hollywood," Bob Bristol said, "but you really stink."

"Sorry, guys," Doug said. "I usually don't get seasick."

They helped him remove his overcoat, and he stowed it next to the other gear below the table. He found a place alongside Novak in the circle of men.

"They're supposed to feed us again," Sergeant Zoller announced with a glance at his watch. "Should be any time now."

The revelation did little to change their overall mood. Dugan's personality lacked its usual pep as he finished his latest cigarette and crushed it on the edge of the table. He had another going in his mouth before the fire had gone out in the previous one. Bristol's whistling seemed aimless and without melody. Novak tugged at the laces on his boots, while Zoller checked his watch seconds after the last time he looked.

"Anyone notice we keep changing directions?" Doug asked. "When I was up on deck, this tub started making zig-zags."

"They must be worried about U-boats," Novak said.

"How would you know?" Sal scoffed.

"My brother's in the Navy. He says they have the convoys move like that to keep the Germans from sneaking up on them." Novak grabbed Dugan's cigarettes and tapped out a half-dozen from the pack. He arranged all but one of the smokes into a formation that matched the one in which the *Leopoldville* was involved. "Here's our convoy." Novak passed one hand over the cigarette grouping while brandishing the remaining Camel with his other. He placed it outside the configuration. "This lone one here is a U-boat, and the object is to keep the Germans from joining our party."

"I don't get it," Bristol said.

Novak moved the cigarette representing the U-boat inside the rear portion of the formation. "If our convoy keeps going in a straight line towards Cherbourg, a U-boat might be able to slip in unnoticed because of the sound of our propellers. Our sonar has a hard time picking up enemy activity when their noise mixes in with ours. The Krauts could sneak in and get a shot off."

"And the zigzagging motion can prevent that?" Doug asked.

"Well, it helps." Novak adjusted his cigarette convoy into a different position. "If we keep changing our direction all the time, then it increases the possibility that the German sub stays out in open water where sonar has a better chance of finding it. That's good for us, because once they establish the U-boat's position, the destroyers can chase after it."

"I saw that," Doug interrupted. "After I got sick, I was standing at the rail when all of a sudden those English destroyers took off to the left."

"That's *port*, Hollywood," Sal said.

"Thanks," Doug said. "I forgot you were the expert here."

Sal laughed. "Look, boys, all I know is I don't want any Kraut submarines breathing down our necks. If Novak says it's good for us to zigzag, then that's all right by me. Ain't no way we're going to get hit. So just relax and enjoy the ride. That's what I say." Sal leaned back against his duffel bag.

"No way we can get hit, Novak?" Doug asked. "You sure?"

Novak grinned. "What's the matter, Hollywood, you don't like to swim?"

"Let's just say that the sea and I haven't been friends for a few years now," Doug said.

From an entrance behind them a dinner gong sounded.

"Chow time!" Sal said, and leaped to his feet. The others weren't far behind.

Doug stood up slowly and took a deep breath. *You can do this,* he said to himself. *Just stay out of the water, and you'll be fine.*

168

CHAPTER FOURTEEN

24 December 1944

Eight hours before midnight.

"Oh come, all ye faithful ...."

Doug's singing voice was off-key and halting before it drifted away altogether. He
yanked at his collar and shook his head like a drenched collie.
What am I doing? he thought. *Now that song's gonna be stuck
in my head.*

Nearby in the late afternoon winter twilight, a quartet of
GIs belted out the carol. Doug's boots tapped a muffled beat
on the deck, more to warm his feet than to keep time. His decision to join in with the chorus was initially a welcome
diversion, but now it proved just one more element of aggra-
vation. The wind mocked him with icy blows of sleet and
seawater, and the slate sky mirrored his mood. As he clung to
the railing, he turned his shoulders to dull the brunt of the
wintry blasts. It was impossible, however, to escape the sing-
ers, who were in full throat despite the conditions. The
gurgling in his stomach was a portent for more misery.

169

An early dinner had been delivered to his squad down on F Deck fifteen minutes earlier. The meal was an unidentifiable entrée. Mystery meat floated in a dark liquid whose grease-layered surface gave off a purplish glow as it sloshed in the bucket being used as a serving dish. Whether it was the smell from the dinner pail, or just the overall atmosphere in the cramped space, nausea forced him to make a second trip topside.

"Oh come ye, oh come ye, to Bethlehem ... "

The soldier choir continued to sing, but Doug did not join in this time. He picked at paint chips from the rusted railing sticking to his palms. His stomach rumbled again.

"Hate to say it, Hollywood. But you look like crap." Sal uncorked a phlegm-filled wad of spit over the side. "Those morons are unbelievable." He tossed his head in the direction of the carolers. "We're going into battle and they're singing. That would make me sick, too."

"You know, I hate it when you call me Hollywood." Doug's comment was made more with resignation than displeasure, but it was ignored anyway.

"Just like that slop they were trying to serve us. I wasn't gonna eat any of that crap." Sal was a locomotive when his emotions were up, and there was little anyone could do to slow him down. "Not that I would ever take anything from them foreigners anyways."

"Just because those cooks are Belgian? What makes you think you're any better than they are? They're on our side."

"That's the trouble with you, Hollywood. You'll probably feel sorry for those Jerries when we get over there and start to mow 'em down. Not me, brother, not me. I can't wait to start

170

killing me some Krauts." Sal continued his rant, accompanied by bursts from an imaginary machine gun.

It wasn't because of Sal, but Doug's stomach flip-flopped as if he had been sucker-punched in his midsection. He spun from the railing and staggered towards the other side. He flicked at a doughnut scrap trapped in the wool of his overcoat, a reminder not to get seasick upwind as he did before. A gusher of vomit let loose before he could reach the opposite rail, and the residue underfoot sent him skidding on his back until his knees banged against the metal barrier at the rim of the deck.

Sal began to follow his friend, but he quickly stopped when Doug got sick. "Whoa! That's nasty, Hollywood! I'm outta here." The little man spun on his heels and left before he lost it, too.

Doug climbed to his feet and draped his upper torso over the top rail. He stayed motionless for almost five minutes. Sal's departure allowed him to return to his solitude and his dark mood. He glared at the taunting waves below before fumbling inside his shirt to find his medal. He squeezed it with a death grip.

"Hey, Mac, you okay?" A nameless face among the multitude of soldiers onboard walked over. "Looks like you're having a rough time."

"Nah, just a little seasick." Doug pushed the medallion back underneath his clothing. "I'll be okay once we get off this boat."

"You'd think the Army would've let us stick around awhile and celebrate Christmas first, huh?" The soldier was older, early forties at least. He was wrapped in a large over-coat.

"Oh yeah, Christmas." Doug scowled. He stared at the icy Channel bucking beneath them rather than say anything else.

"It's okay, we don't need to talk," the soldier said. "I saw you moving your lips into the wind like you were talking to someone invisible. I just thought you might just like to, you know, talk to someone you can see—share that spirit we're supposed to have at Christmas time and all." The soldier chuckled, not unkindly.

Doug forced himself to meet the older man's gaze. "Sorry, pal. I'm just not into celebrating any holidays that talk about peace on earth." He turned away a second time.

"You were praying then, weren't you, son?"

Doug looked startled for a moment, then said quickly, "I don't pray."

"It's okay. Lots of soldiers start praying for the first time right before they see action."

"I've prayed lots of times before," Doug told him. "But look, why do you care anyway?"

The man parted his overcoat at the neck and pulled the collar back slightly. Doug could see a chaplain's cross affixed to his lapel. "You might say praying's my thing," the man said.

"Well it isn't mine, sir."

"Hmm, it was once, you said. But not now. Something bad happened to you once, is that it? You blame God, because God could have stopped the bad, but didn't."

"It doesn't seem that simple, sir. It's not solely about blame, I guess. God claims to be so all powerful. He doesn't need to let anything bad happen, if he wanted to. Even this war. He could stop all the fighting if he got involved."

The chaplain nodded and bunched himself up his overcoat. "Seems like a crazy world, doesn't it. Here we are freezing on a washed-up tub in the English Channel. We're all set to stick our rifles in our enemies' faces and pull the trigger. That doesn't seem like the type of world a good God would create, does it?"

"Sure doesn't, sir."

"Let me ask you this, though," the chaplain said. "Supposed you jumped off this railing right now into the water, do you think God would stop you from falling?"

Doug thought a moment. He looked into the sea. "Probably not."

"And—here's the key question—why not? Don't think long about it, son. We're looking for the most obvious answer here."

Doug shrugged and almost chuckled. "Because of gravity?"

"That's right," the chaplain said. "When God created the world he set into motion certain laws that relate to moral and physical realms. Gravity is one of those rules—one of the most basic, in fact. If someone chooses not to heed the law of gravity, like you've just pointed out, then that person suffers the consequences."

"How's that supposed to relate to the war, sir?"

"Mankind chooses to do evil, so wars get started. God allows wars because God respects mankind's decisions, even the bad ones. That's why God isn't the author of evil. You just pointed to the principle yourself—if a soldier jumps off railings into the sea, then the soldier drowns."

"You think I was going to jump, sir? Is that what you're getting at?"

The chaplain smiled. "You looked mighty dejected standing by that rail, that's all. I just wanted to double check to see if you were safe."

"I'm not going to jump, sir. I hate the water."

"Something bad in your past happened with water, then? Something you think was your fault."

Doug's eyes closed and his body shivered. His sorrow, at times, could be overwhelming. The carolers down the deck were still going strong. "My mom drowned, sir." Doug blurted out the words. "That's about all I can say about it. That's why I hate the water. The water started it all off. I don't have anybody left anymore."

"Your father is gone, too?"

Doug nodded his head and closed his eyes tightly, but made no further response. The chaplain had the wisdom not to probe any more deeply. The two men stood together in silence while the *Leopoldville* made another zigzag maneuver. Moments later, two British destroyers peeled away from the convoy. Doug and the chaplain moved farther down the railing to watch the warships race to a point and drop depth charges.

"They must be chasing a U-boat." The chaplain's voice was grave.

Doug pawed at the deck with the toe of his boot.

A whoosh of water rose and fell whenever a charge detonated, and shock waves hit the *Leopoldville* from each explosion beneath the surface. The barrage lasted fifteen minutes. The destroyers returned to the convoy without any success.

Finally, Doug spoke again. "I thought the Germans would be crazy to try anything, but then Novak, uh, one of the guys in my squad, starts talking about all this zigzagging because there might be a U-boat around. Sheesh, what if the Jerries truly are after us?"

"I think we'll be fine, son." The chaplain pointed to the destroyers. "The Brits have it covered, and we're going be docking before you know it. But just in case we're not fine, let me ask you one more question: have you given any thought to making your peace with God."

Doug shook his head. He was silent a while, and then said, "I don't think I'm ready for that yet, sir."

Dusk was falling and the two men could see the lights of Cherbourg twinkling in the distance. The scene looked reassuringly peaceful. Their crossing was almost over.

* * *

"Adeste, fideles, laete triumphante[17]..."

Dan sang in a low tenor as he gazed into the mirror in a makeshift washroom. Cracks fanned out from the center like a spider's web. Several pieces of the glass were missing, freed by some earlier disturbance that knocked it from its perch on a crooked ten-penny nail. His breath fogged the reflection when he moved closer, and his tongue darted in and out from the

---

[17] Latin for *Oh Come, All Ye Faithful.*

side of his mouth as he kept combing and re-combing a cow-lick that refused to be tamed.

His unit had been on break in Ste. Mère Eglise, near Cher-bourg, since their return from Bastogne. They were staying in an abandoned farmhouse they used as their headquarters when they weren't on the move.

The lights flickered, a common reaction whenever the steady stream of trucks and men moving outside created a rumble that would shake the walls. This had become a more frequent occurrence in the time since the Germans launched their offensive. There was little activity outside on this holi-day eve, however, even though the enemy penetration had advanced to within four hundred miles of Cherbourg. Dan should've wondered about the electrical power's lack of sta-bility, but his thoughts were elsewhere.

He had never missed a Christmas with his parents and two brothers, and Eileen was there last year to make it even better. Now they were a world away. He imagined Bud, his little brother, hanging the stockings on the mantel or trying to sneak cookies from a tray as Ma baked in the kitchen. Maybe Tom was bursting through the front door, warning that no one else could place the star atop the tree but him. A cigar in his mouth, Pa would be orchestrating the proceedings from his favorite chair. Nothing remotely resembling that scene was going to happen here in France.

"Snap out of it, you sad sack," he scolded his reflection. "It's Christmas Eve. Make the most of it." He broke back into song.

"What in tarnation are you doing, Sarge?" Reb entered the room from the other side.

"Just getting into the Christmas spirit, my friend. What—you don't like my singing?"

"Is that what y'all call that? Back home, folks might think someone was kicking a dog with all the yelping I heard."

"I'll have you know that my sainted mother thinks I have a wonderful voice. I expect they'll have me leading the congregation tonight."

"Then say some prayers for everybody that's going to be sitting around you."

Dan chuckled at the putdown and then changed the subject. "Tell me ... what have you heard? Anything new with the 101st?"

"I was just talking with one of the drivers," Reb informed him. "He says Bastogne's still surrounded. Says they're running low on supplies, too."

Dan closed his eyes to contemplate the situation for the men they had left just days earlier. The silence made his young squad mate antsy.

"You think our boys can hold out?"

"They've got to."

Dan glanced out the window at the layers of leaden clouds that had dominated the skies for more than a week. "Maybe when this weather breaks, we can get some air support for the guys."

Reb rubbed the stubble of a beard sprouting on his chin. "I hear ya, Sarge," he said, then made a sudden grin. "Anyway ... I gotta take a leak." He made a mock salute and went off to relieve himself.

Dan glanced back at the fractured mirror and gave another pull on his uniform. He was alone again with his thoughts of missing the family's Christmas celebration. His pronounced exhale would have been noticeable if there were anyone else there to hear it. He reached into a pocket and pulled out the small, black leather pouch. Inside were the wooden rosary and a note. One of the creases on the folded piece of paper had a developing tear. He opened it with care.

Dan,

    First rosary I've ever blessed! A little reminder of God's protection from your big brother the priest. Remember, no matter where you are, I'm always going to be there for you.

    Tom

Dan had missed his brother's ordination into the priesthood. He was boarding a landing craft for the Normandy assault on that late spring day.

The small page went back into the pouch and he turned his attention to the rosary beads. They were just small bits of wood linked together by a simple string. The cheap black paint covering them was already wearing in spots. Still, he couldn't think of any gift that meant more to him. With a final stroke of the little metal crucifix at the end of the string, he replaced the rosary in the pouch and sighed again. He longed for his mother's cooking; the smell of his father's cigars; the interaction with his two brothers. The tender feel of a warm embrace from his girlfriend. This Christmas was going to be anything but what he wanted.

Softly, he returned to his singing.

* * *

Herbei, o ihr Gläubigen,Fröhlich triumphiernd...[18]

Willy's gangly frame spasmed as he sang under his breath. Two months in the cramped quarters had taken a toll on his body. Singing his favorite carol was a desperate attempt to keep his mind off his misery. Every muscle seemed to cry out, and the pressure in his damaged ear was unrelenting. The submarine made a violent shake, and he moaned involuntarily.

"Don't be afraid, Beanpole. It's not time to die ... yet." Hesse lay in the bunk directly across from him. "We don't have to worry about the enemy. Our wonderful technology will probably kill us. Or maybe you little boys will do something stupid and send us all to a watery grave."

Willy ignored him. The sub's width was no more than sixteen feet. It was nearly impossible to do anything that was not noticed by someone else. When Willy mustered no response, Hesse turned away and absently scratched himself. Other sailors dozed, some read, and a few just stared off at nothing in particular.

The waiting, the interminable waiting, was the real enemy of submariners. For the raw recruits comprising most of this crew, the enemy was winning. Willy sought solace in the silk bag guarding his treasured keepsakes. Ludwig's pages remained in place, but the wooden carving he caressed with a finger as it lay in the palm of his hand. Even at close inspection, it was difficult to discern what it was.

His father was a master woodworker, and his furniture and decorative pieces were in great demand throughout Bavaria.

---

[18] *O Come All Ye Faithful*, in German

In his free time, a handmade Nativity set was the senior Mül-ler's continuing passion. He would add new carvings, or refine the existing ones, whenever he was struck by a new creative spark. His figurines were exquisite, designed with delicate but detailed features and painted in vivid colors. The crèche held the prominent position among all of the family's Christmas decorations. His two sons were going to inherit his woodworking talent; he was determined about that. The treas-ure in Willy's hand had been the first attempt at fulfilling his father's hopes.

It was supposed to be a shepherd, a Christmas gift for his mother when he was six years old. Ludwig teased him that he couldn't tell if the carving was a shepherd ... or one of the sheep. His mother came to his defense, silencing his brother with a withering stare. She placed the gift in the center of the crèche. The memory of that Christmas Eve ten years earlier raised the intensity of his sniffling.

"What's the matter, boy? Crying for Mother? She can't help you here." Hesse cackled only to be interrupted by a fit of coughing. Too many years of tobacco use and inhaling die-sel fumes had taken a toll on him. Gobs of mucus were stuck in his stubbly beard, and a ham-handed attempt to wipe them away only smeared them deeper into his whiskers.

Willy rolled away from his view. He fought back tears and wiped his nose with his forearm. "I know you would help me, Mother, if you could." The words resounded in his head even though they were barely audible. " ... and Ludwig, too."

He often felt his mother was too doting toward him when he was a child, but he ached for her tender protection at this moment. The whole idea of running away from the military was gaining on him. Willy fingered the blob of wood. "Ludwig was right," he sighed softly. "It does look more like one of the sheep."

Willy returned the trinket to the satchel and closed his eyes.

CHAPTER FIFTEEN

24 December 1944

Seven and a half hours before midnight.

U-474 was within a few miles of the harbor's mouth at Cherbourg when Kapitänleutnant Marquardt issued an extreme quiet order. The U-boat crept along in the murky depths of the Channel. Enemy hunts for the German submarine had intensified, and metallic pings from the fleet's sonar resounded in the otherwise silent surroundings.

Essential crewmembers were at their stations; Willy and the rest lay motionless on their bunks. Conditions within the submarine were fragile at best. U-474 had been submerged at more than sixty meters since early in the afternoon, creating a stifling atmosphere from the lack of fresh air. Potassium packs were just distributed to the sailors in their bunks.

"I hate these things," Dieter said. "The smell is awful."

"Be still," Willy said. "You heard the Kaleu."

The potassium packs, small tins filled with the silvery-gray chemical, acted as rudimentary air filters. The cans would slowly heat during use, and a foul odor would often result. A sailor quiet in his bunk used less oxygen, however, and the packs helped conserve the precious commodity.

"This is crazy. What if they find us?" Dieter said with a whine.

"Quit yelping like a frightened puppy." Hesse hissed at him like a cobra. "Or do you want to make it even easier for them?"

"Drop dead," Dieter muttered.

Hesse leapt with a start and pounced on the boy, choking him with a greasy forearm across the throat. Three sailors pulled Hesse away, but the sonar sounds grew in volume, and the gaps between the pings decreased. The commotion had not gone undetected by those listening above.

"Hard to port ... bow down twenty ... stern up five," the Kaleu ordered.

The helmsmen sprang into action, and Burtzlaff rang the alarm.

"All hands forward. Get into diving position."

The men left their bunks and formed a tightly bunched group at the bow to help in the descent. The sonar pings reverberated against the hull like cathedral bells.

"Garbage cans!"[19] came a warning shout from the radio room.

A wallop of water exploded against U-474's outer shell. The sub trembled. Another command was barked, and the sub moved hard to starboard. The dive continued amidst the thunder created by additional depth charges. The detonations went off in a patterned approach: four to port, four to starboard,

---

[19] The submariners' nickname for depth charges

now four more directly ahead of their course. Marquardt kept changing the sub's path, trying to keep the hunters from locking in on their position.

"Ease the bow to ten degrees," Marquardt barked. "Come to one-one-five."

"All watches report," Burtzlaff said.

"Water-tight, everything is in order ... Water-tight, everything is in order." One after another, replies answered the same thing.

The U-boat maintained its unpredictable pattern downward until her depth reached almost one hundred fifty meters. The destroyers above were casting their nets, hoping to snare the German fish swimming beneath. Far under the sea, the shock waves could still be felt, but the intensity diminished.

Marquardt placed a hand on the shoulder of one of the helmsmen. "Zero the planes and all stop. Let's stay here and see if they'll leave us alone."

There was no sound except for the pinging. One minute passed, then another, the apprehension almost more maddening than an actual attack. Three minutes oozed into four. All waited in breathless fear of death from above.

In the early morning hours, U-474 had picked up radio traffic from a convoy of two steamers and three escort destroyers. They maintained contact but stayed far enough behind to avoid detection until they could determine the enemy's destination. By noontime, Richter had the target: the French port of Cherbourg. Now U-474 needed to reach the most advantageous position to be able to make her strike, even at the risk of losing her secrecy. The chess match with the ships above them went on throughout the afternoon.

The commander of the convoy followed protocol. The Allies' standard response to a perceived threat from below was to make a depth charge strike—normally 40 or so underwater bombs—in ten to fifteen minute barrages. Although their efforts had yet to produce a positive result, the attacks continued. This latest assault—like the ones that preceded it—was a failure thanks to Marquardt's expertise at evasion. The pinging, at last, ceased altogether. Still, no one dared move, and the only sounds were the shallow inhalations of the crew from stem to stern.

Burtzlaff broke the silence. "Watches report."

"Water tight, sir ... no damage of consequence."

The all-quiet order was still in place, but whispered words were passed quickly in a collective exhale. The waiting would continue, but the confidence of the inexperienced crew was bolstered by the good news. This wasn't a training exercise in the North Sea; the enemy was actually hunting them ... and they had survived.

With a wary glance upward, Marquardt took the microphone from its holder and cleared his throat. "This is the Kaleu speaking. Men, we stand on the brink of greatness. This is what we have been training for all these months." He clicked off the sound system to let his message be absorbed, and then clicked it on again and continued. "Perhaps the Allies think we are afraid of the challenge. The misguided above us do not know of the courage and ingenuity of the men of U-474."

The sailors quietly clapped and cheered in response until at the direction of their leader they again fell silent. Marquardt walked in a small circle in the control room, tethered by the connecting wire of the microphone. He clicked on the loud-speaker again and looked deeply into the eyes of the men standing closest to him. "Our targets are slowing. They are nearing their destination. This will be our best opportunity to move in and stab them in the heart! We will be in tight quarters and we must be proficient in all of our actions." He paused again to gesture with his free hand. "We will succeed because it is our duty to do so. We will bring glory to the Fatherland!"

The men's enthusiasm bubbled over anew, but Willy did not share in the excitement. Contact with the enemy was the last thing he wanted. He walked back to his bunk from his diving position. Climbing up on the moldy bedding, he lay on his back and stared at the hull. He removed his talisman and caressed the carving, cupping his hands to keep it hidden. Lost in his thoughts, he didn't see Hesse approach.

The seaman pulled on Willy's shoulder, and the boy fell out of the bunk. "Make sure your fat friend doesn't do something stupid that gets us all killed." Hess scowled. "And the same goes for you."

Straightening, Willy stood toe-to-toe with his adversary and looked him in the eye. "Dieter and I will do what we're told. Just worry about yourself."

"Look, things will get crazy once the Kaleu launches the attack." Hesse jabbed a stubby finger into Willy's chest. "To be honest, I'm afraid you little boys won't be able to handle it."

Willy's right hand closed more tightly around his treasure. He placed his left on one of the torpedoes that lay in its rack between the bunks, inadvertently greasing himself from the lubricant on the shell. "To be honest …" Willy glared back at the older seaman. "I am tired of listening to you bray like a mule." Dieter might be afraid of him, but Willy had reached a breaking point with the bully. If Hesse wanted a fight, then Willy was more than ready.

The sea veteran cocked his right arm, but the younger man pushed it away. Hesse fumed and raised his hand again.

"Go ahead," Willy dared, "I've got nothing to lose. But you'd better make it good, because the next sound you hear will be your head hitting this torpedo." Willy thrust his chin forward, challenging Hesse to let a punch fly.

The older man paused and then dropped his arm. He spit at Willy's feet and backed away. "Just make sure you do what I need to have done. And stay out of my way." Hesse shoved a sailor on the return to his position at the forward tubes.

From the shadows, Dieter cautiously watched him pass. When he felt it was safe, he walked over to Willy. "You sure showed the old jerk this time."

"Shut up, Dieter."

Dieter's voice became a fearful squeal. "You're bleeding. Did he cut you?"

Willy wiped away a trickle of blood near the jaw line on his left cheek below his ear. It didn't come from anything Hesse had done. "Nah, I'm fine," he lied. "I must have bumped something when I came out of my bunk." The latest rush to deeper depths had caused more distress to his damaged ear. He was so angry with Hesse he didn't realized it was bleeding.

"You sure everything is all right?"

"Can't you just leave me alone for five minutes? I just want to get out of here."

Dieter waited to see if his friend might soften. When Willy climbed back onto his bunk and rolled away from him, Dieter's face fell. He made a hopeful glance over his shoulder when he returned to his own bunk, but Willy remained in the same position. Dieter covered his face with his hands and sank into the bed.

* * *

"Mr. Richter, what is our time frame to Cherbourg?" Marquardt increased the speed of U-474, and his navigator worked his instruments and checked his stopwatch before responding.

"At this speed, Kaleu, we could be in position in no more than twenty minutes."

"Very good. All ahead full."

Convinced the enemy convoy was more concerned now with putting into port than staying in a holding pattern to the hunt them, the U-boat accelerated through the deeper waters. Marquardt was willing to sacrifice battery power and potential damage to the schnorchel in order to gain a positioning advantage on their prey. Richter's calculations were accurate; nineteen minutes later U-474 sat beneath the waves at the mouth of one of the Allies' largest harbors.

"All stop," Kaleu ordered.

As U-474 sat in quiet suspension in the depths, singing filled the sub, in a soft voice at first but growing as it proceeded forward from the stern.

"Bauer, what're you doing back there?" Marquardt placed his hand on Burtzlaff's arm.

"Let him be, Karl. It is good for them."

The captain turned both fore and aft with his arms outstretched. "It's all right, men, go ahead and sing ... but not too loudly. We don't want our friends to know we are coming."

Most of the men joined in with a whisper and the Kaleu smiled broadly. A small frown, almost imperceptible, creased the face of Burtzlaff. Willy was also unmoved. He had no reason to sing. A quiet cheer ensued when the final lyrics of *Deutschland, Deutschland* drifted away.

"Mister Burtzlaff, position the men and prepare to go to periscope depth."

"Yes, Kaleu. Battle stations, men. Stand by for periscope depth."

The crew moved into position in anticipation of a slow rise back toward the surface.

"Extreme quiet, men."

The men barely breathed. Those who had to move crept quietly on soft-soled shoes.

"Anything, Herr Zimmerman?" Burtzlaff asked after minutes of deafening silence.

The radio operator leaned out of his little cubbyhole, peering down the walkway.

"Nobody but us and the little fishies in the sea."

The lighthearted response seemed inappropriate to the gravity of the situation, but the wachoffizier did not reprimand Zimmerman; there were more important matters to consider. He tilted his head down to the ear of one of the helmsmen as if he felt no one else needed to know their next step. "All ahead slow ... bow planes down five ... stern up five."

The electric motors hummed to life and the submarine's screw churned the water slowly. The bow sloped downward; the angle would help give a gravitational boost to the torpedo loading process.

"Mister Hesse, load the forward tubes. . ."

"Aye, Mister Burtzlaff. All together now, my worthless whelps."

The torpedo crew sprang into action. Armed with winches and chains, they took advantage of the submarine's slant to maneuver the missiles into position. It was a difficult task due to the close quarters and the sheer weight of the weapons. Each torpedo was covered with grease to ease its insertion and then its eventual departure from the tube. The loading didn't take much time, but the effort and the risk levels left the men bathed in sweat. As each torpedo was loaded, Hesse made a final check before closing the tube door. He had whipped these raw recruits into a competent group, but his demand for perfection wouldn't allow him to believe they could complete their tasks without error. Finally, satisfied as much as he could be, he closed the door on tube number four.

"Bow tubes one through four loaded and ready for action, Mister Burtzlaff." He spoke slowly, his voice like the low growl of a guard dog ready to attack. He grabbed a piece of chalk and flipped it to a crewmember nearby. "Make your mark. It's the submariner's way."

It was tradition to leave a name or brief message on the tube doors for luck. Some recognized a wife or girlfriend.

Others paid tribute to their Nazi leaders. Others wished revenge upon the enemy.

With great care, Willy wrote the letters L-U-D-W-I-G.

CHAPTER SIXTEEN

24 December 1944

Six hours and forty minutes before midnight.

The sun set in Ste. Mère Eglise, and darkness fell.

It was going to be a cold night, Dan speculated. He glanced through a grimy windowpane on his way to the main room of the farmhouse where the soldiers were billeted.

"Well, look at you," GMC teased. "A big date with a pretty mademoiselle?"

"You figured out how to get Eileen over here?"

GMC laughed. "Couldn't quite swing it, but there are plenty of pretty girls in France. How about a date with one of them?"

"Not on your life," Dan said. "I've already got a Cadillac at home, why would I want to drive a Chevy?"

"Well at least you're in the General Motors lineup." GMC laughed again. "I had you pegged for a Ford man."

Dan returned the laugh. "Nah, no big dates tonight. It's Christmas Eve, that's all. I just thought I should get dressed for the occasion. And then there's Mass at midnight, too."

"I know you're religious and all ... but didn't you already go to church this morning?" [20]

"That was my regular Sunday obligation. Tonight is going to be for Christmas."

"So you're going to church twice in the same day?"

"I would be happy to give you all of the theological reasons ..."

"No thanks. I'm not in the mood for any deep thinking right now." GMC raised a wine bottle. "Smitty found a bunch of these down in the cellar. Captain says it's okay to celebrate a little. You want some?" GMC took a long pull from the bottle. An empty lay on the table near two more yet to be uncorked. He tipped it again, finishing the remainder with a large swallow, and then smacked his lips in satisfaction. "Now that's some Christmas spirit."

Dan declined the offer and removed the empty bottle from GMC's grip. Even if he wasn't going to church later, he was not much of a drinker. "Slow down, my friend. We've got all night to celebrate."

"Ah, you're such a killjoy, Sarge." The barb was delivered with a feigned look of anger, but was quickly supplanted by another alcohol-fortified smile. "It sure feels good not to have to think about anything but tying one on. Who knows when we'll get the chance again?"

---

[20] Ste. Mère Eglise was a small French town, but like many of its type, a cathedral was the largest building in town in order to serve the heavily Catholic population. St. Mary's Cathedral was already famous in GI lore. A paratrooper from the 82nd Airborne caught his chute on its tower during the early hours of D-Day but survived a battle with German soldiers by pretending he was dead.

Dan took a seat with an affirming nod. He pinched a small piece from a ham that sat in the center of the table. Smitty had won it in a poker game the night before. The canned meat was supposed to have gone to one of the superior officers billeted in the area, and someone in the quartermaster corps was going to catch trouble for it.

"Nice spread, huh?" GMC noted. "Bobby did a quite a job."

Bobby was the squad's unofficial cook, cobbling together meals from their rations when they were in the field, or with what might be available when they were back here. Long loaves of bread from a local bakery sat invitingly to one side of the ham, flanked by a large bowl of runny mashed potatoes. They didn't look like the ones their mothers might have made, but they were a decent substitute. A plate of cheeses stacked into a slapdash pile stood nearby, and the buffet was completed by a container of peas bleached gray from too much time packed in cans.

"Where's everybody else?" Dan asked.

"I'm here, Sarge," Reb broke in, returning from the washroom. "Let's eat."

"Hold your horses, young man. We wait until everyone's here."

With a look of resignation, Reb slumped into one of the chairs. Bobby soon joined the group, carrying a plate of cookies that probably came from the same bakery where he had acquired the bread. Reb tried to sneak one from the stack, and Bobby slapped away his hand.

"I'm starving like y'all can't believe," Reb said. "What's keeping the Captain and Smitty?"

"They were taking inventory earlier ... they must still be finishing up." Dan cleared his throat and clasped his hands like a soloist preparing to belt out an aria. "How about we sing some Christmas carols while we wait?"

"Tarnation, Sarge! Anything but your caterwauling."

"Here, boy, this'll keep you busy," GMC said, handing him the wine bottle he had just opened. "I bet this stuff is better than any of that moonshine crap you were sneaking back home behind the outhouse."

Reb grabbed the bottle and took a hearty swig only to cough from the unfamiliar harshness. The others laughed which made him more determined to prove his manhood. He took an extended drink from the bottle, draining most of its contents. The experience left him breathless until he glanced over at the far side of the room. "Unbelievable. Y'all gotta be kidding me."

Smitty entered with a cheer and a huge grin. Beneath his shirt were two straw-stuffed pillows. Cotton batting from their medical supplies was crudely shaped into a white beard held in place with tape behind his ears. Two red circles painted with mercurochrome adorned his cheeks, and somehow he had gotten a sock to cover most of his head. A large ball of cotton hung from the toe. "Ho, Ho, Ho! Merry Christmas!" Smitty called out. Over one shoulder, he carried a bulging sack. Treasures from the wine cellar clinked from within. In his hand was a small Christmas tree he assembled by hooking scraggly pine branches together with some wire hangers. A string of beer bottle caps was laced around the twigs for decoration. GMC cleared a space for the tree.

"Well done, Smitty," Dan said. "Best Santa Claus I've seen in a long time."

"It's Jolly Old St. Nick himself," chimed in GMC. "What did you bring us?"

Smitty opened his sack and removed the bottles. Returning to the bag, he fumbled around with a mischievous expression on his face. "Let's see what Santa might have in here. Have you all been good little medics?" Each time he seemed ready to reveal a gift, he would go back to rummaging.

"C'mon, Smitty, get on with it. I'm dying here, and y'all are just messing around." Reb had become emboldened by the wine.

"Someone's being naughty," Smitty said. "You looking for coal in your stocking, little boy?"

Before Reb could respond, Dan broke into song. "He's making a list ... he's checking it twice ..."

Reb got down on his knees and folded his hands in prayer. "Please no more singing. I'll be good, I promise."

The rest howled with laughter.

Smitty finally pulled out a present, a rubber hammer the captain used to check reflexes. "To our favorite future lawyer. Sarge, here's your gavel for when they make you a judge."

Dan took the instrument and pounded it on the table with mock authority.

"Only the Army could put a guy headed to law school in with a bunch of loonies like us," Smitty said. "But we're glad we got you."

"Santa, you know why Dan has to work in an ambulance?" The usually mute Bobby had the look of the devil. "Because

196

they know he'll be chasing after them once he becomes a shyster."

As a new round of amusement rang out, Smitty handed Bobby a pair of wooden spoons in recognition of his culinary skills as well as a fistful of Hershey bars to satisfy his sweet tooth. For GMC, the engineering student, it was a slide rule. Even in a war zone, Smitty had the uncanny ability to find something appropriate for each one of them. He tipped the sack on its end to show it was empty. "Well I guess that's it," he called out.

The pronouncement left Reb crestfallen.

"Wait a minute," Smitty said. "It appears there is one more thing in my bag." Smitty paused, prolonging the teenager's angst. At last, he reached deep into the bottom, pulled out a cardboard tube, and handed it over.

"Gee, thanks, Santa. Just what I've always wanted."

"Take a closer look," Smitty said. "It's a magic telescope. When you look inside, you'll find the answer to your dreams."

Reb stepped away from the table, lifted the tube to his eye, and aimed it at an overhead light. "I don't see anything. Wait a minute, there's something in here." He tapped the tube on the floor and that released a paper rolled up inside. It was a pinup of Betty Grable. He stared at the racy photo while the rest applauded Santa Smitty's work.

"Oh, and Captain said something came up," Smitty informed them, tossing the empty bag aside. "Said we should get started without him."

They dished out the holiday feast. Bobby had done a great job. The simple meal was sumptuous compared to the C-rations they had been eating of late.

"How about a Christmas blessing before we start, Dan?" Bobby said.

The four at the table bowed their heads.

"Lord, on this your birthday, thank you for the food we are about to eat. Thank you for your protection and for the friendship we share here at this table. We have only one real Christmas gift we would like to receive ... to celebrate back home with our families next year."

"Amen, well said."

"C'mon, Reb," Dan requested. "Betty won't go anywhere. Join us."

The teenager missed the blessing because he was still mesmerized by the poster. He put it down with some reluctance, and the others made room for him at the table. He piled his plate high with the ham, potatoes, and peas and attacked the meal like someone who hadn't eaten in days. Even with a mouthful of food, he couldn't stay silent. "Smitty ... sorry, excuse me ... Santa. Y'all brought us some great gifts." Food spilled from his lips. He brushed away the overflow with the back of his left hand and shoveled in another forkful with his right. "But how'd y'all ever get that picture? I've been trying to get one for months."

Smitty pulled away some of the cotton from the makeshift beard that kept catching in his mouth. He tilted back his chair and rubbed his belly. "Santa gathers all the information he needs so he knows who is supposed to get what."

"Yeah, yeah, I know. You're making a list and checking it twice."

Smitty brought his chair back to the floor with a bang and drew his face close to Reb. "And do you know why Santa is always jolly?"

Reb, his cheeks stuffed like a squirrel harvesting acorns, shook his head.

"Because knows where all the wine makers live!"

The squad laughed heartily, Reb most of all. Dan raised his coffee cup. "Here's to a Christmas Eve we'll never forget."

CHAPTER SEVENTEEN

24 December 1944

Six hours and twenty-five minutes before midnight.

Sal pulled another Camel from its pack, and after several unsuccessful tries, lit the cigarette. He flicked the spent match over the side of the troop carrier and took a long pull into his lungs. Twin spirals of gray smoke wisped almost invisibly from his nostrils as he stared at the approaching lights of Cherbourg. The barest hint of the moon peeked from thick clouds laying low in the sky.

Leaning with his back against the railing of the ship, Doug hugged himself and stamped his feet to ward off the cold.

Sal kept taking drags until he flung the butt in the direction of a buoy floating beneath them. "What are those things supposed to be?" He pointed to a line of similar-sized objects meandered away from them in the waves.

Doug turned to look. "Not sure. Maybe part of a submarine net."

"Submarine net?"

"I'm guessing those must be the caps for the pipes that hold the net together. You see that line?" Doug pointed to a heavy gauge cable visible in the moonlight between the buoys. "They probably connect that line to a tug or something. Then they drag the net across when they want to close the harbor."

"So where's the boat?"

"Well, it's Christmas Eve. I'm sure they don't expect anything to happen tonight."

Sal absorbed the information, but uncertainty remained in his expression. "How does it work? Do they capture the thing like a fish?"

"More like closing a door. If a U-boat was trying to follow us, they could close the net before it got into the harbor. If it did get in, the net could keep it from escaping."

"And that works?"

"I would think so, otherwise why would they go to all the trouble in the first place?

You hear that, you Krauts!" Sal shouted at the possible enemy below. "You got no chance!" The little soldier thumbed his nose like a prizefighter and bounced on his feet. He flicked his fists rapid-fire, but just as quickly he stopped. "But what if they're underneath us already? It's possible, Hollywood, isn't it?"

Before Doug could answer, Sal grabbed the top rail and leaned out, nearly the length of his diminutive frame. He searched the churning, dark waters, his head turning back and forth, until Doug grabbed the hem of his coat and pulled him back. "Take it easy. If this all works the way it's supposed to, then everything's going to be okay."

"You think so, Doug?"

"There you go again calling me Doug. Is Captain America going soft on me?"

Sal's face turned red. "I know this might be hard to believe, but I'm not really as tough as I talk.

"Really," Doug deadpanned, and then chuckled.

"I can ... I can tell you that..." Sal struggled to find the words. The boy was serious. "Truth be told, I ... I didn't think I was going to make it during basic training. But I watched you doing everything ... even with all the crap you've gone through." The little man fought his emotions. He bit his lip as if the pain would give him the courage to speak his piece. "There's a reason you've gone through all that trouble, I can tell. Maybe you don't know how to put it into words just yet, but the stuff you went through is in your life for a reason. I just figgered that if you could make it through tough times, then so could I." Sal startled Doug with a fierce grip to both of his arms, his eyes blazing. "That's why we gotta stick together ... 'cuz you and me are friends, right?"

"Sure, Sal. We're friends." Doug pulled his arms free and wrapped one around Sal's shoulders. He pointed to the harbor with the other. "We're in good shape. I bet we're not more than ten or twenty minutes from the docks. The Germans would be crazy to try something now."

Sal seemed placated, but he still cast a wary eye at the water below.

* * *

202

At three knots, the U-boat was barely moving, and the same could be said for her crew. Sailors stole glances at the closed curtain to the Kaleu's quarters where he was in conference with his wachoffizier.

The space was cramped for one person, much less two, but that didn't stop Marquardt from pacing. "What do you think?"

"Well ..." Burtzlaff leaned back each time his leader walked by, hesitant to speak. "If you are asking me whether or not I think the men are ready, I believe they are as prepared as can be expected, considering they have no experience."

"I'm not worried about the men," Marquardt scowled. "Their loyalty and effort has never been in question." He slumped into his desk chair and stared with acute purpose at his second-in-command. "You know what I'm talking about. Do we or don't we?"

Releasing his breath with a rush, Burtzlaff began his own pacing. "We have two elements in our favor. Experience tells me they were guessing with their depth charges. The attacks would have been more concentrated if they thought otherwise. I still believe the element of surprise will enable us to hit our target. " He moved his hands like a fish swimming—or a torpedo—before making a motion as if something was exploding. "And, it's Christmas Eve. That's a factor on our side. The harbor appears to be operating at less than full alert, so we couldn't ask for a better situation. This is *war*, after all."

Marquardt scratched at the stubble on his cheek, his lips pursed. It was only a moment, but Burtzlaff agonized as he waited. The Kaleu placed both hands on his knees and leaned forward. "What are the negatives?"

Burtzlaff stepped to the drawn curtain and gave it a quick kick. He did not want a nosy crewmember overhearing anything. For good measure, he did it a second time. "Intelligence reports indicate a net is in use here, although they won't put it into operation until their entire convoy has passed by. It will be tight quarters because the harbor appears close to capacity, and that might compromise our maneuverability somewhat." His pacing recommenced, but less frenetic than before. "Our information also suggests the presence of mines along the outer edges of the harbor. There won't be much of an error margin for us."

"You give me all these concerns. Are you saying there are too many problems?"

"Nothing we couldn't overcome, especially if the nets aren't functioning." Burtzlaff's voice didn't have as much conviction in his answer as he wanted, and he averted his eyes when he finished.

"But what?" the captain demanded.

The wachoffizier leaned close, speaking in halting whispers. "It is the crew ... I know they will do whatever we ask them to ... but most of them are just boys. They shouldn't even be in the service. I just don't know how they're going to react."

Marquardt pressed a hand against Burtzlaff's chest. The action created some space between them, but it was more an expression of affection for his long-time junior officer. "Someone must have felt that way about us at one time, Karl, and we turned out all right." He rose and tapped him on the chest a second time. "Let's go find out, shall we?" U-474's leader pulled back the curtain with a snap, startling the nearby sailors. "Bring her to periscope depth but make sure you stay on the outer perimeter."

The helmsmen began their manipulation of the bow and stern planes, while others worked the bilge pumps to help the submarine ascend. Using the noise from their targets' propellers as a cloak from the sonar, the submarine climbed to a depth of fifteen meters and leveled. Only essential lights were burning, at the lowest level possible, to conserve the battery power that would be needed for their escape. Their red glow gave the control room an eerie ambience.

"Raise the schnorchel," the Kaleu ordered.

Burtzlaff's eyebrow arched, but he echoed the command to deploy the ventilation duct.

"A gulp of French air will do us all a bit of good, don't you think?" Marquardt continued.

Ironically, nearly everyone held their breath as the pipe was raised to the surface. Seconds passed torturously until it became evident the schnorchel was, for the moment, working smoothly. Throughout the sub, the crew inhaled air from the outside world for the first time in hours and many of the men wore a sheepish, uneasy grin.

"Close in. Torpedo tubes stand by," the Kaleu said.

"Maintain total silence, men," Burtzlaff said.

The two senior officers were thinking through the same checklist as they approached the crucial moment of attack.

Marquardt widened his stance for stability. "Raise the periscope. Let's take a look, shall we?" He peered into the scope, his cap turned backward so the brim would not prevent him from getting the best view possible. "Depth, Mister Burtzlaff?"

"Fifteen meters, Kaleu."

"Range?"

"Two hundred eighty meters."

"Good. Flood tubes one and two."

"Tubes flooded," Hesse called back moments later.

"Open bow caps on one and two. Range, Mister Burtz-laff?"

"Two hundred fifty meters."

"Here we go. Ready ... *Fire one!*"

***

Willy sat up in his bunk, or at least as much as the hull would allow. He could hear the swoosh as the armed fish launched itself toward its target. Water rushed into the bilges to keep the submarine from being shot to the surface by the release of the torpedo. The pressure change sent new waves of misery through his damaged ear.

***

"Thirty seconds to target ... " Burtzlaff clicked a stopwatch in his right hand.

"Prepare to fire Tube Two." Kaleu's words shot out at the same velocity as one of his weapons.

"Twenty seconds to impact ..." Burtzlaff spoke without emotion. "Fifteen seconds to target ..."

"Ready ... Fire *two!*"

* * *

Doug slapped at the railing. "Almost there. I'm going back down below."

"Hang on," Sal said. "Let me finish this heater. I just lit it." He puffed furiously.

"Not a chance," Doug shouted over his shoulder to Sal. "We've got to get our gear, and I don't want to be stuck going the wrong way when everybody starts coming up the stairs."

"Oh, crap, you're right." Sal took one more drag on his Camel then tossed it over the side. As he did, he spotted something unusual out of the corner of his eye. "Hey, Hollywood, there's some kinda white line in the water. Come take a look. You think that's more submarine net?"

Doug was already at the top step for his descent down the hatch, and the question was lost to the rising wind.

Looking back into the water, Sal saw the strange white line was moving at an increasing pace ... straight toward the *Leopoldville*.

Sal sprinted for the hatch, racing as fast as his short legs could carry him, but within inches of the entranceway, an incredible blast was unleashed. The first torpedo hit pay dirt.

Sal was knocked face-first into the deck by the giant quake that shook the troopship. Dazed, and with the taste of blood in his mouth, he pinched at the bridge of his nose. "Are you kidding me? Did I just bust my honker?" He might have sat there contemplating his fate if not for the acrid smell, evident even through his injury. The odor and a cloud of black smoke spewed from the hatch that led back down to their area. He crawled across the lurching deck and peered into the murky abyss. "Hollywood ... Doug ... can you hear me?"

The explosion toppled Doug down the stairs to one of the landings. He could feel the rumble below still running its course. The stink in the stairwell was overpowering, a mixture of sulfur and cordite fortified by the unique stench of burning flesh and hair. Debris covered him, and when he attempted to rise, a pain in the small of his back made him scream in agony.

"Hollywood?! You hear me?"

"Sal? Ow ... yeah, I hear you." Doug's eyes burned from the smoke. He combed wood fragments out of his hair and wiped at a bleeding gash on his cheek. A second attempt to stand brought another stab of pain.

"Protect yourself, Sallie," Doug advised. "The Germans usually send more than one."

"Hey, anybody up there?" a voice cried out from below.

"Yeah!" Doug yelled back. "What's happening down there?"

"It's pretty bad. Bodies everywhere. We need help," the voice from below pleaded. "I can't see much of anything from this end. Can we still use these stairs?"

The open hatch was drawing the smoke from the explosion into the stairwell, but Doug could still see enough to know that the flights below him were completely destroyed. His own perch seemed precarious, ready to collapse at any moment. The steps back to the top were hit hard but appeared to be usable. "Hang on," he shouted to his unseen compatriot below. "I'll get some help. Is there another way out down there?"

"Guys are trying to get out at the other end, but there's too many of us. We won't make it out that way in time. Water's coming in fast, and we've got a lot of wounded."

The throbbing in his back was excruciating, but Doug forced himself upright. He reached around his waist and felt a rough piece of wood protruding from his back just to the right of his spine. His fingers moved down the spike's shaft to where it penetrated through his heavy wool overcoat. When he moved, the shrapnel's opposite end caught in the railings around the landing that had not been damaged. The pain shot higher. He climbed towards the light above, placing one foot on a crumbling step and then another. He nearly passed out. Finally, he dragged himself through the hatch and found Sal curled in a defensive posture on the deck. "Get up, Sal. We've got to get help."

Sal peeked over his right arm. Blood flowed into his mouth and over his chin.

"You going to be okay?" Doug asked.

"I busted my schnozz, but look at you. You look like a porky-pine!" Sal butchered the word.

The lighting on the deck was better than in the stairwell, and Doug could see his overcoat was pierced with pieces of wood so that it did appear as if he was covered with quills. Freed from the tight quarters of the hatch, he had room to work on the giant splinter stuck in his back. When he pulled it free, his knees buckled.

"Easy buddy, you got stuck good." Sal picked up the discarded piece; several inches of its tip were covered in blood. He shook his head in disbelief.

"I'll be okay; it's not as bad as it looks." Doug winced, trying hard to cover up his lie. "There must be plenty of guys worse than me right now. We need to find someone in charge to figure out what we need to do." He gave Sal a handkerchief to help stanch the blood from his broken nose. "You're always telling people how tough you are. Well, now you're gonna have a busted beak to prove it."

Sal applied the cloth to his nose, beaming over his new mark of bravery. "You weren't right this time, Hollywood."

"What are you talking about?"

"You said that the Krauts always fire at least two torpedoes."

"That's what I was told."

"Then where's the other one?"

* * *

The sound of the payload hitting its target echoed back toward U-474, only to be quickly supplanted by the crew's cheering. On their maiden voyage, this inexperienced lot had achieved success.

"We did it! We did it!" Dieter left his bunk to celebrate with Willy, who tried his best to put on a happy face. But the cheers from the crew were cut short by a frantic scream from Zimmerman in the radio room.

"CIRCLE RUNNER!"

Wailing, Dieter dove back into his bunk. The second torpedo and its acoustic detection system had fixed on the noise from the propeller of U-474 rather than its intended target.

"Hard to Starboard!" shouted the Kaleu.

The helmsmen turned the U-boat. The submarine clanged against something metallic. It was one of the harbor mines. Miraculously, the collision did not activate the underwater bomb. The fear of setting off one of the other mines, however, left Marquardt unable to make the type of evasive maneuver he needed to escape his own weapon. U-474's screw was fully exposed and its noise drew the torpedo ever closer. "Stand by for impact," he ordered.

Burtzlaff's impassive face contradicted the imminent disaster he was visualizing in his mind. He stared intently at the advancing sweep of his stopwatch. "Five ... Four ... Three ... "

"Hard to Port," the Kaleu yelled in a final, desperate maneuver.

The torpedo creased the stern of the submarine on the starboard side, the collision sending her into a spin. Willy was catapulted from his bunk by the force of the blow. He slammed into a bed railing on the opposite side. Blood dripped now from both ears.

"We've been hit!" A pasty-faced Dieter stuck out his head from his bunk. "We're going to sink." He babbled and made wild gestures. "I DON"T WANT TO DIE."

Willy stared at his friend's contorted face. "What's wrong with you, Dieter? You're acting like a madman."

Their world was in chaos, but his friend was not making any sense. Willy cocked his head, confused, and then asked, "Dieter, why are you whispering?"

CHAPTER EIGHTEEN

24 December 1944

Five hours and fifty-five minutes before midnight.

"ATTENTION. ATTENTION. REMAIN IN YOUR ASSIGNED AREAS. THERE IS NO DANGER OF SINKING. PREPARATIONS ARE BEING MADE FOR ORDERLY DISEMBARKING."

Doug and Sal listened to the blare from a loudspeaker hanging on the wall above them. A group of soldiers stood with them, but none of the men's faces looked familiar. Others wandered the main deck, most looking for answers to what had happened. It had been a half hour since the German torpedo exploded into the hull of the *Leopoldville*, but a consolidated plan of action didn't seem anywhere close to being initiated. Doug could feel the ooze of blood from the wound in his back. Sal dabbed at his broken nose with a bloodstained handkerchief.

"Zoller said this was where we were supposed to meet if there was trouble," Sal whined in his staccato voice. "I don't see nobody, not even that pain-in-the-ass Dugan. I'd give anything to see that jerk right now."

Neither man dared verbalize their worst fears. GI's continued to stream onto the main deck, but there was no sign of anyone from their squad. Doug walked over to a lifeboat padlocked to a large iron ring. His wound forced him to walk with a slight stoop. He rattled the metal tether holding the boat in place. The lock and chain were caked with rust. "I hope someone has a key for this. Otherwise, we're gonna have a long swim."

"Man, don't say crap like that."

A new chorus of cries for help came from the hatch, cutting short the interplay. Doug and Sal joined others in the area in a cluster around the opening. An air of uncertainty dominated the atmosphere. The young soldiers weren't gripped by a paralysis of fear. It was more a reluctance to act without direction. Besides, they didn't have anything—at least they thought so anyway—that might help the trapped men below.

"Hey, look! Here comes Colonel Garrison," someone noticed.

"Hello, sir." Doug managed a sharp salute.

The officer squinted and then returned the gesture. "Tillman ... good to see you, son." He looked over the crowd of soldiers. "Is this your platoon?"

"No, sir ... nobody but myself and Private DiPrimo here."

Sal gave a half-hearted acknowledgement as Doug continued. "Was that really a torpedo that got us?"

"Appears so," Garrison told them. "From what I've learned, the Number Four Hold on F Deck took the brunt of the hit."

Doug swallowed hard. His squad was right where the worst took place.

"What is the status here?" the colonel demanded.

"I was just starting down the stairs," Doug began, ". . . when everything exploded."

"Down this hatch?"

"Yes sir."

Smoke still flowed from the precipitous exit. The hulking officer circled the passageway, calculating the possibilities. "Anybody know what shape it's in?

"There's nothing much we can do, sir," a corporal offered. "The stairs are gone and there isn't anything around here that would help."

"Actually, the stairs aren't completely gone, sir," Doug corrected. "I ended up on a landing part-way down following the explosion, and I was still able to climb out." He reflexively picked at one of the splinters still stuck in his coat. "But as best as I could tell, there's a big gap between that spot and F Deck."

Garrison was silent, shifting his gaze from the hatch to the immediate area around them and then again down the hole.

Doug thought a moment, then added, "A guy below said there's no way they're gonna get everybody out through the other exit down there before the water gets them."

The colonel removed his overcoat and tossed it with such force it nearly slid off the damp deck. Another survey of the surroundings found success this time. His eyes brightened when he spied his target, a winch attached to a set of support pipes and operated by a large hand crank. "You men over there," he barked at a group of soldiers standing at the port rail. "Bring that here, on the double."

Initially, the men didn't understand the directive—or who was giving the order—but the vigorous gestures and the tone of Garrison's repeated command spurred them into action. They wheeled over the winch.

"That's it, men, place it right there," the colonel directed. "See those clamps? They must screw in this piece here. Make sure it's secure."

The *Leopoldville* began to list to her left from the water flowing in through the hole caused by the torpedo. The winch moved out of position several times before it could be affixed. When the ship trembled again, Sal dropped to his knees. "What in the world was that? I think we got hit again. We gotta get outta here."

"Relax, Peewee," a GI chided him, "...it's just the anchor dropping."

Sal rose to his feet to lunge at the man. "Don't call me Pewee."

"Cut the crap!" Garrison's baritone was an instant peacemaker. "Men are dying and you two are acting like children. Pay attention here."

Red-faced, Sal and his heckler backed away. The colonel took the hook at the end of the winch and tossed it in his hand as if he was testing its worth. He looked around for the next item he required. "Tillman, fetch that rope."

Doug hurried to collect a thick braid coiled next to a pile of life jackets.

"How long is it?"

"I'm not sure, sir. Maybe twenty, twenty-five feet."

"Perfect."

Doug brought the rope to the officer who wrapped it around and between his legs and then over his chest in a criss-cross fashion. He repeated the process until the rope was triple-thick around him with a short length hanging free. "Now, which one of you was a Boy Scout?"

"Me, sir ... Eagle Scout," someone volunteered.

"Well, son, I want you to take the rest of this rope here and attach it to that hook with the best knot you've ever tied."

"I see what you have in mind, sir," Doug interrupted, "but is that wise?" The strategy seemed reckless, especially if the colonel was going to be the one to put it into motion.

"Tillman, I like your gumption, but never question a superior officer." The colonel growled. "There are wounded men down there who need our help."

"I know, sir, but have one of us do it instead, and you can oversee everything from here."

Garrison clucked his tongue and waved a finger back and forth. "I never like having someone else do a job I can best do myself." He stepped back and pounded his chest with his fists. "And I'm the biggest one here if any of you jokers think you can change my mind."

No one else objected, leaving the former Eagle Scout to tie his best knot around the hook of the winch. Garrison gave it a yank to make sure it was snug and then began a cautious descent. The soldiers operating the winch's crank gradually let out the line. He had been lowered only a small distance when the *Leopoldville* was bombarded by a water surge. The glass in the portholes on the deck above them rattled. This time, it wasn't just Sal's heart that skipped a beat. "Here they come again ..."

216

"No, look …" Doug said. On the starboard side, a geyser of water shot into the air, followed moments later by another underwater concussion against the hull of the troopship. The *Brilliant* and the *Anthony* had broken away in pursuit of the convoy's attacker and were releasing depth charges.

"It's the Limeys!" Doug shouted. "They've got the sub trapped. They're trying to take them out."

"You Nazi bastards," the emboldened Sal bellowed. "How about a taste of your own medicine!"

CHAPTER NINETEEN

24 December 1944

Five hours and forty minutes before midnight.

The Allies spotted debris on the surface shortly after the circle runner inflicted its damage on the submarine. A counterattack was initiated, and the assault was relentless. Each round seemed to be coming closer and closer.

The wayward torpedo took away U-474's ability to maneuver. With mines all around them and hunters on the surface, Marquardt issued the "all stop" order.

"They are dropping them in a circle around us, Kaleu," Burtzlaff noted. "What do you suggest we do?"

"It's too late to surface. We would move right into the path of their charges." Marquardt scratched his beard at a perpetual itch on the right side of his jaw. The next burst of explosives pitched the U-boat, throwing the officers against the navigator's desk. The emergency lights flickered and went dark before coming back to life. Seepage was everywhere along the outside seams, and water accumulated on the deck. The Kaleu had been through more training exercises than he cared to remember in his long naval career, yet he still felt unprepared for the next decision he needed to make. Sailors not involved in the operation of the U-boat, or involved in the cleanup of the rising water within the submarine, looked expectantly at their commanding officer. He continued to stroke his chin, furiously thinking about what to do next.

Burtzlaff pointed aft to the engine room. "Once the sea hits those batteries…"

"Yes, Karl." Marquardt's voice bore a hint of annoyance. "I am very aware of what will happen." Electric motors are the principal power source when a submarine is submerged, making them vital in U-474's current dilemma. Should the batteries that generate life into those motors come in contact with a significant amount of seawater, however, the result creates a lethal chlorine gas. It would be the final blow to his boat and certain death for his crew. "Mister Burtzlaff." The Kaleu assumed a volume and tone befitting his place at the head of the chain of command. "Have the men stand by to abandon ship."

"Are you certain?" Burtzlaff said. "If we move quickly, perhaps we can still make an escape."

The Kaleu wasn't used his decisions being questioned, but these were extraordinary times and Burtzlaff's loyal service had earned him the right to do so. Marquardt crossed to the helm and his boots crunched on shards of glass from the dials damaged by the Allied barrage. Navigational charts floated in puddles around the desk. He turned fore and aft as if he want-ed to make one more mental picture of the boat and crew that were certain to be his final command. "The enemy must be underway with their own rescue efforts. Our men will have a better chance of survival by being among the many in the water. It is best this way. Now, hurry."

"Yes, Kaleu." Burtzlaff cleared his throat and took the microphone. "Men, Kapitänleutnant Marquardt has ordered us to abandon ship. We have run this drill many times. I know we will execute it properly and with the dignity that befits the men of the Kreigsmarine."

The next depth charge exploded closer to the hull than any of its predecessors, and the shock wave tossed equipment and sailors like rag dolls. Burtzlaff was knocked down, but the microphone, its cord fully extended, remained in his hand. He was issuing the next order before he returned to his feet. "Those assigned to distribute the Dragers,[21] begin the process now. Make certain you secure your own apparatus before you take care of the other men in your group. The rest of you, find your positions for scuttling the ship."

"Beanpole! What in God's name are you doing? Didn't you hear Mister Burtzlaff?" An irate Hesse spat the words at Willy in a breath almost too foul to bear. "Go get our Dragers, immediately!"

A new charge rattled U-474 and seawater sprayed in larger doses from broken seals. The commotion sent Willy and the older sailor to the deck.

---

[21] The Drager was a rudimentary forerunner to scuba gear. A black corrugated tube was connected at one end to a canister of oxygen. The cylinder was about the size of a lunch-pail thermos. A small brass valve at the top of the flask controlled the amount of oxygen released. A rubber and glass facemask was attached to the other end of the hose, and a more pliable piece of rubber formed a mouthpiece at the bottom of the mask. All of the components were fitted into a padded vest made of canvas and coated with a brownish-colored, water-resistant material. First developed to allow repairs to be made on a U-boat while submerged, the Drager now would be the final hope for these submariners to make it to the surface.

"Get off me, you worthless whelp," Hess shouted. He placed his hand on Willy's face and pushed him back against one of the lower bunks. "I knew one of you was going to get me killed if I wasn't careful. Bring me my Drager now before I kill you myself."

Willy shook off the insult, righted himself, and went off to fetch the lifesaving gear, stored in a cabinet mid-ship. With his hearing damaged further after the hit by the circle runner, he had only been able to make out the word *Drager* and that was only because Hesse was right in his face. The throbbing in his head was out of control, as was his fear. Men moved by him in both directions in the same state of panic. He sloshed in water above his ankles. When he reached the storage bin, it was difficult to unlatch since the rising water acted like a weight against its doors. The door wouldn't stay open unless he braced it with a knee. The awkward position forced him to bend over in order to retrieve the Dragers, and the pressure that caused in his damaged ears should have stopped him from moving. He pressed on because there was no other option if he wanted to stay alive. Unless the pressure inside matched the seawater's outside, U-474's escape hatch could not be opened. Valves would have to be released to flood the compartments and equalize the pressure. If the crew was to have any chance at survival, the escape lungs needed to be distributed before their time was gone.

Willy slid one arm through the life vest and then the other. He had been self-conscious wearing a Drager during training exercises because its length was too short for his tall frame. There were no concerns now. Placing the mask over his face, he adjusted the straps to make it snug, although the action increased the pain in his head. He opened the valve on his oxygen tank for just a moment, and it seemed to relieve some of the pressure. Satisfied everything was in order, he grabbed jackets for the others in his assigned group.

Hesse, hands on hips and a scowl on his face, stood at the entrance to the bow room.

"Relax, old man ... I'll get there when I get there." Willy shouted the words from behind his mask, confident they wouldn't be heard. His remarks fogged the glass. Before the vapor could dissipate, another blast hit. U-474 was jolted more strongly than it had been by any of the previous blasts.

The interior of the submarine went completely black, and a wild scream rose in Willy's throat.

CHAPTER TWENTY

24 December 1944

Five hours before midnight.

"I gotta apologize, Sarge," Reb said. "Y'all sound like Bing Crosby compared to Bobby."

The medics' Christmas Eve celebration was well into its second hour, and Reb seemed to be having the most fun. He was beyond tipsy, headed towards roaring drunk, but no one looked concerned. They were off-duty. "Sure you don't want some, Sarge?" he asked with a wave of a bottle.

"Thanks, but no thanks. I'll just stick with the lousy coffee."

"So now everybody's a critic," Bobby groaned. "I ought to make you feed yourselves, and then we'd see who'd be complaining."

As the banter ping-ponged among them, Captain Levine briskly walked into the room, his brow furrowed. "Dan, can I see you for a minute?"

"Hey, it's the Captain," Reb said. "It's about time. I thought y'all were gonna to stiff us." The wine was doing more and more of Reb's talking. Levine gave the inebriated teenager a terse acknowledgement, ignored the disrespect, and again directed his focus at his noncom. Dan hurried to join him on the far side of the room. While GMC and Bobby tried to calm their rambunctious cohort, Smitty was all business. His makeshift Santa beard was crumpled in his fist, and he cast a questioning eye at the squad's two leaders.

"What is it, sir?" Dan asked.

"I just received word from Cherbourg," Levine said. "A troopship was torpedoed as it was about to enter the harbor area."

Dan inhaled sharply. "When?"

"More than an hour ago. I don't know who or what got screwed up, but we're just hearing about it now." The captain was always so precise in everything he did, and the breakdown in the communication chain did not sit well with him. "It was a large ship ... there may be as many as twenty-five hundred men on board."

Dan let out a long whistle, and now everyone's attention was directed at the pair. Not wanting to reveal too much, the captain dropped his voice low. "I'm awaiting more information, but it doesn't sound good. Have the boys ready to move." He nodded and quickly returned to the office area in the farmhouse.

Dan rejoined the others at the table and took a deep breath before he spoke. "One of our troopships was just torpedoed over at Cherbourg."

"Those stinking Nazis." Smitty pounded a fist on the table. An empty bottle rolled off and smashed on the flagstone floor. "Leave it to Hitler to pull some crap like that."

"On Christmas Eve, no less ... " Bobby said.

"Smitty, go make sure the wagon's gassed and warmed up," Dan said. "As for the rest of us, let's get our kits and gather all the extra supplies ... as much as we can fit on the truck."

"Is it bad?" Bobby asked.

"Captain didn't have many details, but he said there were about twenty-five hundred of our men onboard."

"Twenty-five hundred! What are we supposed to do?"

"The best we can, Bobby ... the best we can. Now let's get moving, and don't forget your overcoats. It's going to be even colder down by the water."

The men sprang into action, all except for Reb. His equilibrium was shot, thanks to the wine, and he fell down when he came out of his chair. Dan picked him up by the collar of his jacket. "You going to be okay?"

"I'm just fine, Sarge. This stuff's just different from what I'm used to." Reb lifted a wine bottle in a salute to Dan and put it to his lips before he could be stopped. "Y'all don't have to worry about me," he gurgled through his final swallow of burgundy.

* * *

Doug was exhausted from blood loss. He sank with a thump onto a crate, his back screaming for mercy. Colonel Garrison's rescue efforts continued at the hatch to the left of where Doug sat. The improvised use of the winch had achieved some success. Time after time Garrison was lowered into the darkness of the decimated stairwell to return with an

225

injured soldier under each of his powerful arms. The men handling the winch's crank uncoiled him down the hole again.

Sal didn't much care for manual tasks, so when it became obvious more men wanted to help than were actually needed, he left for another part of the ship. Doug remained to offer his assistance, but his injury was becoming more problematic. The loudspeaker on the wall above him squawked for the first time in more than an hour. It was a message from the *Leopoldville*'s captain, but it was impossible to understand. The soldiers stared at the amplifier as if that might help their predicament. Additional instructions followed.

"Anybody get that?" someone hollered.

"Sounded like German ..."

"No, you idiot, that's Belgian. We're on a Belgian boat, stupid."

Doug smiled, and then winced at the pain. Although he didn't understand the message any more than the others did, he knew there wasn't a Belgian language. It was called Flemish, and it was more similar to Dutch than German. Whatever the language, it wasn't helping them find out what to do next.

"Pull, men. The colonel's got two more." A cry from a corporal who had taken over control of the winch brought the group's attention back to elevating Garrison and more of their buddies. Doug rose to help. His breathing was forced and his stride unsteady as he moved to the winch.

"Hey, pal, if you're wounded, go sit down."

"I'm okay." Doug's face contorted. "I'll get checked out once we get done helping the colonel here." Doug took the far end of the handle, but he couldn't exert much force to help spin the crank.

"I said go sit down. You ain't no help to anybody in your condition."

Doug wanted to protest, but he realized the truth of what the man said. He stepped aside and another GI took his place.

Conditions were worsening. Blasts of cold air continued to drop the temperature and brought a chop to the waves below. Doug pulled up the collar of his coat around his neck. The *Leopoldville* wrenched awkwardly to her left, causing the soldiers to lose control of the winch's handle. "Watch it," one of them yelled.

A twinge of panic shot through Doug. An image of him and Sal making an icy swim in the frigid waters of the Channel flashed through his mind. The two were a sorry sight, bloody and beaten, gasping and straining toward the shore.

The image left him as quickly as it came, but a remembrance came and stayed. He held on to it, recalling it with wistful fondness.

* * *

The Tillmans had finished a picnic supper aboard Kate's sailboat, and thirteen-year old Doug was interrogating his father. His mother snuggled under her husband's brawny arm.

"I'm still trying to figure something out, Dad?" Doug said.

"I'm all ears," Big Jim responded in voice that sounded like he had gargled glass.

"How come you never go with Mom and me when we take out the boat?"

"I'm not much of a water man," his father answered after some hesitation.

227

"You afraid or something?"

Kate started to protest, but Jim waved her away. "I wouldn't call it being afraid," Jim said to Doug. "Let's just say I prefer to stay on dry land." He grabbed a beer icing in a nearby pail, and, after popping the cap, took a hearty swallow of the foamy liquid, nearly draining the bottle. He swiped at his lips to wipe off the excess. "There is something *you* should be afraid of, though," he cautioned his son."

"What's that?"

"W-W-A-A-T-C-H-H-I-T-T!" Big Jim's belch was incredibly loud and long to the delight of his teenage son.

* * *

Doug held the image stationary in his mind. He knew there was more to come. His mind flitted to the darker part under duress, but he held off the rest of the memory as best he could. "I am trying to watch it, Dad," Doug said, looking skyward. "... But things aren't looking so good right now."

The deck of the floundering troopship beneath him rumbled and quaked, new plumes of black smoke streamed from the hatch. Moments later, the process repeated itself, the vibrations strong enough to knock men off their feet.

Garrison had returned, and he dangled helplessly from the winch's cable until he was pulled safely to one side. He tugged at his self-made harness. It was still doing its job. "Men, I think the boilers are starting to go." His body seemed to be sapped of all strength, but he spoke with rugged determination. "There isn't much time left ... let's get me down there again."

They fed out the winch's line and Garrison stepped back into what remained of the stairwell. Doug's mind went to the darker place. He couldn't fight the image off this time. He swallowed dryly, the blood seeping from the wound in his back.

CHAPTER TWENTY-ONE

24 December 1944

Four hours and thirty-five minutes before midnight.

Without much traffic on the road, Smitty had the ambulance at full throttle. Ste. Mère Eglise was only twenty-five miles from Cherbourg Harbor, and country roads soon gave way to darkened city streets as the medics neared their destination. Levine was at his usual position on the passenger side of the cab, oblivious to the jostling from the truck's wild pace. He held a small flashlight and looked over the notes he hastily jotted down during his conversation with headquarters. The rest of the medics pinballed against each other or the rigid canvas walls in the back. Smitty wasn't making any attempts to avoid potholes, and the jolts were too much for Reb. He kept opening the rear flap to vomit.

"You gonna make it, kid?" Bobby asked, sincerely concerned.

Reb wiped his mouth with the back of his hand. "Why didn't y'all warn me? I'm sicker than a coon dog that ate some road kill."

"I did tell you," GMC said. "But you said you were fine. Besides, we didn't figure there'd be any action tonight, so we let you have your fun."

Reb leaned his head against the canvas, his eyes clamped shut. "Next time, y'all need to keep me from having so much fun. Nobody could feel as bad as I do right now."

"I can think of guys trying to stay alive on a sinking ship," Dan said in a low voice.

Reb pursed his lips and the rest fell silent. Dan went back to the beads of his rosary, praying for those they wouldn't be able to help. A few minutes later, Smitty made a sharp turn and slammed on the brakes. A shard of bright light broke through the slit in the canvas behind the cab.

"We're just about there, men ... time to get ready," Levine called from the front while pulling back the curtain completely so they all could see what was happening.

"That's unbelievable!" Bobby said. "Look at that!"

The ambulance idled at the crest of a hill on the road leading into the harbor. A line of trucks and jeeps stretched out in front of them, drivers honking their horns in a chorus of frustration. Giant searchlights mounted on the roof of Cherbourg's marine terminal were scanning the sky for even the remotest possibility of an air raid. The headlamps from the trucks and jeeps created a montage of spotlight bursts and motorized silhouettes. Portable illumination devices were trained on a large pier being utilized as the main clearing station for the rescue operations. Men and equipment were everywhere, but if there was organization, some kind of plan, it was not readily apparent. But then, who would have considered having a plan for something like this?

Bobby found his voice again the soonest. "Looks a lot different than the last time we were here," he murmured in a voice so soft it might not have been heard if the rest were not struck mute by the sight. "This is the nightmare before Christmas."

The line of vehicles moved forward at a pace not any faster than a faucet with a slow leak. The group's desire to help—like the others who had rushed to the scene—was being held up by the logistical realities of the harbor. The ingress and egress were not designed to handle this volume of traffic. Smitty's patience disappeared as the ambulance waited in the queue. Despite the apparent desperation of the situation, the military policeman checking identification papers did not seem to share the same sense of urgency.

"C'mon, pal," Smitty said out the window. "They need us down there. Let's get a move on."

"We need to make certain only authorized personnel are permitted into this area," the MP replied without emotion as he checked the ambulance's registration.

"Fantastic." Smitty's voice dripped with sarcasm. "While you pencil pushers do your duty, our boys are dying out there."

The face of the policeman flushed purple and he reached into the cab. Smitty cocked a fist in response only to be stopped by the captain.

"Gentlemen, please." Levine leaned over his driver to speak directly to the MP. "Corporal, I know you've been taught to follow procedure, but time is precious. Every minute is crucial for those soldiers on that ship. You can see as plain as day we're part of the medical corps." He fixed a hopeful gaze at the guard and gestured with his head in the direction of the activity down on the pier. "You might help save some lives if you could speed up the process a little bit."

With a shamefaced expression, the MP handed back Smith's papers, and addressed the captain. "Sorry, sir. Go right ahead."

Smitty muttered unintelligible obscenities and put the ambulance back into gear. The captain ignored him; he was already thinking about what his squad would need to do once they were in action. The pier where the rescue operations were underway was home to the *Normandie*, a large transatlantic liner, during peacetime. Despite its immense size, a conglomeration of people and vehicles choked the space. Somehow, Smitty was able to maneuver to the far end of the dock without having to stop. His constant mashing on the truck's horn and a steady stream of vulgar shouts to get out of the way helped the process. He yanked the hand brake into position but left the motor running to keep the headlamps lit.

"Stay in the area, men," Levine ordered, dismounting from the truck's cab. "Let me see if I can find out who's in charge."

The squad descended from the rear as the captain hurried down a wide ramp extending from the pier. A barge, at least one hundred fifty feet in length, had been moved below the main landing area to create additional space for the recovery efforts. Two Army tugboats, with oversized searchlights mounted on them, were stationed at each end of the barge.

"Where are you going, Reb?" Bobby said. "Captain says we're supposed to stay here."

Reb waved in acknowledgement but kept moving anyway to the opposite side of the pier. He stopped at a large, rusting stanchion and grabbed a thick rope for support. He leaned over the black water and spit up more from his churning stomach. When he was done, he staggered back to the rest of the group with the gait of a codger.

"Maybe you should lie down until you feel better?" Dan said.

"Don't y'all worry. I'll be fine."

Dan didn't believe him, and he took Reb by his arm to guide him into the back of the ambulance.

Captain Levine reappeared. "Leave most of the gear here, men. They'll be coming in so fast we won't have time to do much. Just bring all the morphine we've got." He poked his head into the cab. "Corporal Smith, we've been assigned to the 280th. You know where that is, don't you?"

There were three hospitals in the immediate vicinity, and the decision had been made to keep those operations fully manned. Levine's squad and the other rescuers on hand would assist in speeding the injured to the hospitals. "No problem, Captain," Smitty said. "I was there day before yesterday. If the rest of these idiots stay out of my way, I can get there in no time."

"Great," Levine said. "The rest of you, come with me."

With a worried glance at Reb, Dan led his mates down to the barge where the initial flurry of rescue boats began to arrive. Surprisingly, there weren't as many onboard as they expected. Dan reached for the soldier closest to him and assisted him onto the makeshift dock. The GI's clothes were soaked but stiff from being in the icy wind. Dan took a blanket from a monstrous pile and wrapped it around the man. "You'll be okay. How are you feeling?"

"I-I-I'm-m-m f-f-fr-ee-eez-ing."

The soldier didn't answer any additional questions, but Dan figured it was just the cold that was keeping him silent. When they reached the ambulance, two other survivors were already seated on one of the benches. "How many do you think you can haul, Smitty?" Dan asked.

"At least ten, I would think, as long as they can sit up. It might be a little tight, but it'll probably keep them warm."

Dan headed back to the rescue area where he had more luck with his next man. "Say, Bud, what state are you from?"

"Pennsylvania."

"Right next to me ... I'm from Ohio."

The soldier beamed, gratefully pulling on the blanket. His step quickened on the short trip up the gangplank as they talked about home. The ambulance filled in minutes and Smitty sped away as soon as the rear gate slammed shut. Another ambulance moved in to fill the void.

"Sergeant, give me a hand over here." Levine searched for a pulse on a soldier's wrist.

Dan tore open the man's coat. He couldn't believe how cold the wet clothing felt, but when he reached beneath the man's undershirt to massage his chest, the skin had even more of a chill. He inspected the man's I.D. and then moved so the captain could probe with his stethoscope.

"He's gone," the captain sighed after a fruitless search for a heartbeat. "What were you doing with his dog tags?"

"I was looking to see if he was Catholic. I thought I might help him make a final contrition. That's part of our religion, sir."

"I'm quite aware of that. That's a noble thing to do. Was he?"

"No, sir, Protestant. I'll say some prayers for him anyway."

"Good idea, but make it fast. I'm afraid he won't be the last one for us tonight." Levine went off to check on the next soldier, leaving Dan to take care of the body.

"He might not be the last ... but it's the first for me." The squad had been in France since the early days of June, yet unbelievably, this was the first time Dan had dealt with a dead body. With a gentle touch, he made certain the soldier's eyes stayed closed and then lifted him in a fireman's carry. The far end of the main pier had been designated as the assembly area for victims and he set the corpse alongside three others.

He couldn't take much time, but Dan took out his rosary anyway. He whispered a few prayers and made the Sign of the Cross with the beads in his hand for a man he didn't know. He started to put the rosary away before deciding to place it around his neck instead. The small crucifix bounced on his chest as he ran to where the captain was calling for more assistance.

CHAPTER TWENTY-TWO

24 December 1944

Four hours before midnight.

Willy's vision was blurry from the saltwater. There was little feeling in his extremities thanks to the oceans cold. The facemask on his gear was fractured—that explained the brine's harm to his eyes—and the oxygen canister in the outer pocket of the Drager was spent. He spat out the mouthpiece, but the rubbery taste remained. Worst of all, his world was now silent. Thanks to the damage he suffered when the circle runner hit their sub, and then when he was thrown to the surface by the final destruction of U-474, his ability to hear was all but gone. The Drager kept him bobbing chest high in the water except when the chop would wash over him. He tossed the mask aside and wiped his eyes but that only increased the discomfort. Mouthfuls of salty sea mixed with spilled diesel fuel made him gag. He twisted his arm back and forth to shake the moisture out of his watch and brought the timepiece close to his face. Nothing was moving. He shook his arm again and blinked rapidly to clear the cloud-

237

iness from his eyes. The hands on the watch remained fixed in place.

"Six thirty-eight. It's eighteen thirty-eight Hesse would be screaming at me. Hesse? Surely he found a way to survive."

The difference in terminology notwithstanding, the gap in his timeline was troubling. He recalled being on his bunk sometime after 5 p.m., but that was ninety minutes earlier than what his broken watch was showing now. What time was it really? He spun in a circle to assess the immediate surroundings, but the movement was awkward due to the life vest. A sliver of the moon peeked on and off through the clouds and cast an eerie glow on the water when its light bounced off slicks of phosphorus drifting on the surface. Flotsam was everywhere, telling evidence that U-474 must have completely broken apart when the depth charges finally found their mark.

"DIETER, DIETER! HESSE! MISTER BURTZLAFF!"

It was a strange sensation. Willy knew he was yelling, but he could only hear the echo of his voice inside his head. He continued his cries for a familiar face but saw no one. In the distance, he could make out the enemy convoy and the ship they struck with their torpedo. The *Leopoldville* listed to her port side. One of the destroyers was attempting to pull in along the starboard rails. He could see lights moving towards the sinking ship.

Those must be rescue boats. If I can get over there somehow ...

The distance would be difficult, particularly in the cold, but then the lake in Bavaria where he had learned to swim never got very warm. Now that experience might save his life.

He was confident the Drager could keep him afloat. The only question was for how long.

He spied something among the scraps from the submarine and paddled in that direction. The kapok filling inside the Drager, used to provide buoyancy for the jacket, made full strokes impossible. The most Willy could manage were small slaps in the water in front of him. He had little feeling in his legs, and his kicks for additional propulsion were largely ineffectual. Despite that, he reached his target: a large rectangular piece of wood floating in the swells. It was the top of Kapitänleutnant Marquardt's dining table, the one bit of luxury the U-boat leader had allowed himself onboard.

Thank you, Kaleu, thank you. Wherever you are, God have mercy on your soul.

The expensive piece of furniture was not overly large at six feet by twelve, but since it was made of teak, the wood of shipbuilders, it might float forever. It took several attempts to match the timing of the plank's movement, but on his third try, Willy secured a handhold. He could only pull himself halfway out of the water and he was spent from the effort. His exhale produced a small cloud of frost without any staying power. His eyelids clanged together like prison gates.

I'll just rest here for a moment and then I'll swim over to that ship.

* * *

Even in the spotty illumination on the *Leopoldville*'s deck, Sal's flushed face shone like neon. "Them bastards!" His breath billowed and his stubby legs pounded the floorboard with the force of a locomotive barreling down the track.

"What's the matter?" Doug attempted to stand, but a spasm wrenched his insides and he was slammed back into his seat on the deck. He coughed, and a projectile of blood and mucus landed on one of Sal's boots.

The little man was too angry to give it any more than a cursory glance. "You don't look so good, Hollywood. You okay?" Sal paused, but not long enough to allow an answer to his question. "Anyway, you won't believe the crap that's going on. I'm over watching them get some lifeboats ready, figuring you and me would find a place in one of them."

Doug nodded, but with his face pulled tight and his eyes blinking fast from the pain.

"I happen to look over on the port side ... or is it starboard?" Sal continued. "I can never remember which is which." The vein on the side of Sal's neck palpitated. "Anyways, I look over on the LEFT side and I see most of the crew from this tub climbing into lifeboats ... and they're carrying their stinking suitcases."

"You're kidding?"

"So I go over see what's going on, and one of them starts talking to me in that gibberish."

"Flemish."

"Flemish, shmemish, who cares. All I know is I couldn't figure out what he was trying to tell me."

"Could you make out anything he said?" Doug fidgeted on the crate, trying to find a more comfortable position.

"No. He was waving his hands, and the jerk was spitting all over me while he was talking. I couldn't understand any of it. Then he jumps into a boat and they shove off."

"The lifeboats are gone?" Doug pointed to the speaker on the wall above their heads. "They made announcements earlier, but nobody could understand what they were saying. I didn't like the sound of it ... and now this?" He struggled to get to his feet. Walking was becoming an effort.

"Doug, you need help."

"Agreed ... but we should let Colonel Garrison know the boats are gone."

Their commanding officer was at the top of the hatch after another rescue foray, two more soldiers under his arms. One was a member of Third Platoon. When the other GIs took him from Garrison's grasp, the soldier collapsed on the deck. His face became clear in the moonlight. It was Gerry Dugan. Sal and Doug rushed forward to help and crouched beside him. Dugan's face had been seared, his uniform reduced to smoldering fragments. Where his skin wasn't charred, blood dripped from gaping wounds.

"It's ... good ... to ... see ... you ... boys." Each word from Dugan escaped with a rattle.

Doug softly laid a hand on the top of Dugan's head. By the amount of blood evident, it didn't seem like Dugan could hold out much longer. "How about everybody else, Gerry?"

Dugan's voice dropped to a whisper, tears spilled from his eyes. "Gone ... They're all gone." He shivered with such force his tattered clothes flapped like a flag. "I was playing craps on the opposite side from where we had stashed our gear ..."

241

Another shot of pain shook his body and interrupted the narrative.

"Maybe you shouldn't talk," Doug said. "Save your strength."

Dugan shook his head, gritted his teeth, and continued. "I ... I ... I was up big money and figuring I was the luckiest guy in the world. Then suddenly everything exploded. They told me I was thrown against the wall ... and that I was on fire. I don't remember much after we got hit."

"But then how do you know about the rest of the guys?" Sal interrupted.

Dugan sucked in a huge lungful of air. "They were passing me up and over ... to the big man." Dugan rolled of his eyes in Garrison's direction. "When we went by where the squad had been camped out, nothing was there."

"Nothing?" Sal said. "What do you mean?"

"It was just a burned-out hole in the side of the hull. Water pouring in." Dugan's body convulsed and a gasp escaped from his throat.

Sal leaned in close, as if to hear a last word.

A moment later, Dugan was gone.

Doug closed the soldier's eyes.

"Hey, we gotta go, Doug," Sal pleaded. "You heard him. This thing is gonna sink."

"He's right, boys. The ship is going down," Garrison advised over his shoulder. He was at the top of the hatch again, and he studied the men gathered around him with the look a parent would give to his children. "All of you need to find a way off ... on the lifeboats or whatever. Find whatever you can. They won't be able to keep her afloat much longer."

"But what about you, sir?" Doug asked.

"Thanks for the concern, Tillman, but my job is to help as many of those men trapped below as I possibly can."

"But, sir ... "

"That's an order. Now get moving. Good luck, son."

With that, Garrison worked his way back into the darkness of the nightmare below.

"C'mon," Sal pleaded again, tugging at Doug like an impatient four-year old. "You heard him. Let's get out of here."

CHAPTER TWENTY-THREE

24 December 1944

Three and a half hours before midnight.

A trident of veins twitched in the middle of his forehead, and Levine's respiration came in harsh, furious gulps. "What were you thinking? Of all the stupid ..."

"Sorry, sir, we were told to bring back survivors. That's what we did, sir."

"One?! You only brought back one?"

Four sailors in a LCP, a Navy landing craft, dropped their heads, not wanting to meet Levine's fiery stare.

"Now get back out there and I want this thing so loaded you'll be afraid YOU'RE going to sink. Go, before I report you to your superiors."

The sailors gratefully put their boat into motion again.

"That's why everything gets all screwed up," Levine said to Dan, who had come back down the gangplank after escorting the sole survivor brought in by the LCP crew to one of the waiting ambulances. "I practically had to beg to join the Army. Me, a practicing physician with all kinds of experience, had to plead to get in." His right arm was upraised, his index finger extended slightly from a closed fist. Dan knew the pose. It meant the listener should pay careful attention. "... and then they turn around and take these kids and put them in charge of things they know nothing about. Half of them don't even shave, and we expect them to know what they're supposed to do?" He shook his head in disgust and began to walk in the direction of the next survivor awaiting help.

Silently, Dan fell in place alongside.

"Speaking of kids," Levine said, "... where's our Dixie drinker?"

"Aw, don't be too hard on Reb. He'll be okay."

"I understand, Sergeant, but he's not much help in this mess now, is he?" He rarely called Dan by his rank. Levine wasn't happy they had been left short-handed in what had developed into a major crisis.

Dan's brow furrowed. "With the barge moving all around the place, it was keeping his stomach pretty queasy."

"So where is he?"

"Well, since he couldn't stay here, I put him in with Smitty." Dan angled his head to the side and gave the captain a mischievous look. "I figured if nothing else, having to sit and listen to Smitty give him crap ought to sober him up in no time."

Levine unsuccessfully tried to stifle a chuckle, and then playfully punched him in the shoulder.

The discussion over, they returned to their duties. Dan greeted a survivor wearing nothing but splotches of diesel fuel on his shivering body. "What's your name, buddy?" Dan asked, placing a blanket around the soldier.

"Eckels ... like freckles."

"And you've got a bunch of them. Here." Dan gave him a cloth to wipe the oily smudges off his face. Eckels began to scrub vigorously, only to lose his grip on the blanket. He dropped the cloth to retrieve the blanket, but when he started to wipe his face again, the process repeated itself.

"Let me have that," Dan intervened, taking the rag. "The nurses at the hospital will be able to clean you up properly."

"Thanks. You guys have been terrific. I thought I was a goner."

"What happened out there?"

"Not sure. We were jammed everywhere in these cargo holds. I was grabbing some shut-eye under a table when things got crazy."

They walked up the gangplank at a cautious pace since the young man didn't have anything on his feet. Debris was everywhere.

"The explosion woke me," Eckels explained with a shiver, "and the next thing I knew I was getting blasted by the water. But that wasn't the biggest problem. It was the backwash."

"Backwash?"

"Yeah. The water that sucked back out through the hole. It took me with it."

Dan shivered at the thought of being pulled out into the ocean. He knew the terror of being underwater.

"I'm a decent swimmer so I made it to the top okay," Eckels continued, "but I didn't have a life jacket. It was tough staying afloat because I was weighted down."

"From your clothes?"

"My overcoat, my boots, everything. I figured I had to ditch all of my stuff if I was going to have any chance."

"That was smart."

"Except I was afraid I was gonna freeze to death before somebody would find me. Thank God for those swabbies."

They reached the ambulance and Dan helped him into the back with several other survivors. Eckels began to remove the blanket.

"No, you hang onto that," Dan said. "We've got enough. Besides, if you walk into that hospital without it, the nurses won't be able to keep their hands off of you."

Eckels' eyes lit up at the remark.

* * *

"Go!" Doug shouted. "You need to go now."

A large group was gathered at the bow of the *Leopoldville*, including Doug and Sal, trying to escape to the *Brilliant*. A soldier had a foot on the top railing, the other on the rung below. Two GIs stood by to lend support. The soldier's shoulder patch bore the ferocious profile of a black panther, but his face showed nothing but terror.

Thick, twisted hemp ropes had been exchanged between the troopship and the destroyer. The two ships were lashed together in the surging seas and buffeting wind. Waves, some swelling as high as eight feet, separated the ships by the entire length of the attached lines, and then just as quickly, brought them back together in violent contact. Nevertheless, the boats stayed connected and that allowed men to attempt to jump to safety on the destroyer. The troopship sat much higher in the water than her escort; they were close to the same level only when the destroyer caught a swell. Much of the time, the drop-off from the *Leopoldville* could be as much as twenty to thirty feet, and that didn't take into account the vacillating space between the ships. A jumper needed to go at just the right moment for his best chance at success. This timid private missed his opportunity. The *Brilliant* rammed into the side of the *Leopoldville*, rejecting the would-be jumper into the mob of hopefuls awaiting their chance behind him.

"Look, kid ... either do it or get out of the way. I ain't gonna stand around waiting for you to get some nerve." An impatient soldier with burly shoulders shoved his way past the others and climbed the railing, tossing his helmet into the water. "So long, suckers. Maybe, I'll let you have some of those French girls after I'm done."

"Wait ... not yet." Doug had become like a coxswain, counting out the beats and judging the movement of the two boats. His warning went unheeded as the soldier leaped toward the destroyer. Turbulence pushed the *Brilliant* beyond his effort, and the soldier disappeared beneath the waves.

"Do you see him?" Doug called.

"There he is ..." Sal shouted.

"Where?"

"Over there. See ... there's his Mae West."

The life vest, named in honor of the buxom movie star, was bright yellow, making the soldier easy to see when the preserver brought him back to the surface. The man was disoriented from his plunge into the Channel and didn't appreciate the approaching peril. The rest did.

"Swim, swim fast!" A man shouted from the deck.

"For God's sakes, Turner, get out of there!" came another shout.

"Hurry! Here she comes ..."

The life jacket was keeping him afloat, but the GI's progress to get clear of the destroyer was not matching the speed at which the open space was diminishing. Doug turned away. He couldn't bear to watch. The ships rammed together with a thud, and the soldier met his fate.

Doug slumped to the deck, the pain in his heart as troublesome as his back. "Why didn't he wait like I told him? Why didn't he wait?"

"It's not your fault. The jerk didn't want to listen to nobody no how." There was little machismo in Sal's response despite the tough words. He knelt down alongside his friend. Doug's condition was deteriorating. Summoning a vestige of courage, Sal tried to raise him to his feet. "Just fuhgeddaboud that last guy. We gotta get back in line before it's too late."

Doug did not react to the pull on his arm, and Sal's face grew taut. "Please! We gotta back in line or we won't have no time to make the jump."

Doug's body slumped as if every bone in his body had lost its desire to remain firm. "Look at me ... I can barely move. Do you really think I could make that jump?"

"Then what are we gonna do?"

"You should get back in line. You can make it."

Sal's face momentarily lost color, and then a tinge of red bloomed on his cheeks, growing full flower into purple. "What the matter with you, Hollywood? You're the only reason I've gotten this far. Do you really think I'd leave you? That hurts ... that really hurts."

Doug gave him a tight-lipped grin and extended his arm to Sal for an assist to get back on his feet. "You're right, buddy ... I'm sorry. We need to stick together. What do you say we find us a way off of this tub?"

The decision by the captain of the *Leopoldville* to drop anchor after she was torpedoed turned out to be the wrong choice. Incapacitated by the mooring, as well as by the lines that kept her attached to the *Brilliant*, the troopship bounced in great, heaving movements in the wind-whipped crests. The action grew the hole in the hull on F Deck, and more of the Channel poured into her lower levels. The ship's list toward the left was pronounced; she wouldn't stay afloat much longer. The *Brilliant* was taking on as many men as she could, but each time the British destroyer collided with the larger ship, she sustained damage to her own hull. Rescue craft hovered on the perimeter, but they were stymied from being of much use by the *Brilliant*'s position and the increasing tilt of the torpedoed steamer. Finally, it was too much for the destroyer to remain. Her sailors wielded axes and cut the lifelines between them. For Doug, Sal, and the other soldiers gathered near the bow of the *Leopoldville*, their last hope for survival appeared to be drifting away with the *Brilliant*.

"What are we gonna do now?" Sal whined.

Doug draped an arm across Sal's shoulders to comfort him. "We'll think of something. I probably wouldn't have made it anyway."

The bow of the troopship was rising from the water filling the lower compartments. The steep angle, combined with the tilt to port, made walking difficult. The pair inched along the starboard railing towards the stern.

"Maybe if we hadn't stayed with the colonel," Sal said. "Maybe we would've made it."

"Forget about it," Doug said. "Isn't that what you're always telling me? We'll be okay."

Sal ignored the attempt to buttress his confidence. He pulled away and went to a nearby lifeboat still hanging in its storage position. Sal gave the boat's chain some furious yanks before trying to pull apart the padlock that held it in place.

"Please ... please, Sal. Stop."

The little man kept clawing at the tether, and then collapsed to the deck, sobbing. "We're gonna die."

Doug hugged his friend's heaving shoulders and let the frightened man cry even as his own fears continued to grow. Their demise was never closer to being realized.

CHAPTER TWENTY-FOUR

24 December 1944

Three hours and fifteen minutes before midnight.

A large wave lifted the dining table. It caught Willy on his chin as squarely as a haymaker from Max Schmeling.[22] He was thrown off the makeshift raft and swamped by the frigid water. Pools of spilled diesel fuel from his destroyed submarine made the water murky and seemed to be taking away the buoyancy of his Drager. He gagged at the petroleum taste, and his eyes burned because couldn't keep his head above the salty crests of the Channel. Remnants of U-474 banged against him even though he couldn't see what they were. Something hard and sharp cracked Willy across his thighs. The pain sent shock waves through every part of his body ... except his feet.

They must be so cold they've gone numb, he told himself. The lack of feeling in them distracted his thoughts until he was whacked from behind by some other piece of submarine detritus. His whole body trembled from shock. He shivered

---

[22] German world heavyweight champion boxer.

violently in the water and thrashed helplessly. Willy was certain that this was the end.

Somehow, the Drager lifejacket did its job and brought the helpless sailor back to the surface. Kapitänleutnant Marquardt's teak dining table continued to bob near him, only now it was a few meters beyond his reach. Willy spat out a mouthful of seawater.

Don't panic, he thought. *They destroyed the sub, not you. Keep calm. What did Ludwig always tell you?*

Learning how to swim had been difficult for Willy. Children from his village swam in a small lake near the town's mill. The pond was cut out by a glacier during the Ice Age, and fed by an underground spring, its water always remained cold. The pond had a muddy bottom that would envelop their feet when they entered, but it disappeared in quick fashion. Willy found it a swim or sink proposition once he got away from the shore. The combination of the water's temperature and his lack of experience would fatigue him in short order. Worse, fear would overwhelm his efforts, and too often, he would need his brother's help. Red-faced—from embarrassment and the cold—he would feel equal parts of resentment and relief whenever Ludwig came to his rescue.

This situation in the Channel was frighteningly similar. Willy slapped and kicked at the icy water, but he was like a boat without a rudder or propulsion. Try as he might, he couldn't seem to get any traction in the water. He moved like a submarine without any screws.

Willy's breathing became ragged, and the heaving gasps drained oxygen from his lungs. He stopped paddling and lay back, letting the Drager keep him afloat. He could barely feel his fingertips. The rest of his body had the same sensation. A strange, thick film seemed to be all about him. He wasn't sure how much longer he could keep treading water.

Through small breaks in the clouds, the moon illuminated the water, but the light was harsh rather than comforting. He recalled those childhood days at the lake, and he made a silent plea to his brother. Without warning, something banged against the back of his head. The Kaleu's table had floated within reach.

"Thank you, Ludwig!" he shouted to the sky. "I knew you would help."

He rolled over with caution. A hasty move might push the furniture-turned-life raft beyond his reach. Whether it was his brother's hand from above, or just another gust of wind, the next wave lifted U-474's lone survivor to where he could grasp the slab. He clamped his hands to the sides and pulled himself up as far as he could. His bottom half remained in the water. The table still floated amidst the debris from the demolished submarine. Luck struck again when a crate that might prove useful came into view. Unfortunately, it would mean having to move with the table over to where the wooden box bobbed in the waves. He took several deep breaths to build his strength and resolve, and then willed himself to sink further into the water. With one hand clutched on the Kaleu's table, and with what little propulsion he could generate with his legs, Willy stroked with his free hand, attempting to provide as much forward progress as the awkward positioning would allow.

It took about five minutes of full exertion. Willy was spent when he reached the wooden container that somehow was still intact except for its top. That proved to be another break. The wooden slats of the lid had been fractured, which would allow him to reach inside. He would have been hard-pressed to undo the latch with his cold fingers.

The stamp on its side confirmed the value of the contents within. He hung on to the raft with one hand and picked through the fractured slats on the lid with the other. He removed a half dozen sou'westers, long waterproof coats the sailors of U-474 wore topside during foul weather. Their yellow color was in sharp contrast to the gray his world had become. He piled the coats on the table. A second reach produced a handful of Tyrolean sweaters, and they joined the oilskins in the pile.

Hopeful again, Willy surveyed the horizon. He could see nothing but a black void in front of him. All the activity, and his best chance to be rescued, was taking place in the opposite direction. He kicked fiercely to swing the table back toward the action of the harbor. Each movement sent fire through his left leg, even in the frigid water. His right leg didn't seem to be providing any thrust at all, and that was an added complication to his dilemma.

Maybe my right leg's caught in something. Maybe it's just that my feet are too cold to feel what the problem is.

It was difficult to maintain a grip on the sides of the board, and his progress was erratic at best. Fatigue was regaining its advantage and the cold appeared to be accelerating his energy loss. It wouldn't be long before he would lose all control of his raft. He decided he needed to be completely atop his floating sanctuary rather than his current half-in/half-out of the water position. With a burst of strength, he pulled himself onboard and fell on his back.

The biting December wind was painful, even for someone with his Bavarian upbringing. He could see a spread of blue growing in his fingernails, and he didn't want to think what his toes must look like. Turning his head, he saw the pile of rescued clothing. A distant memory brought a smile to his face, even if the smile was short lived.

* * *

Nine-year old Willy and his friends were on another adventure. Snow, heavy with moisture, seemed to be everywhere thanks to a strong, swirling wind. They were testing their skiing skills on Kreuzberg, the highest peak in the area.

Their village of Waldberg was situated in the foothills of the Alps where elevations weren't as significant as in Austria or Switzerland. Still, at more than 900 meters, the mountain was more than anything they had tackled before. These Bavarian boys were as comfortable on skis as they were in their shoes, and Willy was the best of the group.

Several successful runs were already completed, and he was leading his friends up the mountain for another attempt. A few of the boys complained they were cold and wanted to take a break, so Willy reluctantly agreed. They skied over to a monastery, built centuries earlier, that stood at the top of the summit. The thick, wooden door at the entrance, although weathered, was still formidable. Long iron straps held the planks of it together, with a giant ring of the same material serving as both a handle and a knocker. Willy needed to use both hands to swing it hard enough to make a noise. He was about to do it again when the door moved. Its bottom scraped across a worn flagstone and the noise made the boys step back in fear.

"What are you children doing here?"

A large Franciscan monk loomed in the doorway. He wore a rubber apron over his cleric's robes and sandals on bare feet, even though it was the middle of winter. A St. Bernard, with a small keg hanging from its collar, stood guard at his side. The boys cowered in silence. When the cleric fixed his gaze on Willy—perhaps because he was the tallest one of the group—the rest shoved him forward. Ludwig had told him once that the priests and brothers at the monastery were friendly and generous, but Willy was getting no sense of that from the hulk glaring down at him.

"P-p-pardon me, Father, b-b-but we're cold and … and hungry … and we were told you would give us … give us something to eat and drink."

"And who told you that?" the friar thundered.

Now Willy could barely make his mouth work at all. "M-m-my b-b-br-other," he answered in a whisper.

The incessant panting of the St. Bernard sounded like the tick-tock of a giant timepiece. The boys were petrified. They stared down at the snow until the silence was broken by a bellow of laughter from the Franciscan. "Well, your brother is correct! But not some of this, I'm afraid." He hoisted a clay stein filled with the latest sample from their brewery. A life of prayer was not the only thing with which the order was involved. The Kreuzberg brewery had a national reputation, even in a country where beer was as plentiful as water. "I think your parents would feel better if we gave you some cocoa. How does that sound to you, boys?"

Willy mumbled some thanks. The rest of the group was still speechless.

The cleric led the boys into a large dining room and over to a roaring fireplace in the far corner. They were cold and jostled for the best position in front of the fire. The friar left but returned in short order with a tray filled with mugs, a loaf of bread, and some cheese and sausage. Willy and his friends eagerly snatched the steaming cups of hot chocolate and then did the same with the chunks of food. He asked them about their homes, their parents, and families and they regaled their host with stories of their skiing exploits as well as discussions over which of them was the best performer. Willy was the top choice, although it wasn't a unanimous opinion.

The Franciscan grabbed a handful of the wool sweater Willy was wearing and, with a laugh, lifted him as if he was a doll. "Whether or not this young man is your best skier, his mother, at least, makes certain he is the warmest."

His friends laughed at the sight of Willy dangling off the floor in the giant's grasp, but the looks on their faces showed they didn't know exactly what to make of the monk's comment. All their mothers had bundled them to deal with the biting winds that were a daily reality where they lived, especially in the winter. What did Willy have that the rest of them didn't?

"It's not always the heaviest coat that keeps you warm," the friar explained. "It's knowing what will offer the most protection when you get wet and cold."

The others wore coats or large jackets, but not Willy. By the time she was the same age as these boys, his mother had been taught already by her shepherd father how best to handle the cold when out in the open. The wool sheared from his flock was boiled before being made into the yarn for sweaters. The lanolin from the wool gave that yarn the ability to retain warmth even when wet. Combine thinner layers of under-clothing with the outer shell protection of a wool sweater she was trained, and you will stay warm. Willy's sweater might seem as bulky as their coats and jackets, but it was lighter and gave him better maneuverability. He had good skiing tech-nique, but every little advantage helped make the difference when he raced against them.

"Layers, gentlemen," the Franciscan instructed as he lifted Willy's sweater to reveal what he was wearing underneath. "The secret is in layers."

* * *

It's all about layers, Willy. That's what is going to help keep you alive out here.

Willy reached to his left to arrange the clothing into a shell to protect against the harbor's winter bite. When he did, his legs barked in complaint. He pressed his forearms into the table to raise himself up more to see what the problem was.

Must be still tangled in something, he thought. *Maybe I can pull myself free somehow—*

The sight of his lower body hit him harder than anything he had ever experienced.

His left leg was a mangled mess. All he could see was that his leg was now bent in directions it wasn't supposed to go. It looked like the tibia had been fractured in at least three places.

That was a gift in comparison to its partner.

The frigid water had deluded him when the Allies' depth charges cracked open U-474 and sent him to the surface.

Willy's right foot was completely gone.

CHAPTER TWENTY-FIVE

24 December 1944

Three hours before midnight.

The stream of returning rescue boats was unending. Victims were left in a pile on the pier because there was no place to store the bodies yet. During a lull in the pace, Levine assigned Dan and GMC to organize the dead bodies into rows. The captain wanted to show proper respect to those that had perished ... and to provide room for the others yet to come.

"You notice something about all of these guys?" Dan asked.

GMC shook his head. He held the feet of a soldier, with Dan at the head, as they carried a casualty to a free spot on the pier.

"Look at all the stuff they're wearing." Dan removed a waterlogged overcoat from the victim and tossed it onto a fast-growing mound of unneeded equipment. They laid the soldier down with the others. "There's no way they could have survived dressed like this. Too much weight in the water. You'd think they would have known better."

"Not if they figured they'd catch it if they didn't have all their gear with them." GMC pulled apart the man's criss-crossed arms.

"But stuff like this?" Dan said. "This is crazy." A solitary box of C-rations was frozen against the soldier's chest.

"Hey, guys!" Bobby yelled from the gangway. "More boats are coming in. Captain needs one of you down here."

"Your call, Sarge," GMC said. "Either way is fine with me."

"Go ahead, you take it."

"You sure?"

"Go on, before I change my mind."

GMC went off to assist on the barge. Dan watched him until he was out of sight before getting back to the grim task at hand. Eight men remained in the pile. He rolled over one of the bodies that had been placed face down.

"Oh, my God!"

The dead infantryman had bitten into his life jacket as if to stifle a scream, and the piece was still lodged in his mouth. Stuffing leaked from a jagged tear and he was covered with it. Dan removed the wedged scrap and brushed off as much of the fluff as he could, although it wouldn't make any difference to the man's situation. He placed the soldier alongside one of the other victims, whispered a silent prayer, and moved to the next body.

This latest round of losses had common features beyond wearing too much gear. Their exposed skin was frosty and translucent blue in color. For most, exposure to the elements had been their undoing more than the torpedo. Their eyes—at least those still open—were glassy, like his mother's porcelain dolls back home. The death stares were troubling, and he closed them whenever possible.

Dan reached down to close the eyes on a private whose face was bloated and blue from his fatal swim. A spurt of water shot out of the man's mouth, a reflex of compressing air. Dan fell backward into the pile of remaining bodies and then made a panicked scramble away on all fours. It was several minutes before he was calm enough to get back into action. This time, when he reached to close the man's eyes, nothing happened. Hoisting him by the belt of his overcoat, he carried him to the rows of bodies. The process continued until only one soldier remained. He was the first arrival; the others had been tossed on top of him.

"We should've been able to help you," Dan murmured. He wiped away moisture that silently glistened on the dead man's cheeks.

"Dan!"

It was Bobby again. "More boats! We need you down here, too."

Dan hurried to finish his task but was surprised to see a new tear of water trickling down this victim's face. The man's stare seemed less opaque and his skin did not have quite the same ghostly transparency, but otherwise he seemed like the rest of his buddies.

There it is again, Dan thought. A tear, and then another, and yet one more. Dan reached inside the man's uniform and placed his hand against the soldier's chest. He bolted upright a moment later. "Captain Levine!" he screamed. "I've got a live one here!"

263

Dan tore apart the man's shirt; the buttons danced away like popcorn shooting from a heated pot. He vigorously massaged the man's chest and felt the slight beat continue to strengthen. He looked into living eyes as tears pooled beneath them. He wiped them away gently. The other bodies covering the soldier must have provided enough warmth to reignite the spark of life.

"Small details," Dan whispered to the man. "Small details."

* * *

The tilt to port was now so pronounced that the starboard side of the *Leopoldville's* hull looked more like the main deck than the deck itself. The settling of the stern was quickening, and waves washed over the railings. The harbor was inexorably pulling the ship to her death.

"What are we doing?" Sal had lost all pretenses. He was like a small child, in total fear. "We gotta go to the other end. We gotta go the other way!"

A rush of men hurried by them, but Sal's persistent tug on Doug's sleeve was not slowing their move in the opposite direction, toward the rising water at the stern. The little man might be terrorized, but the increasingly dire circumstances seemed to have energized Doug.

"It's okay, believe me," Doug said. "We want to be going this way." They stopped for a moment when they came upon a scattered pile of life jackets. "Here, take this," he said, passing a preserver to Sal and then taking one for himself.

He passed his right arm through the jacket, only to have a spasm bend him in two. Sal had the presence to say nothing, even though his fear was spiking. He shifted his gaze away and pawed at the ground, watching his boot make a figure eight in a puddle. He tied and then retied the straps on the front of the preserver. Sal was going to make certain it stayed secure. The pain eased to a manageable level for Doug, and he was able to put on his jacket. Before they could resume their escape to the stern, an explosion below deck sent a ferocious growl through the ship. The *Leopoldville* yawed even more sharply to port and her bow rose farther into the black night. Another quake echoed the first.

"Will you listen to me now, Hollywood?" Sal yanked harder on his friend's arm, desperate to follow the fleeing crowd to the bow.

"Do you trust me?" Doug asked.

"Of course, but, we're gonna drown."

"I'm telling you, we need to go *this* way," Doug persisted. It took all of his remaining strength to keep Sal from joining the pell-mell dash of the other soldiers still onboard. "We're not going to drown ... I won't let you. But we are going to end up in the water." He made his own pull on his resistant partner to bring them to the starboard rail, close to the stern. It was like walking up a steep hill, but Doug was unwavering. "Look down there," he instructed. "This is why we don't want to follow those guys to the front of the boat."

Sal's eyes were cemented closed, his head turned away from the agitated harbor.

"LOOK!"

The ferocity of Doug's command startled Sal. His eyes popped open and his body went stiff except for his cheeks, which sucked inward as he stared at the waves beneath them. The harbor was a maelstrom of white caps.

"Think for a moment. How far is it to the water?" Doug asked.

"...I, er ... guess ... uh ... about fifty, maybe seventy-five feet."

"Now how far do you think it will be for those guys up there?"

The rush of the sea into the lower levels had become a torrent. The bow of the *Leopoldville* appeared to be rising right before their eyes.

"I dunno ... a lot higher than we are. So what are you saying?"

"I'm telling you when we go into the water—and we gotta go now—I'd rather be doing it from right here."

"You know I ain't that much of a swimmer."

"It's the only way, Sal, if we want to live."

The little man looked unconvinced, but his shoulders slumped in resignation. Doug was his only hope. He would need to follow his lead wherever it was going to take them.

The hull below their position looked like an ivy-covered garden wall. Heavy ropes, more than a dozen of them, were tied to the starboard railing, and the mess of tangled cords reached to within feet of the water. Soldiers were rappelling down the side to escape. The pool of men in the inky wetness below increased in direct proportion to each downward movement by the *Leopoldville*'s stern.

Doug swung a leg over the railing, and with his back to the water, he placed his feet against the hull. "Wait until I get halfway before you start. That'll let me settle in the water before you get there. It will be easier for me to help you."

"If you say so ..."

Doug began his descent, making incremental movements to minimize the strain on his back. Still, he needed to stop several times. Sal's panic at being separated, meanwhile, superseded his fear of the water, and he followed almost immediately. He fell on his friend mere seconds after Doug slipped into the harbor. They both sank below the waves until their life preservers brought them back to the surface. Sal made frenzied splashes as he fought to stay above the breakers.

"It's freezing and my—"

His words were lost to the next wave. When he resurfaced, his blubbering was from more than just the water he swallowed. The life jacket was bunched around his neck, cutting off his air supply. Each time he reached to pull the float down, the weight shift caused the water to cover him. The Channel soaked his overcoat, and the increased weight was turning him into a sinker. With each dunking, it got worse.

"Help me!" Sal cried. "PLEASE!"

Only a couple feet separated them, but Doug was still cautious. Sal wasn't going to drown; the life jacket should do its job. Sal's lack of control, however, could prove troublesome. When his desperate arm waving and the churning harbor sent him below the surface a fifth time, realities outweighed the risks. Doug needed to help him. He swam with small strokes. His own overcoat was retaining water and he could feel the heavy drag. He grabbed at the collar of Sal's preserver just as he was about to go under again.

"I've gotcha!"

Doug kept his words slow and measured in his instructions for what they needed to do next, although he had to shout because of the noise coming from the *Leopoldville*. Men continued to stream over the side to join those who had already abandoned ship. Cries for help echoed through the area. Meanwhile, the flooding below deck ran unchecked. The rushing water collapsed section after section of the inner structure, and the action produced metallic groans that had an eerie, human quality to it. Sal continued to flail his arms, and Doug looked like an exasperated parent trying to handle an uncooperative child. Underwater, Sal accidentally kicked him in the groin, and he lost his hold on the life jacket. Sal slipped under the water. When the preserver returned the little man to the top, Doug punched his already broken nose.

Sal hollered in pain. "What are you doing?"

"Trying to keep you from kicking me in the privates again."

Sal swiped at the rush of blood and tenderly pressed his nose to see if he could stop the flow.

The distraction enabled Doug to get into a position where he could better control him if there was another panic attack. "Now listen to me carefully. If you're going to fight me on this, we're both gonna die."

Sal forgot about his nose and looked at the ship. "She is ready to go," Doug continued. "... and when she does, it's gonna pull everything down with it."

His arms were quiet in the hold he had around Sal, but his legs kicked furiously. The cold water provided an initial numbing effect to the pain in his back, but now the increased activity made his wound howl. The whirlpool that would be produced when the ship went under was an approaching reality, and they wouldn't make enough progress away from it if he only used his legs. Still, he hesitated before releasing one of his hands. He made awkward strokes but maintained his grip on the life jacket. Sal stayed frozen with fear.

CHAPTER TWENTY-SIX

24 December 1944

Two hours fifty minutes before midnight.

W illy remained on his back on the table. Enraged thoughts raced through his mind.
   A cripple!
It was a life difficult to comprehend.

A wave drenched him, and instinctively, he sat up which put his damaged legs in plain sight. The water's temperature had produced a tourniquet-like effect on them. The color of his legs, especially in the shredded tissue and tendons where his right foot had been severed, was a combination of blues. The flesh was pale, almost chalky in spots, while in the areas where the veins had been mangled, the clotted blood was blackish in hue. One of the fractured pieces of his tibia had broken through the skin, and it shown a brilliant white thanks to a cleansing from the harbor. His body shook with revulsion and wonder ... and from the cold.

Layers. Remember?

The self-admonishment spurred him to action. He wrapped each leg with the recovered sweaters. He tied the sleeves together to ensure they would remain in place. The sweaters were wet but he felt their insulating warmth in short order. The sou'westers came next. He arranged them like a large blanket, several laid atop the sweaters, two others across his upper torso as he stretched out.

The *Leopoldville* was more than a thousand meters away, but she drew Willy's attention when the table went into a series of bucks and rolls. The agitation in the harbor grew with every dying movement made by the troopship. The stern was almost completely submerged, raising her bow. Most of the hull, four hundred ninety feet in length from fore to aft, was exposed. The ship weighed nearly twelve tons, but she climbed into the night as if constructed of balsa wood. Had his hearing not been lost, Willy would have been struck by the screech of overstressed metal and the cries from the men still trapped onboard.

* * *

It was bedlam in the water around the *Leopoldville*. Pleading voices—some cursing, others crying—reverberated against the side of the sinking ship. The desperate strokes of hundreds of soldiers made the churning sea even more intemperate.

An exhausted Doug broke through the surface after a third dive, flashing a small smile of success. "Now if you kick me, at least it won't hurt as much," he said as he raised his prize: Sal's boots. With a heave he immediately regretted because of the pain it caused to his back, he tossed aside the sodden

271

hunks of leather. His next step was to untie the straps on Sal's preserver.

"What are you doing?" Sal's eyes widened.

"Your boots weighed you down, and your overcoat will, too. I thought if I got rid of it, you'd float better."

Sal folded his arms across his chest. "Fuhgeddaboudit! I know you think you're looking out for me, but there's no way I'm taking off anything else until I get on some land."

Doug didn't want to make it an issue, but he knew their soaked clothes could become a fatal problem. Since Sal wouldn't cooperate, he would have to take care of his things to be able to maneuver for both of them. He moved off a short distance, ignoring a grunt of fear from Sal, and dropped below the water. It was difficult to bend, but he managed to unlace his own boots. The watery pull on his legs eased immediately. He untied the belts on his preserver, letting the device float in front of him where he could still retrieve it easily. He wriggled out of his overcoat, and as the discarded garment sank, he placed his arms back through the openings of the life jacket. The process had been more of an ordeal than he thought it would be. He lay back and closed his eyes, his body drifting in the tide.

"Hollywood? What are you doing?"

"Just gimme a minute!" Doug spat out the words and then floated silently. His only movement was the rise and fall of his chest, barely discernible underneath the preserver.

Sal dog-paddled closer. "You okay?"

"Sorry, I punched your broken nose. My back is killing me and I didn't know I could get this tired."

"Fuhgeddaboudit," Sal replied, his voice brightening. "You'll be—"

His words were swamped by a deafening noise from the *Leopoldville*. Steel beams in the bowels of the ship collapsed like toothpicks, the sound like the cry of banshees. She climbed to a nearly vertical position, hesitating as if the ship was uncertain what was to come next. With a screech of metal on metal, the *S.S. Leopoldville* made her final move. Unlike the slow motion rise, her descent was going to be rapid.

"Swim, Sallie ... SWIM!" Doug hooked an arm around him, and they struggled to move from the chaos of the hundreds of GIs also trying to escape.

With a final gasp, the *S. S. Leopoldville* disappeared. The undertow was strong, but Doug and Sal swam beyond the perimeter of the deadly draw. Others weren't as fortunate.

"I can't friggin' believe it. It's gone ... it's really gone." Sal's words were barely above a whisper, and then he flailed in panic like a madman. "We're gonna be goners, too if we don't find ..."

"Knock it off, Sal—" A coughing fit interrupted Doug's explanation. He was certain the bleeding in his back had resumed. Sal was fighting him, even if the little man didn't realize it, and the effort pushed him to his limit. "If you keep this up, I'm not gonna be ... able to keep us ..." Each word needled his back and tortured his lungs. "... going, if we don't ... find something for me ... to rest on soon."

Providence stepped forward. Several yards away from them, a large lid popped up amid the wreckage expelled by their now-gone transport.

"There's something we can use," Sal exclaimed. "C'mon. I gotcha." It was the first time since they went into the water that he had taken the lead. His crude strokes weren't overly efficient, but the distance to the floating top was not far. The lid was about five feet in length but no more than three feet wide. Sal slid himself on and was able to drag Doug onboard. He fell on his back while Doug slumped face down.

"I know you might've been scared," Sal said after catching his breath. "... but, hey, there wasn't nothing to worry about. I had it all the way."

It hurt to laugh, but Doug had to anyway. The braggadocio was welcome with how he was feeling. Maybe they could hang on until a rescue boat found them.

Other survivors paddled closer, attempting to join them on the lid. Their efforts, and the counter moves by Sal to prevent it, pitched the chunk of wood about. "Screw you guys!" Sal hollered. We was here first. Go find your own!"

The lid began to break apart under the strain. Other men clambered to get out of the water. Sal swung wildly at the invaders but hit nothing but air. The lid separated into two and plunged Sal and Doug plunged back into the freezing water.

In the bedlam, Doug lost his grip on Sal. A man without a life jacket grasped at Sal, and the two submerged. Doug stroked closer, probing the waves in front of him with an outstretched arm. His back was on fire.

"Sal!" he shouted. "Sal, where are you?!" Doug couldn't see his friend anywhere. "Jesus," he said. The word was a desperate prayer.

Sal splashed to the surface. A second later the other soldier splashed up, made a frantic grab for Sal, missed, and caught hold of a piece of the broken lid.

"Hollywood!" Sal called. "Hollywood—you gotta help me. My life jacket's gone."

CHAPTER TWENTY-SEVEN

24 December 1944

Two hours twenty-five minutes before midnight.

Dan was back on the pier, stacking more of the bodies retrieved too late to be saved. A shrill whistle, three notes in rapid succession, cut through the night, the signal from the captain. Dan hurried down the gangway to the far end of the barge where Levine stood with a pasty-white Reb alongside.

"Yes, sir," Dan said.

"This isn't working like I hoped," the captain said. "Too many of these men are already gone before we get a chance to help them."

A small tug steamed away from the barge and headed back toward the open water. The tug had just brought in forty men, but all but nine of them had succumbed before they could be given any medical attention. It was becoming a too-familiar scenario as the rescue efforts progressed.

"The shock, the exposure ... we have to get to them sooner."

"Whatever you say, Captain. What's the plan?"

276

"Smitty is hauling as many survivors as he can to the 280th, and I want him to keep at it even if it means putting some of those men in the cab with him."

That explains Reb being back, Dan thought to himself. Nearby, two lonely boats were tied to a small, rickety quay. The boats' condition matched their parking space. It seemed as if every other usable craft in Cherbourg was involved in the rescue effort.

Levine tugged on the rope that connected one of the boats to the dock. "Maybe if we could get out to where the men actually are, it would give some of them a better chance. I sent GMC and Jepson out a few minutes ago, and I think we need to go, too."

Dan swallowed, thought a moment, and then said, "Okay, let's do it."

"One problem." The captain placed an arm around Dan and lowered his voice to a whisper. Reb drew closer, straining to hear what was being said. "Two boats. Three men. These boats are awfully small. If we all go in one boat, it won't leave much room for the men we're trying to help." He cleared his throat with a nervous cough, his eyes narrowing. "And if we split up, one of us will have to go alone."

Dan didn't hesitate. "You take Reb with you, sir. You're too valuable to go out there alone. You can have him do whatever you need."

"Y'all talking about me? What can I do?" The teenager leaned in close to hear the pair's conversation, and he caught the captain's shoulder on his chin when the doctor spun to answer his question.

Dan reached out and kept him from falling backward. "You can help the Captain get our guys out of the water so he can work on them."

"Y'all can count on that," Reb replied, happy to be doing anything other than riding shotgun with Smitty.

"You sure?" Levine raised an eyebrow. "Maybe I should just stay here and the two of you could pair up in one of these boats."

"There are other doctors here," Dan replied. "Like you said, going to the where that ship sank may make all the difference."

"Okay, but be smart out there." The captain gave Reb a push on the shoulder. The two moved back down the pier to collect what they would need out on the water. Dan did the same.

The boats had been left for a reason. Their condition was questionable at best, and their size didn't allow much space for supplies or for those to be rescued. Dan worked over the plan in his mind. *Every little bit could help; the captain was right.* He tossed blankets, bandages, and other medical necessities into his boat. Reb and Levine did the same to theirs.

The small fishing skiffs were approximately ten feet wide and about thirty feet long. Their bows came to a sharp upraised point while the sides angled out before straightening as they approached the stern. An outboard engine rested in the middle of the backboard, a small handle attached to the motor to serve as a tiller. Benches were positioned in the middle, and rusted brackets sat on the gunwales, remnants from the long-ago use of oars instead of motorized power.

"You know how to operate one of these?" Levine asked as he tugged at the rope starter on his skiff.

Dan grabbed the wooden handle knotted to the ignition cable on his outboard and gave it a mighty tug. The motor roared to life. "Piece of cake," he beamed. "I'm an old pro when it comes to these things."

Reb gave him a look of surprise. He was going to say something but was distracted by the captain's effort to get their outboard going. It took multiple pulls—with Levine's exasperated grunts as accompanying sound effects—but eventually the engine kicked into action. They finished organizing the gear in their craft, and Dan did the same with his.

"We'll meet back here at 2300 hours," Levine yelled. He flashed the watch on his left wrist in Dan's direction.

Dan returned a salute and watched their boat speed away. He put his own skiff into gear and was startled when it jerked forward. He quickly throttled down to idling speed and floated aimlessly for twenty yards in the oily water. The moon, unshackled for a moment from the gathering clouds, cast foreboding beams of light across the harbor. He struck himself with disgust on his forehead with the base of his palm. *What are you thinking? The only boat you've ever piloted was in a bathtub. How are you going make this work?*

The risks of going solo would have been difficult for an experienced sailor in the current conditions, and Dan knew he was nowhere close to being one. Still, as reckless as his decision might have been, he knew it was the only choice he could make if they were to accomplish what the captain had in mind. With his mouth closed, he drew a deep breath through his nostrils, holding it for a long time before it was released slowly through his pursed lips. His shoulders slumped momentarily, but then with renewed resolve, he straightened and pushed the motor's throttle into its forward gear. The bow of the boat rose from the acceleration.

Dan's speed remained relatively slow, no more than ten knots. The size of the skiff made it virtually invisible to the larger boats, and he selected a cautious route, away from the heavier traffic. Only as he moved farther away from the pier, did he ease the throttle farther forward. The parade of boats returning with victims and survivors was steady, and most paid scant attention to him. A larger-than-anticipated wave took the skiff airborne for a few seconds after one of the Navy tugs passed, and several more swells soon followed from the wake of the larger boat. He bounced around at the rear of the skiff and lost his grip on the tiller. Regaining command, a chilling realization struck. "YOU ARE AN IDIOT!"

His screaming reproach was gone on the wind in an instant, but its implication was a lingering reality. The skiff was loaded with blankets and medical supplies, but in the haste to search for survivors, he'd left without a life jacket.

Dan throttled down a little too abruptly, and the outboard sputtered and shut down. The boat rocked in the wind-driven chop, the wakes from other boats. He regained his composure and yanked on the starter rope. Nothing. He yanked again. The engine coughed to life for a few seconds then died. He yanked again and again. The engine remained lifeless. He fumbled with the choke. He squeezed the bulb of the gas line, desperate to try any variation that might start the engine. Dan pulled and pulled and pulled with increasing frustration and desperation.

The engine stayed unresponsive.

The moon showed a sliver on the dark night on the sea. The wind whipped the water around him into a snow-white lather. Dan trembled, shook off the dark thought that passed through his mind, and returned to the engine, urgently trying to flog a dead horse back to life.

* * *

Doug swam over to where he was three feet away from Sal. "Do exactly what I say!" Doug hollered, treading water. "You need to trust me now like you've never trusted me before." Other men could be seen in the distance. Their cries of help rose in the night wind. "Listen to me! Listen *only* to me!"

Sal's eyes were wide. The little man was on the verge of panic. "Tell me what to do!" he shouted, and sank beneath the waves a moment. He flayed his arms and sprang to the surface. "Anything!"

"I'm going to grab you around your chest from behind. When I do that, you have to stop moving. Understand?"

Sal nodded.

Doug swam behind Sal, caught him by the chest, and leaned back. The added weight nearly submerged them both, but between Doug's leg kicks and the one life jacket, they managed to stay on the surface.

"Hollywood, I'm so … so scared." Sal's teeth were chattering.

"You're going to be just fine," Doug said. "I've got you, and I'm not going to let go. But you can't panic. You gotta keep trusting me. If you panic, you'll take us both down, and I'll punch you in the nose again and let go. Agreed?"

"I get it," Sal said. "You see anything around here that can help us?"

"It's too dark to see much." Doug coughed, the shakes racked them both. "There are a lot of other hungry soldiers out here, too."

Sal craned his neck around and looked at his savior. "Your lips are blue, buddy. You going to be all right."

"We're not done yet, Sallie," Doug gasped, "but we don't have the strength to fight with these guys every time we find something that might help us. We need to get away from this area if we're going to make it."

"Okay, I surrender," Sal said. "You're the boss."

Doug nodded. He was too cold to talk further. They broke away from the others and swam in the direction of the outer reaches of the harbor, looking like an inverted three-legged racer with their crude dog-paddling. Their progress versus the energy expended wasn't coming close to matching their hopes, but they remained undaunted. They needed to find something from the wreckage, anything that would help keep them alive until they could be rescued.

"What's our plan?" Sal asked. "Swim all the way back to Limey Land?"

Doug almost laughed at Sal's sarcasm, but the pain and fatigue wouldn't allow him to do anything but use his diminishing faculties to concentrate on their search. "Remember when we passed the submarine net coming in?"

"I think so," Sal gulped between mouthfuls of seawater.

"It should be out here someplace. If we can find it, maybe we could use its cable for support until we get some of our strength back. You a praying man, Sal?"

"Not really, no. You?"

"I haven't been for a long while. But now would seem a good a time as any to start again."

"You want me to pray? Seriously? I don't know nothing about praying."

"Then shut up and let me." Doug paused a moment while a wave broke over their heads, then continued, "God. I know we haven't talked in a while, and I know I've got a lot of questions still. But I'm willing to put all that aside now if you are too. Here's what I'm asking: if ever you cared about us, we need to find that cable."

"Uh ... *amen*," Sal added.

"Amen," Doug said.

"You think that's gonna work?"

Doug shot water out of his nose. He would have laughed except for their predicament. "I don't know what I believe anymore, buddy. I just know that God—if there is a God—sure doesn't answer prayers the way we always want him to. I guess we just have to trust in him like I need you to keep trusting me."

"I can live with that." Sal almost smiled.

Neither man had any idea where the defense enclosure was, but it seemed as worthwhile a target as anything did. They swam for several more minutes, but even with a target determined, their efforts didn't appear to be taking them any-where closer. Doug stopped his stroking and floated on his back.

"What's the matter?" The concern in Sal's voice raised its pitch to a squeaky timbre like the yelp of a puppy.

"This is stupid." Doug wheezed. "It's all stupid."

"Don't give me that crap. We're gonna make it. We're both gonna make it! We just prayed! That's gotta count for something." Panic rose in Sal's voice.

Doug didn't respond. He closed his eyes and wondered if his mother knew what was happening before she had been taken by the sea. *Was this what it was like just before the end?*

As they drifted farther from the others, Sal dog paddled, spinning in an agitated circle, searching for anything that might change their plight. "Hey ... there's something."

"Nice try." Doug panted with eyes still closed. "I doubt we're anywhere close to the cable."

"Fuhgeddaboudit. I ain't talking about that stupid net. Look over there."

Sal continued to paddle while Doug raised himself for a better look. In the distance, an object, bigger than the lid they had tried to use earlier, was moving in the swells. Doug was struck by the bright yellow color of something that sat on top of it. Their potential salvation brought his body back to life.

"That thing'll be perfect ... plenty of room for both of us." Sal gasped, but with the promise of survival keeping him energized. "And I bet somebody's gonna find us in no time."

CHAPTER TWENTY-EIGHT

24 December 1944

Two hours before midnight.

F ace down, Willy gripped the edges of the Kaleu's table with all of his remaining strength. His hands were
the only things from under the pile of sou'westers that
were visible. The oilskins helped keep the harbor's waters
from making him any wetter, and the sweaters around his legs
provided warmth, but he was helpless when it came to ma-
neuvering his life raft. The ebbing tide continued to carry him
toward the open water of the English Channel and away from
where he wanted to be.

Just let this end. There is nothing left for me.

Those thoughts and his progress came to a sudden halt
when the tabletop crashed into a steel column. It was one of
the support beams for the submarine net. The table floated up
and down in the constant surging action of the tide and the
activity in the harbor, but, now wedged under a circular cap
affixed to the metal beam, it held firm. Willy poked his head
out from the mound of clothes as if he was a turtle and let
loose a throaty laugh. "You just won't let me give up, will

you, Ludwig?" He raised his arms to the sky. "I am in your hands, as always. Take me home, my brother."

His celebration initiated a slide down the angled table, and he was waist-deep in the water before he stopped the descent by regaining his grip on the sides. His arms burned from the awkward angle, but he managed to inch back to the top. Holding the end of the table with one hand, he reset his clothing cocoon with the other. Exhausted, he closed his eyes.

* * *

"Look!" Sal proclaimed. "There's somebody on that thing already!" He cupped one hand to his mouth and yelled, "Hey! HEY! Are you deaf? We're over here."

Willy was scrambling to keep his place on the table when Sal called out, and both he and Doug were puzzled by the lack of a reaction to the yelling. The two Allied soldiers used their crude swimming strokes as best they could and reached the bottom edge. Doug breathed heavily and winced in pain.

"What's up with this guy?" Sal said. "He ain't moving now. Doesn't he know we're here? Gimme a little boost and I'll find out."

Doug shoved Sal onto the table and he crawled alongside its immobile passenger. After a moment's pause, he lightly tapped him. When nothing happened, he did it again with more authority. Willy's arm jerked and the sudden movement caught Sal across his chest. Knocked off-balance, he tumbled back into the water next to Doug. Willy flipped over and stared at the two men who had found him. His pale blue eyes were wide with fear.

"What wrong with you, pal?" Sal demanded as he splashed the water in anger. "Didn't you hear us yelling?"

Willy made no sound or movement; his trepidation was incapacitating. He had visitors ... and they weren't from U-474. Doug gave him a once over and grabbed one of the sou'westers that slid down the table when Willy reacted to being touched.

"I don't think this stuff is ours. At least it doesn't look like what I saw on the ship."

"This guy's a Kraut," Sal screamed.

Willy couldn't hear what was being said, and he wouldn't have understood the words even if he could.

"Please, help me," he begged in his native tongue.

"Listen to that," Sal said. "I told you he was a Kraut. He's a dead man, Hollywood."

Sal climbed onto the table again, but his rush towards the German was stopped when Doug grabbed him by the ankle. Sal twisted to pull free, but Doug hung onto him with desperate strength. Willy watched them struggle. It appeared the man in the water would not be able to maintain his advantage much longer. With a guttural scream, Sal pried himself loose. He was now free to make this German pay for all of his troubles. He extended his hands towards Willy's throat.

"BENNY GOODMAN! GLENN MILLER!"

Sal stopped in disbelief.

"Benny Goodman ... Glenn Miller," Willy repeated.

Doug and Sal recognized the bandleaders' names, even through the heavy accent, but neither man knew how to respond. Given a reprieve, Willy made a wry smile. *Swing music. Who knew?*

287

"Don't do anything to him, Sallie," Doug said. "Come back here and give me a hand." Doug groaned as he attempted to climb onto the tabletop.

Sal hesitated. "I don't know, Hollywood. This jerk is why we're in the drink in the first place."

"Please ... I don't know how much longer I can hang on." Doug shivered in the water.

Sal shook his head in annoyance and eased down the sloping table. The waves kept sweeping over the slab. He grasped Doug's hand and pulled. He couldn't bring the bigger man up. Doug's eyes suddenly rolled up in his head, and he slumped within his life jacket.

"Hollywood, you stay with me, you hear?" Sal slapped him on the side of the head and grabbed the preserver for extra grip. With no response, he splashed water at him. He pulled his arm back to do it again, but something got in his way. Willy had left the opposite end of the table and had moved in alongside Sal. The German reached for a piece of the preserver.

"Don't try nothing cute, you hear me?" Sal threatened, still not realizing Willy couldn't hear or understand his words.

Willy's clumsy pulls didn't accomplish anything more than bang Doug's body against the bottom of the table.

"Watch what you're doing, Adolf." Sal punched him in the shoulder.

Willy read Sal's lips. He shook his head and patted his chest with his free hand while still keeping a grip on Doug. "*Nicht Adolf. Mein name ist Willy*[23]," he said, his teeth gritted.

---

[23] Not Adolf. My name is Willy.

"Adolf, Willy ... fuhgeddaboudit. Look, when we go to pull my friend again, I'm gonna count to three and then you're gonna yank harder than you ever have in your life. Got it?" Sal counted out the numbers with his fingers and mimicked pulling with maximum effort.

"Ein, Zwei, Drei," Willy said in German for the numbers one, two, three.

Sal was peeved but didn't want to waste any more time by getting into a war of words with someone that wouldn't understand what he was saying anyway. He reclaimed as tight a grip as he could on Doug's jacket and Willy followed suit. "Okay then," Sal called out. ". . . one ... two ... three ... pull!"

The two men hauled Doug part way up the table. The tabled groaned in the waves, snapped away from its makeshift mooring, and plunged all of them into the water.

* * *

Dan was helpless in the waves. He moved farther and farther away from the area of the sinking. He continued to pull on the starter cord, but time and time again the engine refused to come to life.

He looked at his watch. How long had he been drifting out in the water? Half an hour? Forty-five minutes? Dan slapped at the top of the motor in disgust. His overcoat, drenched from the waves, was oppressively heavy, and his body wouldn't stop shivering. To his far right, he could see the spotlights in use by the other boats involved in the rescue effort, but in his current situation, they might as well have been a hundred miles away. He bowed his head in self-pity, and then shook himself out of it.

Quit feeling sorry for yourself. At least you've got a boat. Think of those poor guys in the water. C'mon, figure out a different solution.

Almost immediately, he remembered placing a flashlight in the skiff when they loaded provisions back at the pier. The supplies, stowed at the bow, had been tossed into a jumbled mess from his erratic steering, but after digging through a pile of blankets, he found the light. He took aim off the starboard side and waved the yellow beacon back and forth. He stopped after a few passes. *Who am I kidding? They're not going to see me over here.*

Dan shook his head and sighted the beam again. This time he moved it slowly in a circle around the immediate perimeter of the skiff. Clothing, chunks of broken equipment, and other bits of refuse floated by in aimless patterns at the whim of the wind and the waves. He pulled up a fragment of wooden paneling with German words written on its face.

This has to be from the sub. Our boys must have taken them out.

He pumped a fist in the air in celebration and then dropped it, catching himself, his face flushing red. He had seen too much death this Christmas Eve, and celebrating the demise of more men, no matter which side they were on, wasn't right. He clicked off the flashlight and it slipped from his grasp as he sat down next to the silent motor. He threw a punch at the engine and it twisted away from him. That's when he saw the one thing he'd missed. The engine was still in gear.

You are such a moron. No wonder it wouldn't turn over.

Placing the outboard into neutral, he gave a forceful tug to the starter cord. The engine immediately regained life. He took the tiller and set the throttle forward. The skiff kicked into motion with more power than he anticipated due to the amount of fuel sitting in the carburetor from the earlier false starts. The rush forward knocked his hand off the control, and the bounce from the waves had him flopping about at the rear of the boat. Controlling his panic, he slid his hands around the motor until he found the throttle switch. The outboard coughed but didn't lose all power as he decelerated it. His relief was momentary. The skiff crashed into something, and the contact extinguished the engine.

Taking the flashlight, he crawled to the bow. The skiff had collided with a large metal post. The impact cracked several boards, but the boat was otherwise intact. The water was too cloudy to see anything directly beneath the post, but when he shined the flashlight, Dan spied a cable floating near the surface. He extended the beam slowly along the wire's path and found a second pole about twenty yards away.

Why would they have buoys here?

The light's intensity diminished the farther its spot lengthened from the skiff, but he thought he could make out the cap of another pole along the cable line.

Must be a submarine net ... what else could it be? I guess it didn't do its job this time.

He crawled back to the stern, afraid he would fall if he tried to stand up while the skiff was banging against the post. He made sure to set the outboard in neutral before pulling on the starter cord. On his third yank, the motor responded. His push into gear was so slight the boat's movement wasn't much more than when it was drifting. The skiff crept along-side the cable as if it was attached to it, passing one post and then another. After a hundred yards or so, and with the motor back in neutral, Dan re-lit the flashlight for another pass. There was nothing there. The site of the *Leopoldville*'s sink-ing was off to his right, a large stretch of open water between him and the other boats. He gently pressed the off switch and set the light next to him on the bench.

"What are you going to do, Dan?" He'd said the words aloud, and he blushed at his comment. "Of course, talking to yourself is the first sign of insanity."

He hunched over, his elbows resting on his knees. His fear of the water and the lack of a life jacket had slipped momen-tarily from his consciousness. He was left with two choices. Have the courage to make a dash to the rescue site, or follow the net's cable and then the shoreline back to the pier without picking up any GIs. Straightening, he took the rosary, still around his neck, in his hand.

"Okay, Lord," he prayed aloud. "What do I do?"

A wave breached the starboard side and soaked him. He laughed nonetheless.

"That's an interesting answer, but I hear you loud and clear."

He aimed the tiller to his right. Once the throttle engaged, the skiff sped off in the direction of the other rescuers.

Dan glanced to his left at the disappearing cable. Far off, something yellow caught his eye. He tried to turn quickly, but it was hard to maintain control in the frenzied whitecaps of the harbor. He needed to make a sweeping arc to maneuver the small craft back toward the opening to the Channel. Once properly aligned, he idled the outboard. He stood for a better look, only to lose his balance. He wedged his feet underneath one of the benches, and although he wasn't always steady, he was able to stay upright.

"I saw something. I know I did. Rats, I wish I had binoculars."

Twinkling lights were visible on the shoreline, but there was nothing but an inky sea in front of him. He couldn't even see the line of the submarine net he left moments earlier. He sat next to the outboard and looked back over his shoulder. Boats were circling slowly, spotlights making passes over each wave, hoping to find at least one more body, alive or dead. Others in the rescue fleet were scurrying back to the pier with their latest load. Turning away from that scene, he contemplated what might be in the dark unknown ahead. The skiff rocked in the harbor's relentless motion, but he sat completely still.

Finally, resolutely, he pushed the throttle into gear and headed toward where he thought he spotted the color yellow.

CHAPTER TWENTY-NINE

24 December 1944

One and a half hours before midnight.

"W-w-we're g-gonna die. You and me and the Kraut. N-n-nobody knows we're here." Sal's words came out in frozen chunks, and his body shook uncontrollably. "We're g-gonna f-f-friggin' freeze to d-death!"

A portion of the tabletop broke off when it dislodged from the post of the submarine net. Its original twelve feet was reduced to no more than ten, barely enough room for the three men. Willy was still, the intermittent movement of his chest the only sign of life as he sprawled on his side. He led the return to their floating haven and paid the price for the effort. Sal and Doug huddled on opposite sides of the German.

"Sal, we've gotta help this guy. Look at his legs."

"G-G-Get r-rid of h-h-him. W-w-what can we d-do anyway?"

"You know we can't. He and this chunk of wood are probably the only reason you and me are still alive. Now, are you going to help me or not?"

Sal harrumphed. They had been able to salvage two of the sou'westers that were still floating nearby when they got back to the table. Doug placed one of them around his friend. Sal hugged his knees to his chest to keep warm. The other was for Willy. Doug bent close to the German's chest to check for a heartbeat. The steady wind and the lapping of the water against the table made it hard to hear, but he thought he could detect a faint rhythm. He pushed Willy's damaged legs closer to his midsection, and the German's eyes opened in reaction. He pulled himself into a tightly curled ball. A wrenching coughing fit suddenly overcame Doug. With a gasp, he collapsed and fell on the submariner. Terrified screams in German roused the pouting Sal. Doug rolled off Willy and slid onto his back. Instinctively, the other two reached for him and their arms bumped in the process.

"You crazy Kraut," Sal said. "Watch what you're doing."

"I'm glad the two of you get along so well." Doug's eyes opened, and although his breathing was herky-jerky, color came back to his face. He was able to force a small grin. "I'm not leaving yet, if that's what you're worrying about."

They helped him into an upright position. Doug offered his hand to Willy, who shook it with as much strength as he had. Sal turned away, his face purple with jealousy. The constant pounding from the waves was taking a toll on the table, even if it was made of teak. Cracks were everywhere on its surface. When the next wave raised the raft and then dropped it, some of the gaps grew wider.

"This doesn't look good, boys." Doug stuck his finger into an expanding split. Another fissure snaked from underneath Willy, and it showed signs of major distress. Sal could care less about the cracks. He was upset that his friend seemed more concerned about someone who helped put them into this predicament.

"I bet our chances would be better if we got rid of the Fuehrer here," Sal said.

"C'mon, get over it," Doug said. "You wouldn't be here without his help."

"I don't remember him doing nothing for me. I hope he dies."

Doug shook off the comment, launched into a new volley of shivers, and scanned the harbor and the ongoing rescue efforts in the distance. "Something's coming toward us." His voice was low, and he wiped his eyes in disbelief before taking another look. The object, whatever it was, was still there. "Sallie, you've got to see this."

"Show your new pal," Sal muttered. "I bet he'd be interested."

"Don't be a jerk. If I'm right, it's just about the best thing you'll ever see."

There was no mistaking it now. Sal cocked his ear to the wind. Doug waved both hands over top his head. The unmistakable steady whine of an outboard could be heard. A boat appeared in the splotchy moonlight and roared toward them. The driver cut the throttle when he got closer and pulled up short of the makeshift raft.

"Hey! Everybody okay over there?" Dan yelled.

"This guy's in bad shape!" Doug said, gesturing in Willy's direction. "We're all frozen!"

"Fuhgeddaboud him," Sal muttered and rose to one knee, struggling to stand. He reached toward the skiff with one arm and yelled, "Get me outta here! He's a Kraut!"

A wave hit the boat and Dan sat down with a thud, stunned by the information. He knew he needed to act fast. The largest of the table's widening seams made a loud pop. The split in the wood was now almost to one of the edges.

"This thing is falling apart!" Sal shouted. "Get over here NOW."

Dan crawled to the bow of the skiff. *This little guy is too hysterical to be of any help,* he decided, and he focused his attention on the other soldier. "Can your injured man move at all?"

Before he could answer, a coughing spasm dropped Doug on all fours.

"Are you all right?" Dan called.

It took several long, slow inhales and exhales before Doug could respond. "Caught something in my back when the torpedo hit us. But I can make it." He again pointed at Willy. "We're gonna have to help him though. He messed his legs up bad."

Dan could make out that they had something wrapped around the injured man, but in the dim light he couldn't determine exactly what. "You'll have to bear with me," he called out. "This is the first time I've ever driven a boat."

"Are you friggin' nuts?" Sal shouted.

"For the love of God," Doug said. "Shut up, Sallie."

Dan ignored the bickering and laid out his plan. "I've cut back the engine because I don't want to crash into you," he explained. "These things don't have brakes." Neither Doug

297

nor Sally reacted to his attempt at some mood-lightening humor. "I'm going to slowly come over and see how close I can get. With these waves, it's gonna be tough. Can you swim for it if there's a gap?"

"Get as close as you can get," Doug replied. "We'll figure it out then."

Dan reached for the gear lever again, then paused and considered the plan more fully. If the little man of the threesome didn't stop the raft from bouncing, Dan knew it would be difficult to get them all into the skiff. With the sloping sides on his boat, it also was apparent that the only way he could get them over the gunwales would be if he were standing. He knew he could wedge his feet underneath one of the benches—as he had done earlier—but still it would be difficult to stay upright. He counted to himself to time the gaps between each crest. Maybe he could find a pattern to the movement that would allow him to keep his balance more effectively. He put the boat in gear and inched forward. The one GI was back down on all fours, clutching at the small of his back. The man on the far side of the table wasn't moving at all. Dan was stuck with the crazy one.

"What's your name, soldier?"

"Sal. And this here's Hollywood. I think the Kraut said his name was Willy. What's yours?"

"Sergeant Dan Gibbons. I'm a medic. Look, Sal, you're the man over there. You need to follow my plan. We're both swaying pretty good here." He mimicked the motion with his hands and then showed them, palms out. "We'll all be fine if we take the slow approach. I think the best idea is for you to help me get your injured friends into my boat, and then I'll grab you."

"No way are you taking the Kraut before me!" Sal shouted. "I want off now!"

"Listen to me!" Dan's voice rose. "Look at them. They can't help. You're all I've got if we're going to figure out a way to get all of us out of here."

After a moment's reflection, the color faded in the little man's face. He ran a sleeve across his mouth and his expression was transformed when he dropped his arm. "All right, Sarge, whatever you say."

It was a surprising change in attitude, but Dan was hopeful that Sal appeared ready to cooperate at last. He spoke quickly before the little man might lose his resolve. "Okay. I don't have an anchor, and it doesn't look like you have anything over there that I can hook a rope on. So, when the boat gets close enough, I want you to grab my arm and pull me toward you. Then you and your friends can climb aboard."

Sal nodded.

Dan lashed one end of a rope he had brought with him to the tiller and swung the rest around one of the benches. If he could keep the steering device in a fixed position while the motor idled, he might be able to manipulate the force of the tide to get the skiff to drift in the direction he needed. He pulled the rope tight to keep the handle pointed at the table and clambered over the benches along the starboard side. All he needed was a push from the harbor to bring them together. When the distance between them closed to within ten feet, he cautiously stood behind the front bench, holding the gunwale with one hand.

"Can you stand?" Dan called.

It seemed to take forever, but Sal got to his feet.

"Perfect. The way the water is moving this thing, I should be close enough any minute now. It's tough keeping my balance, so don't grab my arm until I give you the okay. You got that?"

"Sure thing boss."

Dan kept shifting his weight, trying to see what would work best. He couldn't help but look down at the water, and he silently cursed himself again for his lack of a life jacket. He decided to put his right leg over the gunwale while hooking his left foot under the bench. This position would maximize his reach and yet maintain some stability. He took a deep breath and tentatively lifted his leg. "Okay, here we go. Try to grab my arm. I should be able to guide my boat closer by pulling it with my leg."

Their fingertips were inches apart. Sal strained for his extended hand. The waves bobbed the table in a different rhythm than the skiff. On the next upward surge of the board, Sal jumped, wrapping himself around Dan's arm at the elbow.

"What're you doing?" Dan exclaimed. "I can't hold you like this!"

Sal tightened his grip and tried to climb farther up his rescuer's arm.

Their combined weight put them out of balance, and Dan could feel his left foot slipping. "You gotta let go. I can't hold you." His face distorted from the incredible strain. Sal was practically pulling his arm out of its socket. Dan shook his arm. "Drop into the water, swim back, and we'll try again."

Sal, eyes wide, refused to release his grip. Dan's foot pulled free. Both men fell into the harbor with a splash. In an instant, Dan felt the icy water close about him. He tried to yell, but salt water filled his mouth and airway. He flailed his arms and legs, desperate to touch something solid.

Even underwater, Sal wouldn't release his arm. He climbed Dan like a ladder to get back to the surface. Only when he felt he could make it on his own did he let go. Dan's saturated clothes began to pull him under. He pushed at the water with his hands and feet, not knowing how far he needed to go, or if he was even going in the right direction. Suddenly, he surfaced. He sucked in the welcome air.

"Take my hand!" a voice called.

The scrap of wood was floating only a few yards away. Doug, still kneeling but not in the same distress as before, extended an arm toward him. Dan's eyes burned from the salt. His head ached from the pressure inhaled water had created in his sinuses. He struggled to keep his head above the waves. The distance to the table might as well have been five miles with his lack of swimming ability, but he churned the water with clumsy dog-paddle strokes and furious kicks.

"Keep coming," Doug encouraged.

With all his might, Dan tried to swim. A wave crashed into him, and he felt his nose go below the surface. His energy was slipping away. A scream rose in his throat.

The hand that clasped his was icy cold. Dan gripped the hand and pulled himself to the table.

It was the German's hand.

Dan was exhausted. He tried to haul himself up out of the freezing water. He slipped and plunged under the waves. The

301

hand held him fast. "Ich habe Sie,"[24]Willy grunted. Again Dan tried, only to fall. On his third dip, Doug grabbed him by the collar of his coat, and with surprising strength, catapulted him to safety.

"Hey, Hollywood!"

They turned to see Sal hanging from the skiff, which had floated away after he and Dan went into the water. Sal scaled the side, disappearing from view until he popped up with his arms raised in triumph. He made an exaggerated bow and went to the motor at the stern of the boat.

"Hey, buddy," Sal shouted. "How do you work this?"

"Don't touch anything." Dan called back. "Let me guide you through it."

"The engine's still on. What do I do? Push this lever?"

Sal shoved the throttle forward as far as it would go. The transmission snapped into gear, and the skiff jolted forward. The momentum knocked him off his feet. The boat gained speed. The tiller was still tied fast. Sal reemerged, his face ashen, and peered over the side. The skiff raced by the tabletop on a circular route, its circumference growing ever wider.

"Untie the rope!" Dan shouted. "Listen to me! You've got to untie the rope!"

Sal didn't move. The boat made a second pass.

"UNTIE THE ROPE!" Dan shouted again.

With rediscovered energy, Sal worked his way back to the outboard. "How do you stop this thing? Where's the brake?" The skiff was roaring now. It made an even wider arc on its third lap. When the boat reached a nine o'clock position from

---

[24] "I've got you."

their vantage point, they could see Sal tugging at rope made inflexible by the cold and damp.

"FUGGEDABOUDIT, HOLLYWOOD!" Sal shouted. His head was turned, looking at the raft. "I GOT IT FIGURED OUT!" Off to the right, now at about two o'clock in the skiff's counter-clockwise circle, they could see Sal holding up one end of the rope.

Sal turned his head forward again. At first, there was a quick grin on the young soldier's face, a look of determination and triumph. But the grin instantly changed to horror.

The speeding skiff slammed into one of the heavy columns of the submarine net. A piece of metal splintered off, caught the gas tank, and sparked.

The boat exploded, disintegrating in a giant fireball.

CHAPTER THIRTY

24 December 1944

One hour ten minutes before midnight.

S ilence hung over the three men on the raft as heavily as the rain-filled clouds above them.

Willy didn't say anything. He stared a few moments, and then sank into unconsciousness.

Dan was like a cigar store Indian, his face transfixed. His only movement was his hand working the beads of the rosary that he had removed from around his neck.

Doug sat cross-legged, his chin tucked on his chest as he wiped at his eyes and nose. His periodic howls were as painful as any mourner's keening. The wailing eventually became whimpers, but his sorrow remained acute.

Sal was dead. Their means to a rescue destroyed.

The only sounds were the wind and the waves crashing all about them and the whimpers and bursts of spasmodic coughing from Doug.

Finally, Doug lifted his head and cleared his throat. "It's my fault. It's always my fault." His words were spoken to no one in particular. They trailed off on the wind.

The plaintive cry roused Dan from his stupor. His shook himself, as much to push blood to his extremities as to snap back to the moment. "It's not your fault."

"I was the one who convinced Sal we needed to go out on our own rather than follow everybody else like he wanted." Doug wiped at his dripping nose with an angry swipe. "Maybe none of this would have happened if I hadn't been so sure I had all the answers."

"You don't know that," Dan said. "Besides, if he had listened to me, we'd all be back on shore by now."

Doug turned away to stare at the spot where the skiff had broken apart. He clutched at another spasm, moaning from the pain in his back ... and in his heart. "It's this cursed water ... it's always the water!" Doug reached over the side and smacked the waves. Something snapped in his mind, and again and again, he struck at the water. His raving might have become a new tragedy if Dan had not eased him away from the edge.

"Easy there soldier," Dan said. "I know you're hurting. What's all this about the water?"

Doug bared his teeth and his words came out like a growl. "My last name's Tillman ... TILL-MAN!"

Dan's eyes narrowed in recognition at the name and the resemblance he now saw in Doug to his late, famous father. Dan read the news regularly. He was always looking to stay on top of current events. He knew the tragic story of the two popular movie stars and the son they left behind.

Doug rolled up his right sleeve as if he was peeling back the skin on his arm. A red scar ran from wrist to elbow, its hue made more prominent by the absence of color on the rest of his chilled limb. He clawed at the disfigurement and muttered, "This is my constant reminder of how I screwed everything up. I was just a stupid kid. They told me not to climb the trees in our yard. But did I listen to them?" He stopped his attack on the scar, but he wasn't finished with his confession. "If I hadn't fallen and got this stupid cut on my arm, my parents wouldn't have had to come back to the mainland when they did. They would've missed the storm and ..." He couldn't finish and broke down again into tears.

Dan responded by doing something he hadn't done with any male other than his father and brothers. He pulled Doug to his chest and hugged him tightly. "Nothing happened because of you," he said with a steady voice while rocking him back and forth. "Not with your parents, not with your friend."

"If it's not my fault, then why has everyone I've ever cared about been taken away from me?"

Dan leaned back to look him in the eyes. "I can't answer that. But I do know there's a reason for everything. God's plan is perfect. Even to the point where he allows bad things to happen to good people."

Doug's upper lip curled. "You actually believe that crap?"

"Every day," he responded. "It's kept me going for a long time."

Doug cast his eyes downward; the certainty of Dan's answer surprised him. When he raised them, they were filled with puzzlement more than anger. "Sometimes I think I believe, but too often lately I don't. You can't tell me everything's been perfect in your life."

"No ... of course not. There have been plenty of times when things haven't gone my way."

"So, what did you do?"

"I had faith."

Doug shook his head. "I haven't been in church since my mother's funeral."

"That doesn't mean you can't have faith." He waved the rosary in his hand as if the prayer beads proved his point.

Doug ran a hand across his mouth with a slow, exaggerated sweep before abruptly reaching inside the collar of his shirt. A wave sprayed up against the raft, and he wiped away the mist with the back of his sleeve. He extracted the dolphin and frog medallion hanging around his neck and gave it to Dan.

"What's this?"

"It was a present from my mother to my father. An anniversary gift. You could say it's my one last reminder of better times."

* * *

When the family arrived at Cabrillo Beach in San Pedro, Big Jim pulled a long, silk kerchief out of a picnic basket and said a flourish, "Mrs. Tillman, if you please." He wrapped the scarf around Kate's eyes as a blindfold.

"Is this really necessary?" Kate asked.

"Can't spoil the surprise," Jim said.

They marched to the dock of a nearby yacht club. Confident everything was the way he wanted it, Jim removed the blindfold. "Happy birthday, my K-K-K-Katie, beautiful K-K-K-Katie!" Jim mimicked the popular WWI-era song.

"Oh, Jim ... it's gorgeous."

"Wow, Dad." Doug's mouth hung open. "That's the sharpest thing I've ever seen."

The Tillmans stood in admiration of a sailboat as it glistened in the blue water and sun like a white jewel against the sky.

"I can't believe this," Kate said. "You of all people, bought me a sailboat?"

"Nothing but the best for my best girl." Jim wrapped his arm around her waist and pulled her close. "I know how much you've missed being out on the water, so I thought why not."

"She's beautiful," Kate gushed.

"How do you know it's a girl, Mom?"

"Dougie, they always call boats 'shes'. It's been that way forever."

Kate jumped aboard and landed with cat's paws on floorboards layered with lacquer. She took a seat at the tiller, and rubbed one hand across its polished wood while the other caressed the top rail above it. The only thing more brilliant than the boat's accoutrements was the delight in her expression.

"Since I don't know anything about sailing," Big Jim continued, "I wasn't sure if you could handle a boat like this one."

Kate smiled and put her hands on her hips. But her eyes blazed. "Handle her? Sounds like a challenge to me, Tillman."

"And I know only too well that you do love a challenge. Happy birthday, my sweet Kate."

Doug walked to the rear of the boat to see if she had been christened like the others docked there. His face screwed in puzzlement. "What kind of name is this?"

Kate suppressed a giggle when she saw the boat's moniker, leaving Doug more perplexed.

"I don't get it, Dad. *The Dolphin and The Frog?*"

"Ask your mother; she'll explain it to you." He looked expectantly at Kate, but she had other ideas.

"Later, sweetie," Kate said. "Wouldn't you rather take her out and see what she can do?"

"Yeah," Doug exclaimed with a vigorous shake of his head. "Can we, Dad? Can we please?"

"Not me. But go on. You and your mother take her out."

"Please, Dad. It won't be the same without you."

Big Jim put his arm around his son, not yet a teenager but already close to his height. "Your mother is the sailor in the family. I'm just a landlubber. You two go and I'll be here when you get back. You can tell me all about it."

Kate and Doug reluctantly left him on the dock and prepared to set sail on their maiden voyage. Kate spent a few moments reacquainting herself with the controls. Soon she was piloting the boat through the harbor and out into the open water of the Pacific. The wind sent the boat on an effortless glide through the waves. Doug was an eager first mate, scrambling to follow his mother's instructions.

"You're really good at this," Doug yelled with delight.

"I love sailing," Kate told him. "I think I spent more time on the water than onshore when I was little."

The breeze continued to freshen as it often did in these waters, but she maneuvered the craft expertly, guiding the tiller in one direction, pulling the sail's line in another to take the best advantage of the wind.

"I wish Dad was with us."

"Me, too, sweetie."

"Dad never goes in the water. How come?"

She relaxed her grip slightly on the mainsail line, allowing the canvas to grab all of the available wind. She took a moment before answering. "When Dad was a small boy, not much more than three, he had an accident."

"What happened?"

"Tack first. Then we'll talk. Prepare to come about." Kate changed the tack she was following, and Doug ducked to allow the boom to pass from the port to the starboard side. "Your Grandmother Sarah was giving him a bath. She was gone from the bathroom for only a moment, but somehow your father hit his head on the tub's faucet."

"Oh, no."

"He was only under the water for a minute but that was enough to give him a real scare, one he never forgot. Fortunately she returned in time to save him, but ever since, being in water has been a problem."

Doug leaned back against the starboard railing, lost in the image of his father nearly drowning. His contemplation lasted several minutes while his mother continued to sail the boat through the cobalt waves. He climbed to his feet, ducked under the swinging boom again, and changed the subject. "Where did Dad come up with such a silly name as *The Dolphin and The Frog?*"

Kate smiled. "When your father and I first started dating, I used to tease him that I expected him to be my Prince Charming. Dad would come right back and warn me that I might end up with a frog."

"Why did he say he was a frog? Because of his voice?"

"Your father's been making fun of how he sounds for as long as I've known him."

"It doesn't bother him he's not making movies anymore?" Doug asked. Big Jim had damaged his vocal chords in a football injury during college. He'd croaked ever since. His voice had never been an issue in his acting career until sound was added to movies. Audiences did not want their heroes sounding like amphibians.

"I don't know if it was ever that important to him," Kate said. "I think he's quite content just taking care of you and me."

Okay, that explains the frog part. Are you the dolphin?"

Kate blushed, although it was hard to tell in the color on her cheeks from the wind. "When I was a little, dolphins would come up alongside our sailboat and race with us. I just loved watching them; they're so beautiful. Your father has heard to me tell that story so often he makes a face whenever I do."

"And that's why you're The Dolphin?"

"At least for your father anyway."

* * *

"That's quite a story." Dan shivered on the raft. He ran a finger across the imprint of the animals on the medal's face. "I understand the frog part—a reference to your dad's damaged voice. But your mother was the dolphin just because she liked them as a little girl?"

311

"Well, that was part of it. Dad used to say he called her that because she was just like a dolphin: beautiful, smart, and unpredictable."

Dan flipped over the medal and read the inscription on the back. "'To my Hero. I Will Be With You Forever.' That's beautiful." He waved the trinket. "Here's a thought for you to always hold on to—the way your parents loved each other. I bet they loved you the same way, too."

The light went out in Doug's eyes. His voice became almost inaudible. "For my mother, I know it was true. But, as for Dad ... things kinda fell apart between him and me after Mom died. " His hands trembled as the words spilled out. "He blamed me at first for what happened. Then he started drinking. We drifted farther and farther apart until there wasn't much left between us. I guess at the end, he decided he couldn't live anymore without her."

An awkward silence ensued. Dan went back to examining the medal, not sure if he should probe for more details or not.

Minutes elapsed. Doug spoke again. "He had that medallion in his hand in the bathtub when I found him."

Another wave hit the raft. "You were the first to find him?"

"Sometimes I think that was the way he planned it," Doug said. "He wanted me to hurt just as bad as he was hurting."

"I'm sorry. I didn't know," Dan said. "They don't report those things in the newspaper."

"They sure tried to."

"It was pretty rough for you, huh?"

"Unbelievable. Dad couldn't swim. He never wanted to learn. When Mom got knocked overboard, Dad couldn't save her. He hated himself for letting her die. And he hated me for being the catalyst that caused them to return home early. He'd get to drinking at nights. Sometimes he'd look straight at me and say, 'If only you hadn't fallen out of that tree in the first place.' When I found him in the tub, he was already dead. He'd slit his wrists. The tub was full of blood."

Dan attempted to return the medallion, but Doug waved it away. "You keep it. It's just like the faith I once had. It reminds me now of how everything has gone wrong." He turned his back and stared at the night sky stuffed with storm clouds. His shoulders sagged as if the world's problems had taken up residence there. "Mom drowns, Dad kills himself in a bathtub, and now I'm floating on a toothpick heading into the English Channel with no hope. It's always the water."

"It might be hard to believe at a time like this," Dan said, "but there really is a purpose for everything. That's why you're still here. Your faith can be renewed."

Dan made a second attempt at returning the keepsake, but Doug again shook his head. Dan shrugged and put the medallion in a pocket along with his rosary.

"Okay then, in the meantime, let me see if I can do some doctoring. It'll be a good distraction from our situation. Let's take a closer look at that wound of yours."

Doug untied his life jacket with some reluctance, tossed it to the deck for a pillow, and lay on his stomach. His uniform shirt had been made darker by the water it had absorbed, but the harbor could not wash away the even darker stain his blood left behind. Although Dan tried not to react, he gasped when he pulled the shirt away. The shrapnel had left a hole three to four inches in diameter. The rim of the wound was a hideous purple, dotted with chalky salt crystals. Blood oozed out in thin, red droplets diluted by a clear liquid. Dan knew that was the sign an infection had gained a foothold. The blood flow might have been stronger, but much of it had clotted in the cold water.

"It doesn't look so bad," Dan lied.

"Be honest," Doug said.

"You've lost a lot of blood." Dan ran his eyes around the edge of the wound. "I just wish I had my kit to keep this from getting any more infected."

Doug inched his body to get on his knees. The pain in his lower back made it difficult, but he turned his head so Dan could see his face. "I know I'm not in good shape, but just tell me what you need me to do."

"Just stay alive," Dan answered. "Someone will find us before long. We'll have a great story to tell our grandkids someday."

Doug made a small grin, the first glimmer of hope in his expression since Sal's death. He slid back down on his stomach, and Dan turned his attention to Willy. He untied the sweaters wrapped around the German's legs. The thrice-fractured tibia was hard to look at, but it was in better shape than the German's stump of a right leg. Tendrils of tendons and ligaments dangled where the destruction of U-474 had amputated his foot. The surrounding skin was the same ugly color as the hole in Doug's back. Some color returned to the unconscious man's cheeks and he opened his eyes and moved like he was trying to sit up.

Dan pointed to the Red Cross on his armband and then gestured at the boy with both hands, palms down, to tell him to relax. Willy nodded. The wind's shriek grew louder, and the water's turbulence matched the intensity. The crunch of wood in the table's cracks grew more ominous with each rise and fall. Dan turned to Doug and spoke, "If we can get him in a seated position, maybe you could wrap your arms around him and keep both of you steady. The body heat should help you both, too."

The words had just come out of Dan's mouth when one side of the table snapped off with a loud pop. He fell backward into the water. As he struggled to stay on the surface, the freed section from the table rammed into him. He raised both arms out of the water, draped them over the shard, and floundered forward. After several panicky minutes, he reached the side of the table. He hefted the broken portion out of the water and on deck, thinking they'd need all the buoyancy possible, and Doug placed it alongside Willy. The section was nearly split lengthwise again, and its top was ragged. The effort to handle the cumbersome piece sparked more pain in Doug's back, but that didn't stop him from extending his hands to help Dan.

"You're too heavy," Doug grunted after several unsuccessful pulls. "You've gotta get rid of your coat. Your boots, too. They're gonna pull you under."

Dan reached below the surface of the waves, and with some difficulty, unlaced his boots. Still not feeling very buoyant, he unbuttoned his overcoat and worked to get his left arm out of its sleeve. Doug grabbed onto the collar, and Dan briefly submerged when he came out of the coat. With the weight lessened, Dan was able to put both hands on the table, and with a strong press, he pushed himself out of the water.

The table was now even smaller. It was still rectangular, but it had shrunk to about four feet wide by about nine feet in length. Willy remained on his back in the center; Dan and Doug were squatting on each end.

Doug pulled Dan's coat out of the water. The wind lifted it and it shook in the breeze. "Here, take it back," Doug said. "Anything helps against this wind."

"What's that you said?" Dan asked.

"I said anything helps against this wind."

A flicker of light flashed over Dan's face. "Hang on a moment. That just gave me an idea that might get us to where someone can find us. But we've all got to work as a team."

Anything," Doug said. "What do you want me to do?"

"First of all, we need that section that just broke off of the raft. Hand it over." Doug complied. Dan took the piece, grabbed the jagged top, and with more strength than he thought he could possibly have, split it lengthwise. He shoved one piece gently under Willy's thighs to keep it from going anywhere; the other section he placed by his side. Next, he took one of the Tyrolean sweaters and helped put it on Doug. He ripped two small vertical slits in the back of it, and then threaded one of the pieces of wood through the two openings. The section looked like a long curtain rod sticking straight out from Doug's shoulders.

"Now, we need to turn our friend here over onto his stomach." Dan made eye contact with Willy and gestured with some twisting motions what he wanted to do. The German remained conscious when they flipped him. Dan grasped Willy's arms and carefully pulled him closer to the far edge of the raft that pointed closest toward the open water of the Channel.

Willy's arms could touch the water, but Dan folded them beneath the man's head for the time being.

"Now, give me my overcoat," Dan said.

Doug opened the heavy coat to help Dan into it.

"Actually, it's not for me—it's for you."

Doug raised his eyebrows quizzically. Dan spread the arms of the overcoat over the length of wood sticking out from across Doug's back and tied the cuffs off so they held. The wind caught the overcoat, and it flapped in the breeze. "Sit on the bottom of the coat so you hold it tight," Dan said. "Good. You're going to be our mast. The coat will be our sail."

The faintest hints of a smile twitched at Doug's lips. "I see what you're trying to do," he said. "But I don't think one overcoat will be enough to propel us back to shore."

"Agreed," Dan said. "But you're overlooking the details. Ask yourself, what other resources do we have?"

Doug shrugged. "I don't see anything at all. One life jacket, that's it."

Dan grabbed the other split section of table and handed it over to Doug. "This will hurt your back a bit, I know, but it shouldn't be for too long and the movement will help warm you up. What we're going to need are three engines if we're going to make it back to shore. Take this and use it like an oar for a rowboat. You think you can do that?"

Doug picked up the remaining length of the chunky shard. He dipped one end into the water and made a few rudimentary strokes. Its thickness, more than the handle of an oar, made the rowing awkward and slow, but it was doable. With the wind in his coat and the paddling motion, the raft actually began to make some headway against the waves.

317

"You said three engines," Doug asked. "The sail and the paddle are two. Where's the third?"

"I'll show you," Dan said. "But first I need you to sit at the middle of the raft, at the end of this guy's legs."

"What are you going to do?" Doug asked.

"I'm going to be our third engine off the back."

"Are you nuts?" Doug asked. "You said you can't swim."

"I can't swim, but I can kick. We need to use something to push back against the tide, and I don't think either one of you could be much help there."

Doug took his position at the end of Willy's stumps, the makeshift oar laying across his lap. "How are you going to hang on?" Doug asked. "This thing's awful slick, and your hands are going to get cold in a hurry."

Dan pointed down at Willy. "That's where our German friend will help."

Willy's world, of course, was silent, and being on his stomach, he couldn't see much. Dan knelt in front of him and raised the German's head to make eye contact. "Just hold tight to ..." Dan stopped, realizing Willy wouldn't understand what he was saying. Instead, he took the young man's right hand and placed it around his own left upper arm. He repeated the process with Willy's other hand. He prayed Willy would have enough strength to keep him from slipping away.

Before he could his plan into motion, Willy released his right hand from Dan's arm to extract a nondescript piece of wood from a pocket of what was left of his trousers. He gave it to Dan, who held it aloft for a moment, not certain what it was. Willy gave him a smile and a knowing nod that expressed what his words couldn't say. Dan brought out his rosary and Doug's medallion. He joined the three symbols of hope together and put them in his pocket for luck. Willy pumped his clasped hands back and forth, a triumphant look on his young face, before reclaiming his grip on the Dan's arms.

With a grin for Willy and a nod to Doug, the medic dipped his feet into the frigid water and winced at the cold. "All right, men," he called. "Here we go!"

Doug took hold of the splinter-turned-paddle and plunged it into the harbor on the right side of the tabletop. The wind caught the overcoat on his back like a sail. Willy tightened his hands around Dan's upper arms. After a large inhale of breath, the rescuer, who couldn't swim, slipped his body into the water and began to kick with all his strength.

With a groan and a shudder, the raft slowly began to move toward shore.

CHAPTER THIRTY-ONE

24 December 1944

Forty-five minutes before midnight.

Reb stamped his chilled feet, giving them more attention than they deserved, but it was better than having to deal with the captain. Levine checked his watch. GMC and Bobby aimlessly picked at their kits, trying to look busy. The pier was still active but not with the same intensity as earlier.

"I told him when and where we were going to meet," Levine said, each word coming out like a bullet from a muzzle. "It's not like him to be late."

The others said nothing. They all knew Dan was the most thorough among them. There had to be a reason why he wasn't with them, and they didn't want to consider the dark possibilities.

Smitty approached from the ambulance staging area. They hadn't seen their driver since they first went out into the harbor to search for survivors. "A major up there is releasing us," he announced, flipping a thumb over his shoulder. "He wants us out of here. Said we'd just be stepping on each other's toes." The burly driver pulled a cigarette from behind his ear and quickly lit it before the wind could extinguish the match. After a deep inhale, he expelled smoke skyward. "Besides, there can't be anyone left out there who's still alive anyhow."

Not waiting for a response, Smitty spun on his heels to walk back up the small incline to where he parked his truck. The rest of the squad didn't move, which Smith realized only when he had covered about half of the short distance back to the ambulance. "Hey, what's wrong with you guys?"

"It's Sarge," Reb bleated, pointing to the open end of the harbor. "He's out there alone."

"Whaddya mean he's out there by himself? He can't even swim."

Levine's face went white, and he staggered as if the words had punched him. "Did the rest of you know this?"

Bobby and GMC shoved their hands into pockets and looked away while Reb's face went white.

"Private Hardin?" the captain asked Reb with an intensity that demanded an immediate answer.

"Y'all were having trouble starting the motor, sir. I was gonna say something, but I was scared you'd get madder at me than y'all were already." His body trembled as he wiped a forearm across his weepy eyes. "I knew he didn't like the water ... but Sarge said he was a boat expert. I figured that meant everything would be okay, so I didn't say nothing."

Levine wanted to be angry, but the night had been filled with errors by too many people. How could he take it out on a boy whose biggest mistake had been having too much to drink?

321

"Well, we can't just stand around here and do nothing. There should be enough gas left in the boat Private Hardin and I used. Let's go back out and find him."

"I've got a better idea, Captain. Hang on." GMC raced to the far end of the pier where a Navy PT boat was anchored. "Murph! Hey, George."

A lieutenant stepped down from the bridge. He squinted at the man standing on the dock and then widened his eyes in recognition. "Oh, it's you. Something wrong?"

"A guy from our squad hasn't returned. We'd like to go back out and make sure everything's okay with him."

"I wish you'd been here ten minutes ago. I sent everybody in."

"Everybody?"

"Everyone but me and Jonesy."

GMC placed his foot on the opening between the rails of the PT boat and leaned forward as if he was ready to jump aboard. "Yeah, but do you have any gas left?"

"Sure, I guess. Why?"

"There's five of us," GMC went on. "We're not swabbies, but we could do whatever you need. We think our buddy's okay, but we just wanna make sure."

The naval officer was about to reply, but instead came to attention with a salute. "Lieutenant George Murphy, sir."

"Captain Abraham Levine. Can you help?"

The others had trailed after GMC without him realizing it.

"I suppose so."

"Great. What do you want us to do?"

The PT skipper paused briefly and then clapped his hands. "You, big guy. See that line there? Take care of it. And, kid, grab that one in the back."

Smitty moved to untie the bowline while Reb did the same at the stern.

"The rest of you, climb aboard."

"Jonesy," Murphy yelled to his machinist mate down in the engine room. "Fire it up. We're going back out."

* * *

Get up.

Dan's eyes snapped open. He brought his knees closer to his chest and kept kicking. His kicks were slower now. The feeling was gone from his torso and legs, but his hands were burning as if a million sharp needles were jabbing at him. All he could see was Willy, sprawled on his stomach in front of him. The young German appeared unconscious, but he was holding on to Dan for all he was worth. Dan's eyelids drooped once more.

I'm nice and warm, Tom. Dan thought. *You go without me.*

A warmth was spreading throughout his body. His kicks slowed even further.

Do you want me to tell Ma? the voice in his head said.

Go ahead, Dan said to his brother. *I don't care.*

"Sergeant! Wake up!"

The words splashed Dan back to reality. They were from Doug, holding his back with one hand and the makeshift paddle in the other. Pain was etched across his face.

The weather had grown rougher. Waves, higher than any Dan had seen since venturing out in the skiff, crashed over him at a quickening pace. Clouds totally obscured the moon. His hands were all but useless. The icy conditions had turned them into frozen fists, and it hurt to open them, even slightly. He tried to kick his numbed legs into motion, but when they didn't respond, panic washed over him like the waves.

C'mon, Dan, get it into gear.

He closed his eyes and exhaled slowly. His heart rate and respiration made a gradual return to near normalcy. He kicked a few strokes, and then floated quietly. His head cocked to one side as if he was listening to someone.

All was quiet. Just the wind and the waves.

Finally, with a firm nod, Dan went back to work. He kicked twenty paces, and then rested. He kicked fifteen paces, and then rested. He kicked ten, and then five, and then one.

"Hey, Doug," Dan said. His voice was no louder than a whisper. "Do you see anything?"

"No." Doug spoke only the one word. The way he responded told Dan that the pain in the man's back must be excruciating.

"Can you hear anything?" Dan asked. "Anything at all?"

"No." Again, Doug spoke only one word.

"I need to come aboard for a while and see if I can warm up."

Doug made no response this time.

Willy's hands went slack. The German had slipped back into unconsciousness.

Dan summed all his remaining strength. He inched up onto the slab and then hoisted himself fully onboard. He closed his eyes and clung as close as he could to the German soldier, desperate for any body heat. With one of his frozen fists, he reached up and pushed the broken piece of wood out of the sweater that was Doug was wearing. Neither man was shivering anymore. Both men felt cold—completely, deathly cold.

He would never be able to get into the water again. Dan knew that now. His strength was completely gone. All his resources were spent.

Lord God Almighty, he whispered.

It wouldn't be long now.

* * *

The PT boat made tight, slow circles in the area where the *Leopoldville* went down. Pieces of equipment and other materials from the ship floated in large layers of spilled diesel fuel. The ambulance team, armed with flashlights, swept the beams in every direction. They were the only rescue craft in the area at the moment.

"Anything?" the captain shouted.

"No sir," Bobby said. "Nothing."

Levine pushed away from the railing, a frown deepened on his face. On the way to the site of the sinking, they had passed a line of rescue boats returning to the docks, but none of the few men recovered were alive. They were able to discern that Dan was not among the victims. Once on the scene, they would find an occasional body among the debris, but each time it was an unknown soldier who had already met his fate. These men they placed on the rear deck of the PT boat.

"Excuse me, sir." Lt. Murphy walked over to where Levine stood. "We'll stay out here as long as you want, but I have to tell you Jonesy and me are beat. We've been at it since our patrol started at dawn. We're talking almost eighteen hours, sir."

Murphy appreciated why Levine had them searching. He would have done the same for one of his crew. At some point, however, reality needed to take over, and now was the time for the captain to admit his man was lost.

Levine surveyed the deck. Along the railings, the squad searched for their friend, their heads makings patterned swivels back and forth almost is if they were choreographed. "Lieutenant," Levine said softly, "I completely understand your position, I really do. We are all paying a steep price in this war." He pointed to his team. "But do you see these men? Sergeant Dan Gibbons means more to them and to me than I can tell you. We're not ready to give up."

The lieutenant's weariness was evident in the circles beneath his eyes and his slumped stance, but Murphy didn't hesitate in response. He nodded. "Like I said, Captain ... we'll stay out here for as long as you need us to."

Levine gripped him firmly by the shoulders. "Fine. That's fine. Now tell me ... with your experience ... why haven't we seen some evidence of Sergeant Gibbons's boat if something did happen to him?"

"What kind of sailor was your man?"

Levine hesitated, his face turning red, first from embarrassment and then with anger. "Not much at all, I'm afraid. He can't even swim. I never would have let him go out on his own if I had known that."

Murphy thought for a moment, and then said, "If he couldn't swim, he probably would've been afraid of the deeper water here in the middle. He would've stuck closer to the shore."

"That makes sense," Levine said. "But at some point, wouldn't he have needed to come farther out to where the survivors were?"

"You would expect so," Murphy speculated. "So that gets us right back here and asking why he isn't in this area or back at the pier. And why hasn't anyone seen him?"

The questions had no answers. Levine walked to the starboard side, pondering the possibilities. He stopped mid-stride and turned back to Murphy. "What if he had engine trouble? That stupid motor on my boat kept quitting every time we hit a big wave the wrong way."

The captain's question sparked an idea for Murphy, and he held up an index finger for Levine to hold his thought. He climbed to the bridge and was back, moments later, with a handful of papers. "I should've thought of this sooner." He held out a chart and shook it. "The tides. We had low tide beginning around 1800 hours. If your man hung to the shoreline and was too inexperienced to keep his engine running, then the tide would've taken over."

The captain shrugged.

"So he would have drifted with the tide," Murphy persisted.

"But where? Spit it out, man, I don't know anything about tides."

"Out there!" Murphy pointed to the English Channel.

CHAPTER THIRTY-TWO

24 December 1944

Eleven minutes before midnight

I t began to rain harder—icy spears of moisture that stung with rage—and the wind's roar was steady rather than as gusts in its previous spurts of fury.

The table bucked on the large swells like an angry, slow-moving mustang. Dan was the only man still astir.

Doug, slumped over, lay on his side, the makeshift paddle nowhere to be seen. His skin was the same sickly blue Dan had seen on victims back at the pier. As for Willy, he was motionless on his stomach.

Dan fought the urge to close his eyes and sleep. The thought flooded warmth through him and it called to him like a deadly siren's song. He tried to shake the thought from his head, but the desire was persistent. He lay next to the German, but kept his eyes on Doug.

The rise and fall of Doug's chest was unsteady but still evident. The young soldier wasn't dead yet. Dan leaned closer to Willy and put his ear on the man's chest. The storm's rage made it impossible for him to hear a heartbeat. He shook him with as much force as a clumsy hold with his frozen fists allowed. He again dropped his head to listen, but what he heard sounded like someone calling his name. He raised his head abruptly.

"Did one of you say something to me?"

Doug was silent. Willy was too.

"I swear I heard someone," Dan said.

Neither injured man made a sound.

Dan lowered his head onto Willy's chest and once more listened for a heartbeat. Something caused him to sit upright with a start.

"Hello!" he called out to the wind. "Is anybody there?" Dan's voice sounded high and tight. The clatter of a man about to die.

"Hello!"

"Tom!" Dan called. "Dad's already gone inside. Storm's coming. We need to get the football." His eyes felt heavy. His body oozed into a heap next to his fellow passengers.

A boat bounced through the waves. A large spotlight illuminated the men on the raft. "Hello! Hello, Sarge?! Hey Sarge! Is that you?!"

Levine and the men on the PT boat could see bodies on the drifting piece of wood, although there was no movement from them. They couldn't be certain since they were still a little ways off, but one of the people on the raft appeared to be their friend and crewmate. Lieutenant George Murphy eased back the throttle of the PT boat, and although the wake from the boat wasn't strong, it still jostled the raft with enough force to put its riders in jeopardy. "Jonesy! Kill the engines!" he shouted. The PT's power source shut down and she began to drift in the swells less than one hundred yards from the raft.

"Sergeant? Can you hear us?" Levine yelled across the distance. "It's me, Captain Levine. We're all here! You're saved!"

There was no sound from the raft.

"Hang on," Levine called. "We're coming to get you." The captain turned to his Navy escort. "Any ideas, Lieutenant? What can we do?"

Murphy had remained at his position on the bridge. The PT boat did not ride that high out of the water, but her height was going to be an obstacle to a rescue plan. His decision would need to make the most sense in terms of speed and safety. The lack of movement on the raft was a concern, but the young skipper also knew he must take care of the men he had onboard his own boat. "Captain, can you come up here a moment?"

Levine hurried up a small ladder, while the others anxiously waited, dividing their attention between the two officers and their friend and the other two bodies floating in the waves below. Murphy rubbed his hands in a nervous, twisting fashion and his eyes blinked rapidly. "There's nothing to tie off on ... it's just a piece of wood. Plus, I don't think we can risk putting any of your men in the water in this weather."

On cue, the rain increased its intensity.

"I don't have any more experience for something like this than you do, Murphy added. "It's gotta be your call."

Raindrops rolled down Levine's nose and he swiped at them as if they were annoying insects. He stared at the gloomy horizon of leaping waves and falling clouds, seeking an answer that wasn't there. The silence made Murphy uncomfortable.

Then, from out of the darkness, a voice called.

"Captain?"

"It's the Sarge!" Reb shouted. The others joined in. "Dan! We're here! Can you hear us?"

"Loud and clear." Dan's called, although his voice was weak and raspy from the salt water. "Any of you boys seen a rescue boat around here?"

Levine scrambled back down to the deck. He gave his second-in-command his largest grin. "What's your status, Sergeant?"

"Not good," Dan croaked. "The guys I'm with are almost finished. Both injured. One man's lost his foot. I'm just about frozen solid, but take them first."

The captain snapped into action and shouted to Murphy. "Can you ease this thing in any closer to that raft without swamping them?" While the PT skipper worked to comply with the command, Levine turned to the rest of the squad. "Bobby, get that coiled rope and take it to the railing. GMC, put on a life jacket, just in case, and tie yourself off on another line. Let's hope we don't have to, but if that raft tips over, I want you in the drink immediately. Go for Dan first. Understand."

GMC nodded.

The captain returned his focus to the water. "Dan, listen carefully. We're going to throw you a rope. It's our only option. Tie your men to it along with the life jacket I see you have there. You're going to need to come with them to keep their heads above water. We'll reel you all in."

331

Bobby tied a loop in the end of the rope. With the lasso in his right hand, he measured the distance from the PT boat to the table and then let out the right amount of slack with the remaining rope. "Ready, Sarge?"

"More than you know."

Bobby let the rope fly and it easily covered the gap, landing on the far side of the raft.

Dan pressed a knee on the lifeline to keep it from slipping into the water. He gave the okay sign and went into the next phase of the plan. "Time to get outta here," he said, rousing Doug with a nudge on his arm.

"I can't make it." Doug's words were slurred. "Go without me."

"Not a chance, my friend. We're going. All of us."

Using his fists and forearms like a pair of salad tongs, he hooked his arms around Doug and forced him onto his knees. An inaudible protest slipped through Doug's lips, but he was compliant. Dan pawed at the discarded life jacket lying at his feet. "I need you to put this on me. I can't do it with my hands frozen like this." Doug moved in slow motion. It was almost herculean for him just to slip Dan's arms and head through the holes in the vest. Once the jacket was in place, Dan put a frozen fist through the rope's loop, twisting his upper body to get the rope to slide across his shoulders.

"Bobby," he yelled to the PT boat, "take up some of this slack."

The squad aboard the PT boat pulled at the excess, but with too much strength. Dan was dragged to the edge.

"Slow down! You're gonna kill me!" His frightened scream knifed through the wind with such ferocity that two of

the rescuers dropped the rope. Doug, wide-eyed, knelt paralyzed next to the prone Willy. Dan's frosty breath billowed.
His heart raced even faster than his respiration, but he didn't
want Doug to lose his nerve. Dan crawled on all fours back to
his fellow passengers. "That was close, but don't worry," he
said with a reassuring wink. "I've straightened up these
knuckleheads before. They'll get it right. Just loosen this a
little bit. Can you?"

Doug loosened the slipknot as he was directed, and Dan
manipulated his head and shoulders until he had the rope
hanging like an oversized bolo tie.

"What now?" Doug asked.

"We've got to get our friend here. Help me lift him."

The wind blew harder, pushing the rain into horizontal
sheets. Murphy knew his boat could handle the worsening
weather, but the piece of wood carrying their targets was not
going to last much longer.

Doug and Dan managed to get Willy on Dan's right shoulder inside the loop. Doug took up the same position on the
other shoulder. The weight of the men was nearly overwhelming, but with face flushed, Dan he held firm. "C'mon, guys,
I'm getting wet out here," he joked to his buddies on the PT
boat while he snapped the rope impatiently. A wave lifted the
raft into the air and flung the trio into the harbor.

"Pull!" shouted Levine. "Quickly men! Pull with everything you've got!"

The captain's order ignited a frenzy of activity. Even Murphy joined in on the rope. The harbor's turbulence was
working against them. Their muscles yowled with pain as the
six men struggled to draw in the rope. Each time they seemed

to make progress, a wave battered the ship and threw them off-balance. Water splashed on the deck, adding to the difficulty of staying on their feet. The harbor was like a voracious serpent trying to swallow bait at the end of a line. It did not want to give up its quarry.

The combined weight of Dan, Doug, and Willy was more than the life jacket was meant to keep afloat. The trio was spending more time beneath the surface than on it. Dan swallowed huge gulps amounts of seawater, and his two passengers crushed against his chest. When they plunged underneath the next wall of water. Dan wondered if he had drawn his last breath. Suddenly, their descent stopped, almost as if they had found some invisible footing under the foaming sea. In the next moment, they were moving again, upward until they breached the surface. The men on the PT boat had gained a coordinated rhythm to their efforts.

"Keep pulling, men!" Levine screamed. "We've almost got them."

The threesome sank beneath the waves again, but the dunking wasn't as long. Again, the men heaved. Again, the trio plunged and then rose. Finally, they bumped against the side of the PT boat.

"When we have them on board, Reb," Levine instructed, "I need you to get some blankets—chop-chop. Bobby and GMC, you take care of the other two. I'll handle Dan."

The vertical pull tightened the rope painfully around Dan's midsection. GMC and Smitty draped themselves over the railing and grabbed at the lifeline to ease some of the pressure. Bobby and Reb held their partners' legs, while Levine and Murphy braced their feet against the bottom of the railing and tried to keep the rope from slipping. Dan and his two passengers twirled on the line like spent trophy fish.

"We gotcha!" Smitty found a handhold on the back of the life jacket. With one more coordinated yank, the raft survivors were brought safely onboard.

The lasso was loosened. Willy and Doug were gently lifted from Dan's shoulders. Blankets were placed on the deck, and though they were soon soaked by the rain, they were softer than the floorboards. Additional blankets were wrapped around the two injured men. Dan was propped against the wall of the bridge, all but spent, yet with enough energy to smile when his captain offered him a blanket.

"You're crazy, you know that," Levine said. "How're you feeling?"

"Frozen, but I'm the son of a smoke-eater, remember?" Dan said. "Dad taught my brothers and me the fireman's carry long ago. I knew I could do it."

GMC and Smitty were bent over Doug. "Back injury on this one," GMC called over his shoulder. He's lost a lot of blood, but if we get him back to the hospital, he should make it." He continued to work on the injured man. "Hey kid," he added. "Your face looks familiar. Where do I know you from?"

"Captain," Murphy said. "You better come take a look at this other guy." Bobby and Reb were attending to Willy as the PT boat's commander hovered above them. The soldier's body looked lifeless. Levine instantly moved into action. He grabbed the frozen wrist of the young German, but he could feel no pulse. "Reb, bring my kit—double time!" The youngest of the medics was back almost before the words had left the mouth of the doctor.

Levine fumbled through his bag and then extracted a syringe and a small bottle. "The cold has hibernated his bodily functions. He needs a jump-start."

Levine plunged the needle into the vial that contained a dose of adrenaline. He pulled back on the plunger to fill the syringe. A well-placed injection of the drug into the German's heart might be enough to restore his cardiac activity. He held the syringe aloft, tapped its side twice, and then lightly depressed the plunger to let a drop of the liquid escape from the needle's end. Reb tore open Willy's shirt and wiped his chest to remove the excess moisture. Dan's frostbitten hands prevented him from doing much more than cupping his fists on each side of Willy's head.

"That's good enough," Levine said. "Give me some room." Reb quickly moved aside while Levine did some quick calculations, tapping his fingers on Willy's chest to find the proper spot to make the insertion. He deftly thrust the needle around the boy's sternum and eased the adrenaline into his heart.

"A few minutes," Levine said. "It'll start to work, and we'll know for sure."

Dan silently mouthed a prayer.

"A Kraut, huh?" Reb said. "If that was me on that raft, Sarge, I'd have been tempted to push him off."

Dan shook his head. "His submarine caused a lot of pain and suffering, that's true. But it was his hunk of wood that was our salvation. Me and Doug over there ... we owe this German our lives."

The minutes seemed eternal until the captain pulled the stethoscope from his bag. The instrument moved in fits and starts across Willy's upper body, gliding rapidly at times, stopping on other occasions. The intensity of his expression was something Dan had never seen from him before.

"I think I've got something!" Levine said, at last. "He hasn't been out too long. What's the time?"

"Seven minutes after midnight," Bobby said.

A vigorous massage of the boy's chest and another pass with the stethoscope brought a smile to the doctor's face. "It's weak, but it's beating," Levine confirmed as he pulled the ends of the instrument from his ears. "Reb, get that blanket back on him."

Dan scanned the faces of the rain-soaked group huddled around Willy. "It's Christmas day," he said. "Merry Christmas, everybody."

A soft sigh eased from Willy's lips, his lashes fluttered, and his nose twitched involuntarily. When his eyes finally opened, he found Dan smiling down at him. The boy coughed up some sea water, then found his vocal chords.

"Glen Miller . . ." Willy murmured. "Chattanooga Choo-Choo!"

Laughter soared to the heavens.

EPILOGUE

January 15, 2005

A collection of wartime souvenirs from a long-forgotten box had grown into a substantial mound on the kitchen table. It had been several weeks since her husband's passing, and Eileen and one of her children—Dan, like his father—were putting his things in order. Among the treasures was a ribbon-bound stack of all the letters Dan had written from overseas. Each correspondence read during the course of the afternoon sent mother and son on a search through the battered box to find a connection to what Dan had written.

Dan, Jr. toyed with a threadbare pair of woolen mittens. "Remember how Dad would always complain about his fingertips going numb from the cold at those late season football games? At least now, I know why." He put on the gloves and then rubbed one along his mother's cheek.

Eileen smiled. "Your father was a great man. He loved to tell me he had cold hands but a warm heart." Her eyes held a dreamy gaze, her thoughts centered on some distant reminiscence. The clock on the wall snapped her out of her reverie.

"Oh, my goodness, look at the time. My bridge club is coming over tonight."

It was nearly five o'clock. Mother and son had spent the entire afternoon discovering so much more about the man they loved. Dan's eyes took on a mischievous twinkle. "The weekly meeting for the sisterhood of problem-solvers and gossip-mongers?"

"You're terrible," Eileen said with a laugh and an admonishing wave of her hand.

The family home had been built on a cul-de-sac more than forty years ago. The street was a playground for the children who grew up there. Baseball, jump rope, kick the can, a talent show in someone's garage; the dead end road was always alive with something. It was a close-knit neighborhood, and ever since Dan had been a small boy, the mothers used a weekly card party as an opportunity for camaraderie and a bit of sanity away from their kids. Many of the families, their children grown, had moved away, but the bridge club still survived.

"Help me put these things away," Eileen said. "I'm not sure I'm ready to share your father's story with the rest of the girls just yet."

She pulled Dan's uniform jacket from the pile to hang it up. In the process, she uncovered a manila envelope that had been forgotten while they read the other letters. Dan picked at the yellowed adhesive that kept it closed for so many years, and it disintegrated at his touch. The metal hasp fell apart just as easily. Inside, crumpled newspaper had been used as padding, and the newsprint was still remarkably sturdy. On another occasion, he might have spent time reading the stories from the day the newspaper was published, but time was limited and there were more important things to be discovered. He removed the paper and squeezed the sides of the pouch to enlarge the opening. He gasped when he looked inside.

"What's the matter?" Eileen asked, her voice rising in tone.

He pulled out an old rosary, the black paint chipped away from the beads and the string that held them together frayed to the breaking point. The beads were hopelessly tangled with a gold chain that carried a small, badly tarnished medallion. He gave them to his mother, and she ran a finger over the design of two animals on the small keepsake. On its opposite side, discoloration blurred the words, but with her reading glasses, she could make out the inscription.

"To My Hero. I Will Be With You Forever."

Eileen touched one of the onionskin sheets of stationery scattered on the kitchen table. "Just as Daddy wrote in this letter. After all these years."

The packet held one more surprise. Dan removed a piece of wood, not quite the size of his palm. Its edges had been worn smooth, making its shape indistinct, but they knew immediately what it was.

"That's what the German sailor gave to Daddy," Eileen said.

"That's fine, but what is it?" Dan set down the carving, and the two of them searched through the pages of Dan's letter about that Christmas Eve sixty years ago for an answer.

"Daddy didn't know," Eileen said brandishing a page with an exultant shake. "Remember? He wrote that the guy didn't speak any English except for talking about Glenn Miller."

"That was funny, wasn't it?"

Reclaiming the mystery piece, Dan studied some markings carved into one side.

Eileen leaned in for a closer look herself. The etched words they assumed to be German, although neither one of them knew the language. "You know, I've seen something like this before!" She left the kitchen, returning a short time later with a small, ornate box. "Do you remember the man at Daddy's wake?"

"Mom, anybody I've ever known was there, and plenty of people I've never met. What man are you talking about?"

"A man about my age ... with an accent ..."

* * *

The funeral home was a maze of parlors and hallways, and a serpentine line of well-wishers—it just didn't seem right to call them mourners—wound through it.

There were as many smiles as tears, and spontaneous laughter often erupted from one to another. This wasn't a wake; it was a celebration, a final opportunity to remember a man who had lived a rich life.

An elderly man limped up to the area where the family was receiving the visitors that came to pay their respects. He was attired in an elegant European-style suit, and the shoes were of equally expensive stock. A more careful inspection would have revealed that one was slightly larger than the other. He spoke softly.

"You are a son?"

341

Dan leaned forward slightly. "Yes, sir, one of the magnificent seven: three boys and four girls," came the reply to the question. "My name's Dan ... and you are?"

The stranger touched his ear as if he couldn't hear very well in the hubbub of the people attending the wake. Dan repeated his question. Finally the man spoke. "I guess you would say that ... I am an old friend." The words were flavored with a continental accent. "I first came to know your father many years ago, but I haven't seen him since."

The man was tall, even though the ravages of age had curved his spine somewhat, and thanks to the long wait in line, he needed the support of an exquisitely carved walking stick. The hand resting on the knob of the cane was like worn leather, the knuckles gnarled by arthritis. Its mate was similar in appearance, yet the grip was powerful when he shook Dan's hand.

"You can be very proud of your father," the man said. "He saved men's lives."

* * *

"Sure. Now I remember him," Dan recalled after his mother's description. "The man who walked with a limp. I talked with him for just a few moments and then he moved on."

Eileen set the box down on the table. The two stared at it as if it might explode. "It was the same way with me," she said. "The man didn't say much except to tell me how much Daddy had meant to him. It all seemed rather strange." She picked up the small package. "He slipped this into a pocket of the black suit I was wearing that day, and he told me to open

342

it when I had some time. It's beautiful, but rather mysterious don't you think?" She opened the box, although the hinged lid prevented Dan from seeing what was inside. "I had forgotten all about it until I went to take the suit to the cleaners. I haven't shown to anyone until now."

Eileen extracted a superbly carved figurine from its resting place inside.

"Look there," she said, pointing to the inscription etched around the statuette. "Doesn't that look like what's written on that piece of wood you got from the envelope?"

Dan put both pieces side by side, and although the words on the plain piece were not as easy to read as those on the handsome curio, it was clear that they were written in the same language. Some of the words were repeated on both pieces. It was remarkable how the inscription had been incorporated into the design. The words wrapped along the folds of the carving's garment.

"This one looks like Obi-Wan Kenobi from Star Wars," Dan said.

His mother made a clicking noise with her tongue, and she sighed like air gently being released from a balloon. "I always told your father you watched too many movies."

She lifted the trinket, twisting it slowly back and forth, so he could clearly see what it was. "It's a shepherd ... for a Nativity scene," she explained. "But why would a man I don't know give me something like this? And why would he do it at your father's wake?"

"Was there a card or anything with it?"

"Not that I know of. It was just this."

Dan checked the top and sides of the box to see if anything had been written on them. When he turned it over, a silk-covered piece, serving as the bottom of the inside padding, fell to the table. It turned out to be a small envelope for a letter, written on heavy bond parchment with creases sharp enough to draw blood. The words were in English, and the penmanship was as detailed as the box's prize. Dan read the letter aloud.

To the family of Dan Gibbons,

They say that God can work in mysterious ways, and there would be no argument from my perspective. My daughter left Germany to come to school in the United States and never returned to her homeland. She has been living in your hometown for the past twenty years or so. When my wife passed away, I was convinced to come and stay with her and her family. How fortuitous, then, that I would be in your city and would read the notice of your husband and father's death. Despite my infirmities, I was honored to be able to attend his memorial service, although I did not want to make myself known to you fully just then, out of respect for the occasion.

I would imagine that he might have told you about a young soldier he once saved named Douglas Tillman. After the war, I came to learn of Mr. Tillman's fate through the publicity regarding his many business accomplishments as well as his charitable works. He remained in Europe after the war, if you did not know, married an Austrian girl, and became deeply active in his church and community. Mr. Tillman started a charity for war refugees, helped return many displaced people to their homes, and assisted in the rebuilding of their lives.

Thanks to him, people the world over found help and comfort, healing, solace, and rest. When Douglas Tillman died in 1997, his family and friends wrote in his obituary how he had become a man of great faith. A man who was once afflicted became a man who offered great comfort to many.

When I read about your husband and father, I realized Dan Gibbons was the other man on a Christmas Eve long ago, the one who made all the difference.

Much too late, I want to give proper thanks for what he did that night. As a small gesture, the enclosed piece is a shepherd I have created for your Nativity set. Back in Bavaria, this gift would be considered a collector's item, if I am allowed to boast a little. My family has been crafting these Nativity figurines since my father was a small boy.

There once was another statue of a shepherd, created long ago. It was not much in the way of beauty, but it held a particular distinction for my family and me. On one side of it was written: Nehmengebühr! Seien sie nicht ein nachfolger. Translated, that means Take charge! Do not be a follower. I hope you can make out the words on the enclosed carving. They say You took charge so others could follow. This gift was made with loving care, and while I am quite proud of it, I have often wondered what happened to the simple figurine I made as a child. It became my symbol of hope when all seemed lost.

Don set down the letter and picked up the long-forgotten carving. He ran a finger across its inscription and then did the same with the new statuette. With a look of knowing appreciation, he placed them together on the table and reclaimed the letter.

When your husband and father took charge that night in Cherbourg Harbor, he was like the Good Shepherd. As the Gospels tell us, a good shepherd is someone who always willing to lay down his life for his sheep. It didn't matter for what side, Dan Gibbons took charge, even at the risk of his own life, and the grateful others followed. His courage and commitment, and most especially his faith, will never be forgotten. I once thought my life was lost, but I survived to live a life made richer thanks to him. My memory will always be filled with the events of 24 December 1944, a night of destiny.

With eternal appreciation,

Willy Müller

###

ABOUT THE AUTHOR

Jack Corrigan, known popularly as "The Voice of the Rockies," is the radio play-by-play announcer for the Colorado Rockies. Previously, he spent 17 years as the television announcer for the Cleveland Indians. 2014 marks Jack's 29th season as a broadcaster for Major League Baseball.

33149986R00196

Made in the USA
Lexington, KY
15 June 2014